Previous book by the same author

*From Desert Sands to Golden Oranges-The History of the German
Templer Settlement of Sarona in Palestine 1871-1947.*

Trafford Publishing 2005 - ISNBN 1-4120-3506-6.

Shattered Dreams

at

Kilimanjaro

The book's cover design was created by Horst Blaich with technical assistance from Trevor Evans.
Cover photographs by David Fisher.

The book's design and layout was created by Trevor Evans from Tree of Life Publishing,
Ringwood East, Victoria, Australia - email familybookste@optusnet.com.au

Printed in the United States of America.

ISBN: 978-1-4269-5461-0 (sc)
ISBN: 978-1-4269-5473-3 (e)

Trafford rev. 01/13/2011

 www.trafford.com

North America & international
toll-free: 1 888 232 4444 (USA & Canada)
phone: 250 383 6864 ♦ fax: 812 355 4082

SHATTERED DREAMS AT KILIMANJARO

An historical account of German settlers from Palestine who started a new life in German East Africa during the late 19th and early 20th centuries.

WRITTEN BY HELMUT GLENK
IN CONJUNCTION WITH HORST BLAICH AND PEER GATTER

AFRICA

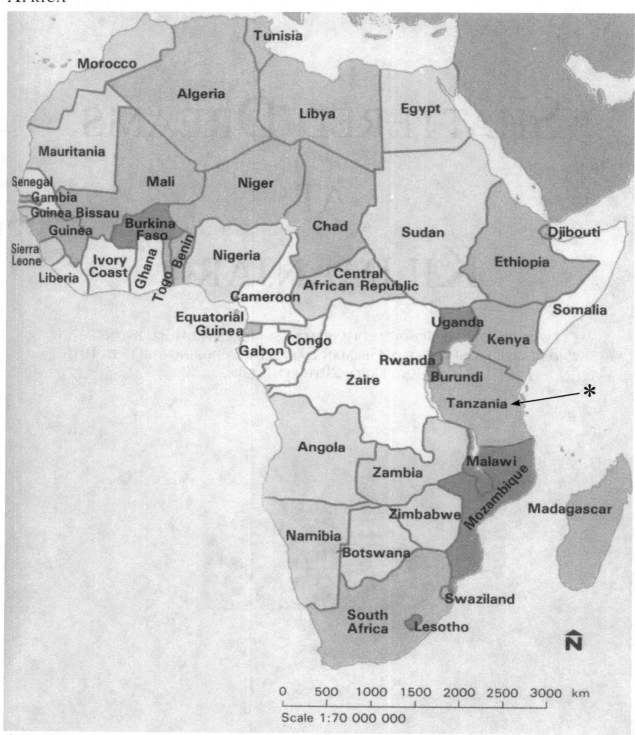

* *Former German East Africa is known as Tanzania today*

INTRODUCTION

Shattered Dreams at Kilimanjaro covers the period from the establishment of the former colony of German East Africa in the late 19th century until the formation of the independent State of Tanganyika in 1961. The book focuses on a small group of German settlers, mainly from the Templer settlements of Jaffa and Sarona in Palestine, who ventured into a new world – German East Africa – to establish farms and plantations near Mt Meru and Mt Kilimanjaro in the interior of the infant colony.

The settlers' decision to emigrate from Palestine was not made lightly. In fact there was bitter debate within the tightly knit Templer communities and much opposition to these young families and individuals leaving their settlements. There was a genuine fear amongst the Templer elders that the departure of young families and individuals to German East Africa might thwart the thrust of the Templer movement in Palestine and place land ownership in and surrounding the Templer settlements in jeopardy. Despite being ostracised, these determined young settlers and their families decided to go to an inhospitable land, firmly believing that it was in their best interests to build a better future for themselves and their families. They never gave up their faith and hoped that the Templer movement would expand to the new colony. Unfortunately, no spiritual, social or financial support was given to them by the Templer Council once they left Palestine. This lack of support for resettlement may well have been a lost opportunity for the Templers to expand their faith to other parts of the world.

Very little has been written about this venture, which ultimately was not successful due, in part, to the tropical diseases contracted by some of the settlers. Other settlers were disillusioned that the economic results were not as great as first envisaged. The main reason for its failure, however, was the outbreak of World War I and the devastating effects this had on the settlers, culminating in dispossession and deportation. During the short time the settlers were in German East Africa they achieved a great deal by clearing virgin land and cultivating it with an array of vegetables and fruits which they had successfully grown in Palestine. Their coffee plantations were just starting to become commercially viable when war broke out. Others started businesses such as building and flour milling.

Only a few of the settlers returned after World War I, when the former German colony became the British Mandate Territory of Tanganyika. Those that did and rebuilt their livelihoods lost everything again when World War II broke out and all German citizens were interned as enemy aliens and their properties confiscated. Many of the settlers were deported to Germany in 1940, whilst some were interned in Africa for the duration of the war.

It is fitting to record the history of these young, adventurous and hard working people. They had to overcome severe personal hardships and disappointments and, in the end, earned little reward for their toils. Nevertheless, they left a lasting legacy because, through their efforts, agriculture was brought to a region in tropical East Africa from which crops are grown and food produced to this day. Similarly, their businesses gave rise to ongoing enterprises in that region.

While an earlier book by the same author, *From Desert Sands to Golden Oranges*, provides a comprehensive history of the German Templer settlement of Sarona in Palestine for the period 1871 to 1947, this book completes the chapter on the families who left Palestine to seek a new life in Africa.

PREFACE

Whilst researching the history of the former German Templer settlement of Sarona in Palestine, I became aware that nothing had been documented about the group of settlers who went from Palestine to German East Africa in the late 19th century and early 20th century. I found this strange, because the families who left Palestine were part of a tightly knit community. Why did these families choose to leave a community that had overcome enormous hardships but, after 30 years, finally had grown into a flourishing community at the beginning of the 20th century?

This book focuses on those families and individuals, who went to German East Africa from Palestine. It shows why the families, several with small children, chose to migrate there; the personal hardships and difficulties they encountered during their journey; the task of starting a new life in the wilderness of Africa; their sense of adventure, their pioneering spirit and probably a sense of national pride in contributing to the establishment of the new German colony.

I must confess a personal interest in this subject because my grandparents, Gottlieb and Paula (née Knoll) Glenk, were amongst those adventurous and dedicated settlers who left. I fondly recall many happy childhood hours sitting on my grandparents' garden bench and listening to my grandfather talk about Africa. This created for me a lifelong fascination with colonial Africa. I am now very pleased to be able to incorporate this part of my family history into a much wider historical context.

After researching and documenting the history and life of the former German Templer settlement of Sarona in Palestine (Sarona is now known as Hakirya in Israel) for the book *From Desert Sands to Golden Oranges*, I turned my attention to the Templers who went from Palestine to German East Africa. I briefly mentioned this subject in my earlier book as most of the families that emigrated from Palestine to German East Africa came from either Sarona or the nearby Templer settlement in Jaffa. This book, a 'stand-alone' historical text, can also be regarded as a sequel to *From Desert Sands to Golden Oranges*.

Both Peter Lange, President of the Temple Society, and Brigitte Kneher, the Society's archivist encouraged me to document this part of the Temple Society's history. They said that virtually nothing had been recorded about the German East Africa venture and agreed that it was a forgotten chapter in Templer history.

When I told Horst Blaich – one of my colleagues who worked with me on my previous book – that I wanted to write this book, he immediately became an enthusiastic supporter of this 'Africa' project. Horst and his wife, Irene, have researched the Blaich family history over many years. Several members of the Blaich family were also amongst the pioneers who went to German East Africa. Horst had amassed much family history and substantial photographic records in the Albert Blaich Family Archives. Our research has uncovered numerous additional images from private collections, many of which are published in the book. Horst took responsibility for the images and cover design, whilst I wrote the text.

So the project began as a joint effort between Horst and myself. I wrote articles in the Templer Record appealing for information; we conducted interviews, researched archives, corresponded with persons in Australia and overseas; and read numerous texts. Our thanks and appreciation is extended to the many persons who helped with information and material. Their contribution is recognised in the Acknowledgements Section at the back of this book.

Peter Lange was a keen supporter of our project. He sent us several life histories and family trees of people who went to Africa, and provided informed comment when proof reading the manuscript. Peter also wrote the Foreword for this book. I thank him sincerely for his support and input.

Brigitte Kneher, the dedicated archivist of the Temple Society in Germany, provided as much assistance as possible for all our requests for information, although the archives only held a small amount of material on German East Africa. I am grateful for her efforts and assistance.

In Germany again, special thanks goes to Dr Jakob Eisler, a well known and respected historian, who specialises in the Temple Society and the Germans who lived in Palestine. Whilst in Australia in early 2004 he identified a number of information sources. He also was one of the proof readers and his comments proved invaluable for historical correctness and detail. Dr Eisler was also instrumental in introducing me to Peer Gatter, a descendant of another pioneering family, the Reinhardts, who went to German East Africa.

I owe Peer Gatter, from Germany, and more recently Cambodia, an enormous amount of thanks and gratitude – his contribution was invaluable! He was willing to share with me information from his own personal family research of German East Africa. Without the input from his personal family archival records and photographic collection, the book would not have been as detailed nor as comprehensive. The personal details he was able to provide added a real 'human dimension' to this historical text. Peer supported the book from the very outset to its completion and I was delighted when he agreed to become a 'co-author'. With his own personal interest of German East Africa, his comments were valued and appreciated. He proof read the book and added substantially to the written text material as well as to the images. I express gratitude to many members of Peer's extended family, especially Irmgard Schoer (née Bauer), Lore Bauer (née Gutekunst) and Dorothea Gatter (née Bauer) for their detailed documentation and information.

In England, Martin Higgins, always responded to any requests, especially those relating to family history matters and relationships.

In the United States of America, I am indebted to a wonderful 100-year-old lady, Luise Kopp (née Bäuerle), who wrote to us several times and sent us her well documented (unpublished) life story. Luise Kopp went to German East Africa with her parents as a six-year-old.

I thank the descendants of the Blaich family in South Africa for providing us with family documentation and written life histories.

In Israel, the interest about the Germans who left the Holy Land to go to East Africa was significant. Dr Danny Goldman's proof reading and comments were welcomed, Dr Yossi Ben-Artzi, Director of the Haifa University, provided personal advice and support throughout the project and Dr Zvi Shilony, Ben Gurion University, provided historical information from his own research. Dr Yaron Perry, Haifa University and Professor Dr David Kushner, Head of the Schumacher Institute, Haifa University are thanked for their support and comments.

In Australia, I make special mention of Herta Blaich, who was born in German East Africa and grew up in the British mandate territory of Tanganyika. She was a great source of information and an enthusiastic supporter of this book. The special contributions of the Goetze family, Werner Neef and Ilse Meyerheinrich (née Blaich) are also acknowledged with thanks.

Trevor Evans from Tree of Life Publishing again provided the skills and flair in arranging the illustrations and text layout for this book. His expertise and technical competence is highly valued and appreciated. I acknowledge the special effort of Jenny Restarick in indexing the book.

There were many other individuals who contributed to the book, they are all named in the 'Acknowledgements' section..

A thankyou to my Australian proof readers, Dieter Glenk, Peter Hornung and my wife, Lorraine, for their forthright comments, sound advice and time spent in checking the text and details.

A special big sincere thankyou to my dear wife, Lorraine Glenk, to Horst's wife Irene Blaich, and Peer's wife Nathalie Duong Sung for their understanding and ongoing support during the compilation of the book.

Helmut Glenk
Melbourne, Victoria, Australia
December 2006

FOREWORD

Another publication on our Templer heritage has now been added to the ones already on our book shelves. The authors, Helmut Glenk, together with Horst Blaich and Peer Gatter, are to be congratulated on their meticulous research on the migration of Templer families from Palestine to German East Africa at the beginning of the 20th century. This chapter in the Temple Society's history indeed deserves to be presented in detail. The existing Templer chronicles (*The Holy Land Called* by Paul Sauer and *Die Siedlungen der württembergischen Templer in Palästina* by Alex Carmel) had only given a superficial and general outline of this event. This new book now provides members of the Temple Society, as well as professional historians, with a detailed historical account of the fate of the persons involved in the "East African adventure".

The readers gain a thorough knowledge of the discussions that took place within the Temple Society and its central administrative council about the pros and cons of starting new settlements outside of Palestine. The necessity for establishing new Templer settlements at the beginning of the 20th century was a fact that could not be ignored, but obviously there was still a strong feeling among Templers that their aim of striving towards ideal Christian communities would be best achieved by limiting their activities to the Holy Land. The Pietistic belief that Jerusalem was the predicted starting point of a revitalised world based on Christian values was still prevalent.

I admire the authors' capability for finding so many interesting personal accounts of the settlers who ventured to Arusha, Mt Meru and Tanga. Considering that Helmut had to start with only what he had heard from his grandfather, the authors eventually succeeded in obtaining historical information from so many sources which they could not have envisaged nor anticipated. Their research culminated in this substantial historical book. From these oral and written sources the reader can get a clear picture and understanding of the many difficulties encountered by the immigrants to German East Africa in regard to agriculture, transport, building and education. The move to East Africa was not planned nor underwritten by a central authority and the settlers were left without external financial support. Their success depended wholly on their own initiatives, hard work and creative ideas.

The numerous historical photographs and illustrations throughout the text enhance the value of the book. With the help of these images we can imagine what the African countryside looked like when the families arrived. We gain an impression of the extent of their properties and a better understanding of how they worked and lived in a remote region far away from their former homes and communities.

I personally became familiar with the area around Mt Kilimanjaro a number of years ago when I undertook several safari trips through Tanzania visiting the famous national parks with their abundance of wildlife. At that time, I did not realize that the coffee plantations in the area could easily have been started a century before by the daring Templer families from Jaffa and Sarona. What a cruel stroke of fate it was that their hopes of cultivating newly-developed land and providing for a prosperous and secure future eventually ended in "shattered dreams".

Peter Lange
President of the Temple Society

HISTORICAL PERSPECTIVE

A number of research papers and books have been published during the past few decades on various historical facets of the Temple Society.

The pioneer of this research into the achievements of the Swabian settlers in Palestine was Professor Dr Alex Carmel. His work on the significance of the contribution by the Templers to the cultural changes and modernisation of the Holy Land is well known and respected.

Dr Paul Sauer, in his book *The Holy Land Called*, covered the history of the Temple Society including the period onwards from World War I. In his book he touched on the Templers in Russia and the USA. As yet no definitive detailed historical account of the German Templer settlements in Russia has been written. In his doctorate dissertation, Dr Dan Goldman wrote about the architecture and planning aspects of the Templer settlements in the USA. Also in my dissertation, *Der deutsche Beitrag zum Aufstieg Jaffas 1850-1914* (The German Contribution to the Development of Jaffa 1850-1914), I mentioned briefly that a number of families, including the Glenk, Blaich, Reinhardt, Olldorf families and others, went to East Africa but I did not elaborate further on this matter.

The book *Shattered Dreams at Kilimanjaro* is therefore of great significance. Helmut Glenk together with Horst Blaich and Peer Gatter document the commencement of colonisation of German East Africa, the first contacts by the Templers with that continent and their intense interest in East Africa from 1896 onwards. There was naturally a vast difference between establishing settlements in Palestine as compared to East Africa. Glenk writes in chronological sequence, meticulously from many primary sources, such as diaries and written documents from the settlers. They detail the hardships and difficulties the settlers encountered when they migrated to East Africa. The book also includes the periods after both World Wars and is illustrated with many images.

We are indebted to Helmut Glenk, Horst Blaich and Peer Gatter for this book which provides the readers with an important contribution to the history of the Temple Society.

Dr Jakob Eisler
Historian
Landeskirchliches Archiv Stuttgart
und Hochschule Ludwigsburg, Germany

KEY DATES AND EVENTS

19th century – European interest grows in East Africa.

1830s – German Christian Mission Society establishes mission stations at Mombassa in East Africa.

1846 /1848 – German missionaries explore inland East Africa (the first Europeans to do so) – they record sightings of snow-capped Mt Kilimanjaro, Mt Kenya and Lake Victoria. They draw a map of the area.

1854 – A petition is signed by 439 persons at a meeting of 'The Friends of Jerusalem' in Germany. The petition is directed to the German Federal Assembly and urges the establishment of Christian congregations in the Holy Land.

1858 – The Friends of Jerusalem send a commission to the Holy Land to investigate the conditions for future settlement. The commission members meet with Peter Martin Metzler, a missionary who has been to East Africa.

1860 – The Friends of Jerusalem send four representatives to the Holy Land to further the Templer cause.

1850s and 1860s – Extensive exploration of East Africa by European explorers.

19/20 June 1861 – A conference is held at Kirschenhardthof to discuss secession from the State Church. The Temple Society is founded under the name of *Deutscher Tempel* as an independent religious community. Christoph Hoffmann is elected Bishop and twelve others as elders.

1867 – The first Templer groups emigrate, unauthorised, to the Holy Land. This venture ends in disaster as most settlers die from disease.

October 1868 – Christoph Hoffmann and Georg David Hardegg, the two founders of the Temple Society, leave for Haifa in the Holy Land to work out a plan for co-ordinated communities.

1869 – The first Templer settlement is established at Haifa
– The Templers buy land and take over a discontinued American settlement in Jaffa to start another settlement.

August 1871 – 60 hectares of land is purchased by the Templers near Jaffa and the agricultural settlement of Sarona is established.

1875 – Dr. Carl Peters, German explorer, journalist and philosopher, visits German East Africa.

1884 – *The Gesellschaft für deutsche Kolonisation* (Society for German Colonisation) is founded. The Society's aim is to establish overseas colonies for the new German nation.
– Peters returns to East Africa and 'negotiates' treaties with the native chiefs.

27 February 1885 – Kaiser Wilhelm I signs an Imperial charter to give 'Reich Protection' to Germans living in the negotiated territory.

1885 – The *Deutsch-Ostafrika Gesellschaft* (German East Africa Company) is established with Peters as Chairman
– A joint commission, with representatives from Great Britain, Germany and France, is established to discuss partitioning East Africa.

Mid 1880s – Much unrest and uprisings in negotiated territories as native chiefs and Arabs try to regain control.

August 1888 - Johannes Reinhardt is the first Templer to go to German East Africa.

December 1888 – Chancellor Bismarck appoints Major Hermann von Wissmann, Reichskommissar for East Africa.
– Wissmann's role is to put down the uprisings. He establishes the *Schutztruppe* (protection force).

1890 – Great Britain and Germany ratify the Heligoland-Zanzibar Treaty on 1 July to determine the border between German and British territories in East Africa.

KEY DATES AND EVENTS

1 January 1891 – The German Protectorate in East Africa is declared a *Reichskolonie*.

April 1891 – Julius von Soden is appointed the first German Governor of the colony.

1895 – Ulrich Reinhardt and family migrate to German East Africa.

1896 – Christof Reinhardt and family migrate to German East Africa.
– The Chief Clerk of German East Africa visits the German Templer settlements in Palestine to discuss settlement prospects in the new colony.

Mid 1890s to 1907 – Violent uprisings and revolts by native chiefs and tribes occur throughout the German colony.

October 1898 – Kaiser Wilhelm II and Kaiserin Augusta Victoria visit Palestine and the German settlements and see first-hand the achievements of the Templers.

1906 / 07 – Discussion amongst Templer settlers in Palestine about migrating to German East Africa.

16 July 1907 – Karl Knoll travels to German East Africa on a fact finding tour. He is joined a short time later by Paul Egger.

December 1907 – Knoll and Egger return to Palestine. A comprehensive report is published on their travels and settlement opportunities.

1909 – 1912 – 13 families and 10 individuals (totalling over 60 persons) leave Palestine for German East Africa. Nearly all settle in the Arusha/Mt Meru/Mt Kilimanjaro region.

1914 – 1918 – World War I. German men in German East Africa of military age are involved in combat. Those captured are interned in India and Egypt.
– German farms and property are taken over by British authorities. Women, elderly males and children remain on their farms.

1919/1920 – German prisoners of war are repatriated to Germany
– German women, elderly males and children are deported to Germany.
– German properties and possessions are confiscated by British authorities.

1921 – Some former German East Africa settlers go from Germany to Palestine with the returning Templers.
– Other former settlers remain in Germany and try to start a new life there.

1922 – The League of Nations gives Great Britain a mandate over former German East Africa. The territory becomes known as Tanganyika.
– The former provinces of Ruanda and Burundi are placed under Belgian administration.

1925 – Karl Blaich and family are amongst the first of the former settlers from Palestine to return to Tanganyika. Other former settlers follow in the next few years. They are unable to return to their former properties and start afresh in Arusha and at Oldeani and Mt Meru.

1926 – The Bäuerle brothers visit Kenya and prepare a detailed report on resettlement opportunities. Their report is published in the Templer *Warte*.

1929 – Railway line is finally completed to Arusha.

1930s – More former settlers return and other Templers from Palestine go to East Africa.

3 September 1939 – World War II starts. All German males living in East Africa are interned.

November 1939 – Some internees and their families are repatriated to Germany as part of an exchange for civilian prisoners in Germany.

16 January 1940 – Another larger group of internees and their families are repatriated.

Mid 1940s – The remaining German women, elderly and children are interned in several camps in Tanganyika.

March 1941 – German civilian internees are transferred to Tanganyika Internment Camp 2 near Salisbury, Rhodesia.
– German male internees are taken to a camp near Pretoria, South Africa.

1942 – Two groups of internees are exchanged with civilian prisoners from Germany.

March 1944 – Married men are reunited with their wives and families in the Rhodesian camp.

September 1944 – Single men are allowed to visit their families in the Rhodesian camp.

8 May 1945 – War ends but internment continues.

November 1945 – The Rhodesian camp is cleared and the 'internees' are transferred to the Norton Camp in Rhodesia.

Early 1946 – Single men from South Africa are transferred to Norton.

May 1947 – The Germans from Norton are deported to Germany.

1950s – British rule continues in Tanganyika as the independence movement gathers momentum.

1961 – The Goetze family, the last family with connections to the Templers, leaves Tanganyika.

9 December 1961 – Great Britain relinquishes its control and Tanganyika becomes an independent nation.

TABLE OF CONTENTS

TABLE OF CONTENTS

TABLE OF CONTENTS

Deutsch-Ostafrika - a German Colony in East Africa

Before European Settlement

Central East Africa, which includes Tanzania, is regarded as the area where human life began and is often described as "the cradle of Mankind". In 1910 a German entomologist found fossils and bones in the Tanzanian Olduvai Gorge that showed evidence of human activity. The Olduvai Gorge in northern Tanzania on the eastern edge of the Serengeti Plain forms part of the Great Rift Valley. During the 20th century, further archaeological work by Professor Louis Leakey and his wife Mary, who found teeth fragments and a skull dated to be 1.75 to 2 million years old, confirmed the existence of hominids – the earliest forms of human beings. Footprints of hominids discovered at Laetoli, a short distance from Olduvai, were dated to be 3.5 to 4 million years old.[1]

1. Olduvai Gorge where fossil remains of early human activity were discovered

Archaeological finds and rock paintings dating back to the Stone Age show evidence of various tribes and civilisations. Throughout these ancient times, stories of riches in ivory and gold emerged and even the ancient Egyptians penetrated the interior from the north to seek gold and slaves. It is believed that the Bantu people came from western Africa in the 2nd century BC and extended their influence over vast areas both inland and along the coast. The Swahili (Kiswahili) language probably developed as the Bantu mixed with Arab and Shirazi tribes along the coastal areas during the 10th to 15th centuries. The Arabs remained largely in the coastal region from where they were able to control all trade, especially the slave trade.[2]

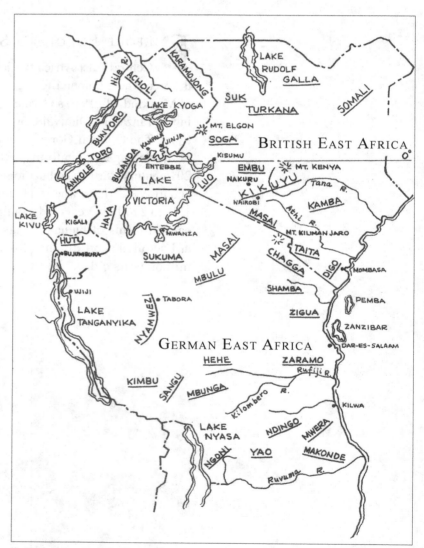

2. Tribal Regions in East Africa

CHAPTER ONE

It was towards the end of this period that the tribes began appointing chiefs. Some of these chiefs (kings) and their descendants were powerful rulers for many years. They fought neighbouring tribes to extend their influence. One such chief was Horombo, also known as "Kilimia – the Conqueror" from the Chagga tribe, who was the first chief to control the whole Kilimanjaro region in the latter 18th century. He was eventually killed by the Massai, a tribe of strong tall people. Another powerful chief at that time was Mbega, who was known as the King of Usambara.[3] At the beginning of the 20th century the settlers from Palestine started their farms and businesses in the Kilimanjaro and Usambara regions in northern German East Africa.

By the middle of the 19th century, Chief Rindi of the Chagga had become the principal chief in the Kilimanjaro region and established his centre of operations at Moshi. Chief Sina, Rindi's main rival, had a large army and regularly carried out cattle raids. Both these chiefs were in power when the Germans arrived in the late 19th century.[4]

THE ARRIVAL OF THE EUROPEANS

On his circumnavigation of the globe in the late 15th century, Vasco de Gama landed in the Mombassa region. Shortly after the first

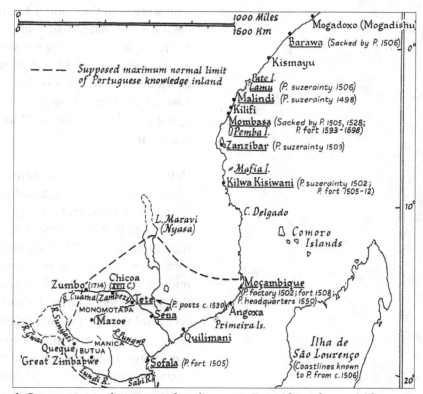

3. Portuguese exploration and settlement in East Africa during 16th century

Europeans, the Portuguese, established ports on the east coast of Africa. They were surprised to find existing well developed settlements, which had been established by Arabs and Persians several centuries earlier. The Portuguese used these settlements primarily as stop-over ports for their ships travelling to and from India and the Spice Islands in South East Asia. In the 16th century, Portugal established colonies on the east coast of Africa – Mozambique – and on the Spice Islands. The Portuguese also established a presence in Mombassa, but had to withdraw when they were defeated by the Arabs in 1727. During their 200-year presence in the region, the Portuguese had not explored the interior because they were predominantly interested in the coastal ports for trade purposes.[5]

Europeans still knew very little about the interior of Central East Africa in the 19th century. The European nations had focussed on the South Pacific, the Far East and the Americas. However, in the mid 19th century, Africa became the centre of geographical and exploration interest. Arab traders had penetrated only a short way into the region, mainly for the slave and ivory trades, but they brought back tales of large lakes and mountains in the interior.[6]

These reports caught the attention of three German missionaries who were with the Church Missionary Society at Mombassa. Dr Johann Ludwig Krapf had studied with *Basler Mission* and joined the Society after completing his studies. He was sent to East Africa by the Society in 1836/37 and started a mission station on the outskirts of Mombassa. Krapf was the first person to translate the Bible into Swahili. Johannes Rebmann and Johann Jacob Erhardt joined Krapf at the German mission in Mombassa. They also had studied at the Basle Mission.[7]

Between 1846 and 1848, Krapf and Rebmann explored the Pangani River valley. This is regarded as the first inland exploration of East Africa by Europeans. As they crossed the plains of Tsavo, they recorded the first sightings of Mt Kilimanjaro and, on a later expedition, of Mt Kenya. Their report of snow-capped mountains, virtually located on the equator, was treated sceptically by the scientific community in Europe. Based on Krapf and Rebmann's sightings and on the Arab traders' stories, Erhardt and Krapf drew a basic map of the area explored by the two missionaries. This map, which achieved fame as the 'slug map', showed two snow-capped mountains and one enormous lake in the shape of a slug. It was used in 1856-58 by Richard Francis Burton and John Hanning Speke when they set out on their famous expeditions which were commissioned by the British Royal Geographical Society to find the source of the Nile River.[8]

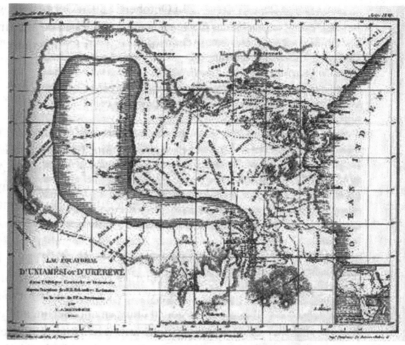

4. The "Slug Map" as drawn by the German missionaries Kraft & Erhard

5. The "Slug Map" already shows Mt Meru, Mt Kilimanjaro and a region called "Arusa"

Several other Germans became involved in the exploration of East Africa. In 1859, Albrecht Roscher (1836-1869) was the first European to land in Mzizma, which later became known as Dar-es-Salaam. In 1861/62, Baron Karl Klaus von der Decken (1833-1865) explored the Mt Kilimanjaro area and established a route from Tanga on the coast to that area. Other explorers from Britain and France were also active in this region during the 1860s and 1870s.[9]

In October 1889, a German geographer, Dr Hans Meyer, after several earlier attempts, became the first man recorded to climb and reach the summit of Mt Kilimanjaro.[10]

THE ACQUISITION OF A COLONY IN EAST AFRICA BY GERMANY

In the second half of the 19th century, the European powers – especially Britain, France and Germany – showed considerable interest in establishing colonies in Africa – sometimes referred to as the 'scramble for Africa'. Germany had only become a unified nation in 1871 after the Franco-German war and had not yet acquired any overseas colonies.

6. *Carl Peters – a German explorer and representative of the Society for German Colonisation. He was one of the key figures to secure German East Africa for Germany*

Dr Carl Peters (1856-1918), a German explorer, journalist and philosopher, is regarded as one of the key figures in the movement to secure overseas colonies for Germany. Peters had studied at Göttingen, Tübingen and Berlin, and graduated with a degree in history. On conclusion of his studies he went to London where he lived for several years. During his time in England he observed how much Great Britain benefited from her overseas colonies. In 1875 Peters briefly visited East Africa for the first time. On his return to Germany from England in early 1884, he was instrumental in forming the *Gesellschaft für deutsche Kolonisation* [Society for German Colonisation]. The Society was founded on 28 March 1884 with 24 members, and its membership grew rapidly. This society's aim was to establish overseas colonies for the new German state. The Society was concerned that Germans emigrating to colonies governed by other nations were losing their German culture and language. It saw the establishment of German colonies as a means of spreading and preserving German culture, language, values and traditions.[11]

Initially, the German government did not support the Society's planned expeditions to overseas countries to arrange and sign land treaties with the local chiefs. The government regarded any expedition planned by the Society as purely a private matter. The Society, however, was determined to pursue its goals and, on 16 September 1884, agreed to send Peters on an expedition to East Africa. The planning was done in secret so as not to arouse any suspicions among the British or Arabs, who might have tried to thwart the desired outcomes of the expedition. In October 1884, Peters left for East Africa. On arrival, he and his team travelled inland from Bagamoyo along the Warni River, utilising the narrow tracks used by slave and ivory traders. There were no roads for carts and all supplies and equipment had to be carried by porters. Peters was accompanied by interpreters and armed mercenaries. Within just a few weeks, Peters was able to reach agreement and have treaties signed with a number of sultans and chiefs in the Usagara, Useguha, Ukami and Uguru regions. The essence of the treaties was to secure the rights of control over the territories (property and trade routes) of the local chiefs and sultans.[12]

These treaties, often misunderstood by the local chiefs, unwittingly gave concessions and property to the Society for German Colonisation. An example of such a treaty is the one Peters concluded with Sultan Mangungu of Msovero in Usagara. That treaty, which became known as 'The Treaty of Eternal Friendship' gave Peters – as representative of the Society for German Colonisation – exclusive rights and all civil and public privileges over the entire territory. A declaration by Peters stated that he, in the name of the Society, was willing to take over the territory. The treaty concluded with *"This contract has been executed legally and is valid for all time"*.[13] In another treaty with Sultan Muinin Sagara in the Usagara region, a clause obliged the Society to do everything within its powers to stop slavery in the Sultan's territory.[14]

When Peters returned to Germany with his treaties, he presented them to the Society for endorsement. The Society agreed to request the German government for the protection of its interests in the territories covered by the treaties. The need to raise capital for the agricultural and economic development of the newly 'acquired' territory was a problem now confronting the Society. The Society's proposal for government protection was supported by Chancellor Otto von Bismarck. On 27 February 1885, Kaiser Wilhelm I signed a formal legal document (an Imperial Charter) to give 'Reich protection' to Germans and their interests in the negotiated territory. This was the first such instrument of protection ever given by the German government. The *Deutsch-Ostafrika Gesellschaft* [German East Africa Society] was established on the same day, with Peters as its chairman. This new society was later incorporated into a company. At the same time, Bismarck announced the creation of the German Protectorate of East Africa.[15]

CONSOLIDATION AND ADMINISTRATION OF GERMAN EAST AFRICA

The granting of protection to German interests by the German Government surprised the other European powers. Great Britain, in particular, was very suspicious of this move, as it was attempting to establish an interest or presence in the East African territory just west

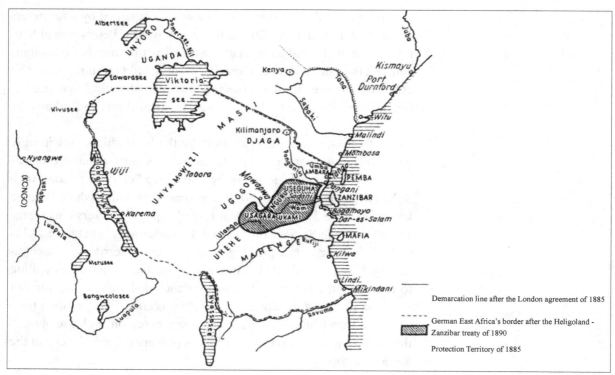

7. German Protectorate in 1885 and borders after various treaties between the European nations

of Zanzibar and already had traders and missionaries in that area. Britain urged the Sultan of Zanzibar to formally protest to Germany about the protection charter. However, neither the Sultan nor Britain had any claim over the interior regions covered by the 'Peters' treaties'. The German response to the Sultan's protest was to approach Zanzibar with a naval force and give the Sultan an ultimatum to withdraw any forces he had in the protected German territory. When the Germans saw how quickly the Sultan caved in to their demands, they saw an opportunity to make further territorial demands for the coastal strip (including the ports), which was still in the Sultan's ownership and control.[16]

The German East Africa Company undertook further expeditions in the interior to gain more territories through treaties. Treaties with local chiefs were concluded in many districts, including the Usambara and Pare Mountain ranges. This resulted in vast areas coming under the protection of the German Reich. However, as the German influence increased, opposition was starting to mount and hostilities towards Europeans intensified. A number of Germans lost their lives in the process.[17]

As these new territories came under German control the German East Africa Company was anxious to utilise and develop them. This attracted a number of geologists, zoologists, botanists and explorers. The company also developed agricultural research stations and appointed officials to administer the local areas. It was difficult to provide for the personal safety of these officials and other Germans, including missionaries, because only a few lightly armed protection personnel were available. The officials were also lightly armed. The Germans developed a system of strategic district administration centres [*Bezirksämter*] also known as *Bomas,* with district commissioners [*Bezirksamtmänner*] – two of these Bomas were located at Arusha and Moshi.[18]

In Germany the company was active in raising capital for its development work in East Africa. It gained the support of a number of leading capitalists, including Alfred Krupp, Karl von der Hendt and Eugen Langen.[19]

On the political front, the German Government became involved in discussions with Britain and France. Britain was concerned with the future control of the Sultan of Zanzibar's territory and also the future areas of influence of other nations in East Africa. In 1885 a joint commission with British, French and German representatives was established. The aim of this commission was to achieve agreement on the partitioning of East Africa and to set the borders for the areas to be administered by each country. The European countries (Britain, Germany and Portugal) also agreed on, and imposed, a blockade against the slave trade and the importation of military equipment from 2 December 1885.[20]

The company, in order to supply and develop the interior areas under its control, needed to have access to the ports along the coast. Peters therefore started negotiations with the Sultan of Zanzibar to secure these ports and the coastal strip for control by the German East Africa Company. Finally, after two years, agreement was reached and a treaty was signed on 24 April 1888 giving control of the coastal strip and, more importantly, of the ports to the Company for 50 years. The company immediately placed officials in strategic locations along the coast. Furthermore, the company was now able to control all trade, providing it with an income base through the imposition of import and export duties. Taxes were also imposed on the native population in the interior. However, the need for security and protection also increased substantially because of these additional measures. During this initial phase, the Company depended on the Sultan's forces for protection, which were often unreliable. Eventually, the coastal strip was purchased outright from the Sultan.[21]

During the mid 1880s resistance to the German presence started to increase with armed clashes and open hostilities. The native chiefs resented the imposition of taxes and having to provide labour; and the Arab traders, especially the slave traders, opposed German control of the ports and trade routes, as well as the taxes. Following serious uprisings in the ports of Tanga and Pangani, German warships were dispatched there with armed landing parties to restore order. With increasing intensity, more and more uprisings and rebellions occurred throughout the area under the control of the German East Africa Company. The armed officials, with virtually no support, struggled to contain outbreaks in their own areas where even missionaries were being attacked and slaughtered. It became impossible for the company to overcome this widespread unrest without further military support.[22]

8. Major Hermann von Wissmann, Reichskommissar for German East Africa

The company sought the help of the German government to regain control of several areas which had been lost and were now in the hands of native chiefs and Arab warlords. Chancellor Bismarck, using the terms of the anti-slavery agreement, sought and obtained the agreement of the German *Reichstag* [parliament] to undertake military intervention to occupy the East African coast, which was under the jurisdiction of the company's treaties. He appointed Major Hermann von Wissmann on 8 February 1888 as *Reichskommissar* [Government Commissioner] to combat the uprisings and regain the lost areas. Wissmann had a sound knowledge of Africa, having explored and twice crossed the African continent – in 1880 and again in 1887.[23]

In order to fulfil his mission, Wissmann established the *Schutztruppe*, a military Protection Force. This force comprised German officers and *askaris* [trained native soldiers]. He then planned a military campaign and requested appropriate transport and supply facilities from Germany. Wissmann and his troops took until 1892, often encountering fierce opposition, to gain full control and to suppress the largely Arab revolt.[24]

On 1 July 1890, Britain and Germany ratified a treaty known as the Heligoland-Zanzibar Treaty [*Helgoland-Sansibar-Vertrag*], which determined the borders for the disputed areas between British and German interests in East Africa. The treaty ceded regions of Uganda (territories for which Peters had signed treaties) to Britain; the islands of Zanzibar and Pemba and the mainland area north of the Umba River also came under British control; the mainland area south of the Umba River and a border taking in Mt Kilimanjaro and extending to Lake Victoria came under German control. The treaty divided Lake

CHAPTER ONE

Victoria across the middle and continued west to the border of the Belgian Congo Free State. Under the terms of the treaty, the British also agreed to allow Germany to control and acquire the coastal strip around Dar-es-Salaam and to transfer to Germany the island of Heligoland at the mouth of the Elbe River just off the coast of Germany. The treaty with England and the finalisation of borders by 'giving up' areas covered by treaties was harshly criticised by a number of figures in Germany. A Belgian-German agreement covered the partition of Lake Tanganyika along a north-south line.[25]

9. Stamp issued by the German Government for the East Africa Colony

On 1 January 1891, the German Protectorate of East Africa was declared a *Reichskolonie* [national colony]. Following this declaration, the German government reduced the German East Africa Company's role to a strictly economic one without any administrative and enforcement (protection) rights. These latter roles had already been curtailed during Wissmann's military operations. The German government reached a financial understanding with the company as it took over the administration of the territory. In March 1891, the *Schutztruppe* became an official Imperial force by law and a new commander, Captain Oskar von Zelewski, was appointed.[26]

10. German East Africa banknotes

In April 1891, the first German Governor of the colony, Julius von Soden, arrived in East Africa to take over the administration. Von Soden had previously been Governor of Cameroon, another German colony in West Africa. Dr Carl Peters was appointed Commissioner to oversee the introduction of law and order in the Kilimanjaro region. In 1895 after continuing reports about him of cruelty and violent attacks on the natives, the German government recalled him to Berlin. During this phase, the natives called him *Milkonowa Damu* [the man with blood on his hands].[27]

An early development during the administration by the German government was the establishment of an internal police force. Police officers were stationed at a number of district centres and protection troops were garrisoned at the *Bomas* throughout the new colony. The new government administration was based on the former administrative centres (districts). It built schools, hospitals and port facilities in quick succession and developed other infrastructure, such as roads and railways. Areas for agricultural purposes were opened up for European settlement, and settlers were encouraged to come to German East Africa.

In 1893 Dr Richard Hindorf brought sisal seeds from the Yucatan region of Mexico to German East Africa. Within a few years, large sisal plantations were established and sisal became a major export crop for the infant colony. Dr Hindorf was also the first German to start a coffee plantation in German East Africa.[28]

11. Dr Richard Hindorf – the first German to start a coffee plantation and who brought sisal plants to German East Africa

The building of two railway lines was important to open up the interior. The line between Dar-es-Salaam and Lake Tanganyika was surveyed in 1894, and construction started in 1906; the second line, in northern German East Africa, extended from Tanga to Moshi by 1911. These railway lines helped to increase trade and facilitated the development of new inland regions remote from the coastal plain and ports.[29]

Although the military had restored order within the colony, peace with the natives and Arab warlords had not been achieved. The ongoing land alienation, the introduction of labour policies and, in some instances, the harsh regime continued to be resented by the native population. From 1891 onwards revolts in the interior continued, there were armed clashes in western German East Africa, led by Chief Isike; with the Chagga tribes in the northern regions; and with the Gogo tribe in the central region. All-out war was waged by the German forces against Mkwawa, the leader of the Hede people who, with his followers, at one stage ambushed a German column and seized enough weapons to resist the Germans for three years. The main rebellion was suppressed in 1894 by a force led by Tom Prince, an English-born officer, serving with the German Protection Force. Mkwawa escaped capture and continued harassing the Germans until 1898 when he was finally cornered and shot himself. The most famous of all rebellions was the Maji Maji rebellion which was widespread and covered nearly a quarter of the colony. The rebellion and associated guerrilla warfare continued in the southern region of the colony until 1907.[30]

There were several positive outcomes from the rebellions in that natives were encouraged to grow cash crops and that an education program was introduced for the native population.[31]

By the end of the first decade of the 20th century the colony was experiencing growth and development. Exports of agricultural products such as sisal, rubber, coffee, skins and hides, cotton, copra, peanuts and beeswax to Germany were increasing and commercial businesses were established to cope with the influx of German immigrants and the development of the colony. Various missionaries had also established a strong foothold in the colony. The main Protestant missions were the *Bethel Mission*, the *Berliner Mission*, the *Brüdergemeinde* and the *Leipziger evangelische und lutheranische Mission*. The Catholic missions included *deutsche und schweizer Benediktiner von St Ottilien, deutsche und schweizer Kapuziner, deutsche und französische weise Väter, italienische Consolata-Missionare* and the *irische und holländische Mission vom Heiligen Geist*.[32]

Before World War I German East Africa covered approximately 950,000 square kilometres, an area far bigger than Germany itself; it was the largest of the German colonies. It had a diverse range of physical features – high snow-capped mountains and several mountain ranges, a fertile high plateau, vast plains in the west, a share of the large lakes of Africa and an Indian Ocean coastline of 500 kilometres with port facilities. There were few permanent rivers, the most notable being the Pangani, with the sources of three of Africa's largest rivers, the Zambesi, the Congo and the Nile defined by the features of the colony's geographical watershed. The colony had an abundance of flora and fauna. It was renowned for its African wildlife. The climate was tropical, with monsoonal rains in October to December (the short rainy season) and again in March to May (the long rainy season). The amount of precipitation and the extent of the rains varied; both were affected by the various geographical features in different parts of German East Africa.

THE GERMAN TEMPLER SETTLEMENTS IN THE HOLY LAND

OVERVIEW

As a prelude to the emigration of German settlers from Palestine to German East Africa in the pre-World War I years, a brief overview of the German Templers in Palestine is set out in this chapter.

The former German settlements in the Holy Land (Palestine) were established between 1869 and 1906. They resulted from a religious movement that began in the Kingdom of Württemberg in southern Germany in the mid 19th century.

The Temple Society was founded by Christoph Hoffmann (1815-1885), a lawyer's son, who – having studied theology – became a teacher and lecturer in Ludwigsburg, Württemberg. For a short time, he was a member of the first democratically elected German Federal Assembly in Frankfurt. He was a man devoted to God and religious

1. Christoph Hoffmann – founder and leader of the Temple Society

2. Georg Hardegg – a co-founder and director of the Temple Society who went with Hoffmann to the Holy Land

principles. He criticized the Church for not solving the social problems of the times and called for a new appreciation of the Scriptures, especially of the Old Testament prophets, which would point the way to how people should interact in Christian communities. He believed that the two principles of Christianity were love of God (an inner, personal belief expressing itself in worship, trust and obedience) and love of one's neighbour as of oneself. Hoffmann believed that God's spiritual kingdom on earth could be achieved by gathering 'God's People' in Jerusalem, as prophesied in Scripture, and by adhering to the above principles. The first group of Hoffmann's followers were therefore known as *Jerusalemsfreunde* [Friends of Jerusalem].[1]

In 1861, Hoffmann and his like-minded followers formed the *Deutscher Tempel* [Temple Society], at a meeting in Kirschenhardthof in southern Germany. Hoffmann was convinced that the Templers should start their work (forming Christian communities as a spiritual Temple) in the Holy Land as soon as possible.[2]

In 1868, Hoffmann and Georg David Hardegg (1812-1879), one of the founders of the Temple Society, left Germany to begin putting their plans into action at Haifa in the Holy Land.[3]

The Temple Society went about establishing their settlements – Haifa in 1869, Jaffa in 1869, Sarona in 1871 and Rephaim near Jerusalem in 1873. These were the original settlements of the Templers in the Holy Land. The settlements of Wilhelma and Betlehem (in the Galilee, not to be confused with Bethlehem, the birthplace of Jesus near Jerusalem) followed at a later stage in 1902 and 1906. The Waldheim settlement was founded by the German Protestant Community, the *Kirchlers,* with the support of the Berlin *Jerusalemverein* in 1907.[4]

The agricultural settlement of Sarona in particular, could be regarded in many ways as the first successful attempts by Europeans to start permanent agricultural enterprises in the Holy Land. During the late 19th and early 20th centuries, the Templers were a major force in the development of Palestine.[5]

The Templers' migration to the Holy Land was not a missionary venture and they did not try to convert the local inhabitants. The Templers believed that by setting examples in family living and community interaction with fellow human beings, they would be able to demonstrate true Christian ideals. Their lifestyle and their agricultural and industrial practices were admired by the local population.[6]

3. Kirschenhardthof today – where the Temple Society was founded in 1861

It should be noted that the Templers who emigrated to the Holy Land in the 19th century should not be confused with the Knights Templar of the Crusader period some 700 years earlier.

Virtually all the Templers who emigrated from Palestine to German East Africa came from the Sarona and Jaffa settlements. A brief overview of these settlements is shown below.

THE JAFFA SETTLEMENT

Immediately after their arrival in the Holy Land conflicting views surfaced between Hoffmann and Hardegg regarding the development of Templer settlements. Hoffmann's goal was a Templer settlement in Jerusalem, whereas Hardegg wanted to develop and concentrate on the infant Haifa settlement. As Hoffmann's relationship with Hardegg worsened, he decided to relocate to Jaffa when, in March 1869, he received and accepted a proposal to purchase several buildings from a former American missionary society, as well as a hotel and a large business and hospital building in the Old City of Jaffa. The Templers considered Jaffa, the port used by pilgrims on their way to

Jerusalem, as a good place to start a second settlement. The Prussian Crown Prince Friedrich Wilhelm visited this infant settlement in November 1869 and through him some financial support for the hospital was obtained. This enabled the Templers to continue to run the hospital not only for themselves, but also for the wider community.[7]

In the beginning, the economic conditions for the Jaffa Templer community were difficult. The settlers were dependent on trade and industry, especially tourism, with growing numbers of pilgrims travelling from Jaffa to Jerusalem. Work opportunities in the community were provided by a steam-driven flourmill, a sawmill and an olive press. Coach building and repair shops, construction and road works offered additional employment and business opportunities for the settlers (Theodor Sandel, a surveyor from the Templer community in Jaffa, had been appointed by the authorities to oversee the improvements to the Jaffa-Jerusalem road). Other businesses included a timber yard, a watchmaker, a saddlery, a joinery workshop, a smithy and a bakery.[8]

By the late 1880s conditions in the original Jaffa settlement had become very crowded. There was a lack of housing and no new land was available within the settlement's confines. Several families therefore

IN THE BEGINNING THE ECONOMIC CONDITIONS FOR THE JAFFA TEMPLER COMMUNITY WERE DIFFICULT

4, Hospital in the Jaffa settlement

purchased property approximately half a kilometre to the north of the Jaffa settlement. The settlers saw development opportunities in this area, especially as a railway was planned from Jaffa to Jerusalem. More and more settlers from Jaffa moved into this area which became known as Walhalla. The Wagner family, who had started a foundry, workshop and motorised pump business in the Old City of Jaffa in the early 1890s, built a new factory at Walhalla in 1901. Hugo Wieland established a factory in Walhalla for cement products that initially produced floor tiles and building blocks. In 1903 the factory was expanded to produce roof tiles and concrete pipes.[9]

By the end of the 19th century the Jaffa settlement's population was 320 inhabitants (234 Templers and 86 members of the German Protestant community). Trades and occupations included bakers, a brewer, a butcher, a wheelwright, hotel keepers, mechanics, merchants, a metal founder, a midwife, a painter, a pharmacist, physicians, a plasterer, a plumber, flourmill operators, restaurateurs, a tanner, teachers, vineyard owners and farmers. The settlement comprised 46 buildings and 30 outbuildings, 15*ha* of arable land, 32*ha* of vineyards and 8*ha* of orange groves. The wealth of the settlement was estimated at 2,059,500 *francs*.[10]

5. The German Templer settlement of Jaffa with church spire, bottom left of photograph

THE SARONA SETTLEMENT

6. Theodor Sandel – the surveyor from the Jaffa settlement

During 1870/71, as the Jaffa settlement grew, there was considerable pressure within the Templer community for a new settlement to be developed. Many of the new settlers in the Holy Land had come from a farming background and wanted the Temple Society to start an agricultural settlement.[11]

In August 1871, the Temple Society acquired approximately 60 hectares of land in the Plain of Saron, three to four kilometres north-east of the Jaffa settlement. Theodor Sandel surveyed the site and laid out a settlement right in the middle of that barren land. Sandel was the son of the Jaffa settlement's physician, Dr Gottlob David Sandel.[12] On 26 August 1871, most people from the Jaffa community and prospective settlers visited the proposed new settlement site and, after a short religious service, lots were drawn for the holdings.[13]

In October 1871, the new settlement was officially named Sarona and the foundation stones were laid for the first buildings .[14]

Sarona suffered extreme hardship during the early years of its existence when many settlers and their families perished. In the period 1871 to 1874 alone, 57 settlers died, mainly from malaria and related diseases. The death rate was higher in Sarona than in any other Templer settlement in the Holy Land and serious doubts were raised as to whether the settlement would continue.[15]

7 . The German Templer settlement of Sarona

Jaffa. Le Village de Sarona.

Jaffa. The Village of Sarona

8. View of the Sarona settlement

9. Main road from the south into the Sarona settlement approx. 1890

With much persistence and hard work, and with an unshakeable faith in what they were doing was ordained, the settlers gradually overcame their difficulties and, due to improvements in scientific and medical knowledge, especially in fighting malaria, the small settlement began to grow and consolidate. By the end of the 19th century, Sarona had overcome its initial hardships and had become a solid and flourishing community. Some Jewish immigrants regarded it as a model agricultural settlement, similar to what they should aspire to.[16]

By the end of the 19th century the population of the Sarona settlement was 243 (54 families of which only two were non-Templers). The settlement had a large co-operative winery; three wine stores with cellars; a producer of sparkling wine and liqueurs; a steam-driven flourmill; a restaurant; a general store; a pharmacy; a baker; a cooper; a blacksmith; bricklayers; a butcher; a carpenter; a wheelwright; a miller; a saddler; teachers; ten winegrowers and 20 farmers. The settlement comprised 42 buildings and 31 outbuildings. The settlers cultivated 300*ha* of arable land, 150*ha* of vineyards, 24*ha* of orange groves and one *ha* of olive groves. The wealth of the settlement was estimated to be 2,673,500 *francs*.[17]

FINANCIAL CONSTRAINTS FOR FURTHER SETTLEMENTS

During the 1890s, the Temple Society, although desirous of increasing the number of its settlements and expanding the existing ones, did not have the financial means to do so. Politically, the German Templers in Palestine were in a difficult situation. Even though the Imperial German Government was sympathetic to the Germans in the Holy Land and saw at first hand the achievements of the Templers, it did not want to upset nor jeopardise its relationship with Turkey. The political implications affected issues such as: questions of nationality, protection of German citizens, financial assistance, education, land ownership and trade relations between Germany and the Holy Land.[18]

As early as the 1870s, the Temple Society had made representations for funding assistance through the German Consulate to overcome its acute financial difficulties. As a result a small financial subsidy for schooling was received.[19]

The lobbying for financial assistance continued through the 1880s and 1890s. The Templers saw an opportunity to strengthen their case by showing Kaiser Wilhelm II their work and achievements first hand during his visit to the Holy Land in 1898. The prime purpose of the visit was to preside over the consecration ceremony of the Evangelical Church of the Redeemer in Jerusalem.[20]

The Kaiser visited the German Templer settlements and was impressed by what they had achieved. He praised the settlers for their work and for upholding German custom and culture and sent a telegram to the King of Württemberg, lauding the Swabian settlers' achievements in the Holy Land.[21]

10. Kaiser Wilhelm II visited the Holy Land in 1898

CHAPTER TWO

The financial concerns of the Germans (not only of the Templers, but also of other religious denominations) in the Holy Land were taken seriously, and resulted in a meeting being convened in Stuttgart to establish the German settlers' needs. This meeting was attended by representatives from the Temple Society.

A committee was formed which met in July 1899, at which time a limited liability company was set up to raise loan funds for the German settlers. An initial capital of 300,000 *marks* was planned. The funds were to be allocated by decision of the board of directors. The board was chaired by Carl, Prince of Urach, Count of Württemberg. The King of Württemberg, who showed an interest in the work of the Templers, supported the initiative.[22]

By early 1900 substantial funds had been subscribed to the company and, at a meeting of subscribers in May 1900, the *Gesellschaft zur Förderung der deutschen Ansiedlungen in Palästina* [Society for the Promotion of German Settlements in Palestine] was formed and a board of directors elected. In August and October 1900 the company advanced the Temple Society a 42-year loan of 80,000 *marks* at 4% interest.[23]

In 1902 the Temple Society used these funds to buy 801*ha* of land near Jaffa to establish a new agricultural settlement, which was named Wilhelma. A further purchase of land was possible near Haifa after the promotion society had provided another loan of 50,000 *marks* in 1906. 703*ha* were acquired in the Upper Galilee and the agricultural settlement of Betlehem was established.[24]

THE DEVELOPMENT OF A 'GATHERING OF THE PEOPLE OF GOD' COMMUNITY IN SOUTH AFRICA

The German Templers, even though they were in no way connected to this movement in Switzerland, took a considerable interest in the attempt by a small number of people from Herisau in Switzerland to develop a 'Gathering of the People of God' community in South Africa. The Temple Society published a number of articles in the *Süddeutsche Warte* about this group.

A religious movement started in Herisau in the Canton of Appenzell, Switzerland in the middle of the 19th century, about the same time as the Friends of Jerusalem was formed in Württemberg, Germany.

The members of this movement had very similar ideals to those of the Templers – they were very pious and deeply concerned about how Church dogma and State interference had destroyed the true meaning of the Holy Scriptures. They, too, believed that the Kingdom of God could be created on Earth in a community living together and supporting each other. They differed from the Templers in that they did not believe that the Kingdom of God had to be established in the Holy Land (Jerusalem). Similar to their Templer counterparts they encountered ridicule and abuse from members of the established church communities in Herisau.[25]

Their efforts to establish a settlement in South Africa in the 1860s mirrored the ventures of the Templers in the Holy Land. This is probably why the Templers took an interest in this group.

The Herisau group, consisting of 20 persons from poor farming and tradesmen's families, left their homes for South Africa in February 1868. Local community members and family members implored their loved ones not to leave. Their journey went via Holland to London, where they embarked on a ship to Cape Town, South Africa. On arrival, they were greeted by a few of their members who had previously moved there in 1860 to establish a community at Wellington on the outskirts of Cape Town.[26]

The Herisau group movement's hopes were short-lived and failed in 1869 mainly due to a lack of financial backing and the deceit and over-commitment of its leaders.[27]

INTEREST IN GERMAN EAST AFRICA GROWS 1896 TO 1907

A MISSIONARY FROM EAST AFRICA

In April 1851, Peter Martin Metzler, a missionary from the *Basler Pilgermission* [Basle Pilgrim Mission], went to the mission station near Mombassa to work with Missionary Krapf. There Metzler also met other missionaries, including Rebmann and Erhardt (see chapter 1). Shortly after his arrival, however, he became very ill and had to return to Europe in early 1852. In August 1853, the *Basler Pilgermission* sent Metzler to the Holy Land where he went to Jerusalem. During the next three years he worked in various locations before he was sent to Jaffa in March 1858, which coincided with the arrival of three members of the Friends of Jerusalem (later the Temple Society), who had come to the Holy Land on an exploratory and fact-finding tour for possible future settlement. They were Christoph Gottlob Hoffmann, Georg David Hardegg and Joseph Bubeck. Metzler and Hoffmann had met previously when Hoffmann was secretary of the Basle Pilgrim Mission in 1852/53. Metzler assisted these three Germans by procuring horses and an armed guard for their journey to Jerusalem.[1]

1. Peter Martin Metzler – the missionary who came from Africa to Palestine

Metzler continued his missionary and social work in Jaffa as well as being actively involved in the establishment of future Christian settlements and in running a shop and a steam-driven flourmill.[2]

In 1865 two Americans – George Washington Adams and Abraham MacKenzie – came to the Holy Land to establish a Christian community. After an exploratory tour of the Holy Land the Americans decided to start a citrus plantation near Jaffa. Before leaving the USA they had instructed an agent to buy some land. When the new settlers, 43 families, arrived from America in September 1866, no land had been purchased. They were, therefore, unable to build houses or start any farms. The prospective settlers lived in tents on the beach, where many of them became ill and died during the first few months. Metzler aided and cared for many of the sick. In early 1867 the settlers were able to acquire some land to build homes and slowly a small community developed. Their leader, Adams, however, was often intoxicated, leading the good life, whilst refusing to release the funds that had been forwarded to him from the United States for development and to assist the struggling settlers, who suffered hardship and hunger.[3]

By late 1867 the settlement project was a complete failure and most of the Americans returned to the United States. Metzler bought several of the houses from the American society. In 1868 he was able to purchase a number of other houses very cheaply as the settlement was finally abandoned. In 1869 Metzler received a request from Baron von Ustinov, for whom he had worked before, to come to Russia and work on the Ustinov estate. It was at this time that Hoffmann, Hardegg and members of the recently formed Temple Society had arrived to settle in the Holy Land. Metzler contacted the leaders of the Templer Society in Haifa and was able to negotiate the sale of the 'American settlement' to the Templers.[4]

Although the Templers knew and had ongoing contact with Metzler, who had spent only a short time in Africa, the period of this contact was well before the German colonisation of East Africa. Therefore no link to the future settlement in East Africa by Templers from Palestine can be attributed to Metzler.

CHAPTER THREE

THE TREIDEL SURVEYS IN EAST AFRICA

In 1908 Joseph Treidel (1876-1927), a Jewish surveyor from Haifa, undertook a short survey in East Africa.[5]

2. Josef Treidel – the Jewish surveyor who went to German East Africa

Treidel had studied at the *Landwirtschaftliche Fakultät* (Agricultural Faculty) at the Bonn University, and in 1898 graduated as a qualified surveyor and civil engineer. Soon afterwards he was contracted by the Jewish Colonization Association to serve as a civil engineer for projects in Palestine. Treidel arrived in Jaffa in late 1898. In conjunction with other agronomists he established the Technical Bureau for Agriculture and Development in Palestine. In 1905 he was employed by the Palestine Committee of the World Zionist Organization and the Jewish National Fund to prepare a detailed map of Palestine. He completed that task in 1911, but was also involved in buying land for Jewish rural settlements and in 1908 he was contracted to build the Kinnereth Lehrefarm (agricultural college).[6]

For his 1908 survey in East Africa Treidel invited Josef Wennagel from the Jaffa Templer community to join him. Wennagel had become friendly with Treidel through the building and construction work Wennagel was doing in the Holy Land. Little is known of the actual area that was surveyed in East Africa, except that it was probably a river valley. On his return after eight months absence, Wennagel was enthralled with what he had seen and experienced, especially the hunting he was able to do. Wennagel had not gone to Africa as a builder but as an assistant to Treidel. His reports may well have struck a chord with some of the young men in Sarona who were looking at opportunities to improve their lives and that of their families.[7]

3. Josef Wennagel went to Africa with Treidel in 1908

Although Wennagel spoke enthusiastically about Africa, he did not move there, but stayed on in the Holy Land where he married and raised a family. There is no evidence to show that the survey work done by Treidel was in the Mt Meru/Usa River region where the Templers from Palestine ultimately settled.

In 1910 Treidel undertook another survey in German East Africa. This survey involved a large irrigation project at the Gomba Farm, near Mtrawanda Swamp and from there to the Wuruni River. Treidel recommended the diversion of the Wuruni River into the Makomasi River and the development of an irrigation project at Gomba. Whilst in German East Africa Treidel was invited to participate in a major expedition of the Ruwu region but declined, probably because of other work commitments in Palestine.[8]

Of interest are Treidel's observations of conditions in German East Africa and a comparison with Palestine. He writes *"[...] from my observations I can clearly recommend the clearing of more bush country for the development of rubber plantations. These plantations require little ongoing maintenance and are yielding a very high return. I am convinced, on the basis of my calculations, that rubber plantations will be a worthwhile business even if the price of rubber falls by 50%. It is evident that this bush country is suitable for rubber plantations, because several neighbouring plantation owners, Gottmann and Rohde, have made a fortune from their plantations in just three years.*

In comparing African plantation work with that in Palestine, I am surprised how easy the work is here. Cheap and disciplined workers are readily available; valuable crops can easily be grown in the fertile soil; building material for houses and sheds is cheap; hunting provides good and cheap food for the farmer; safety concerns from natives is not an issue; a government that builds roads and railways and runs research stations, with a climate no worse than that in Palestine, and even better in large parts of the hinterland. There are also excellent opportunities for businessmen and tradesmen.

How difficult everything seems to be in Palestine, [...] business and trade is so complicated and the returns barely enough to provide a living ... "[9]

THE FIRST SETTLERS DEPART FOR AFRICA

In 1891 the German Government officially took over the control and administration of the newly declared colony of German East Africa. With protection provided by the German military, the colony became an attraction for new settlers, who were encouraged to immigrate with incentives, such as cheap land.

The first known Templer to go to German East Africa was Johannes Reinhardt, born 1857 in Oberkollwangen in the Black Forest, Germany. He was the son of the Templer Elder Philipp Reinhardt of Haifa, and had come to Palestine in late 1869. After his father's early death, Johannes left Palestine in 1874 and returned to Germany. In Hamburg he completed an apprenticeship as a merchant trader and thereafter found work in Berlin. After a brief time in the military, Johannes Reinhardt took up employment as a clerk with the newly created *Gesellschaft für deutsche Kolonisation* [Society for German Colonization].[10]

*4. Johannes Reinhardt (on left) – the first known
Templer to settle in German East Africa in 1890*

Reinhardt's first trip to Africa was during the Arab Revolt that had started in August 1888 after the Colonization Society had leased the coastal mainland areas from the Sultan of Zanzibar.

After another brief stay in Palestine, Johannes Reinhardt took up permanent residence in the new German East Africa colony in 1890. His knowledge of Arabic, which he had acquired during his youth in Palestine, proved very helpful in dealing with the largely Arabic-speaking population in the coastal region of German East Africa. In 1892, due to differences with Carl Peters, who had by then become Imperial Commissioner for the Kilimanjaro area, he terminated his contract with the Colonization Society and settled as merchant trader in Dar-es-Salaam. He exported rubber and ivory to Germany and operated as a sales agent for a German military and expedition outfitter, importing mainly farm gear, steam engines, weapons and ammunition.[11]

5. Ulrich and Caroline Reinhardt with their children Lydia and Gottlieb in German East Africa 1896

6. Ulrich Reinhardt and his wife Caroline in Beirut in the 1880's

7. Christof Reinhardt and his wife Margarethe in Jaffa 1894

8. Christof Reinhardt with his wife Margarethe and their son Philipp Georg in German East Africa in 1896

It is assumed that, stimulated by his letters and tales of African life, his brothers Christof and Ulrich Reinhardt also decided to leave Palestine towards the end of the 19th century, and settle in the new German colony.

Johannes Reinhardt purchased land for his brothers in Tanga and in the Usambara Mountains.

9. Ulrich Reinhardt's farm in the Usambara Mountains circa 1900

Ulrich Reinhardt with wife Caroline (née Besserer) and young children, son Gottlieb (7), and daughter Lydia (5), migrated to East Africa in September 1895. They returned to Jaffa, Palestine for the birth of their daughter, Anna, in 1897 and then went back to Africa.[12]

Christof Reinhardt and wife Margarethe (née Schaible) arrived in German East Africa with their infant daughter Anna (2) in 1896. Christof was a teacher by profession and settled in the port town of Tanga. Here he taught at the local German school and became its Principal. After his death in Tanga in 1908, his family remained in German East Africa, and widowed Margarethe opened a small trading post selling, amongst other things, wine from the Templer settlement of Sarona.[13]

Ulrich Reinhardt was a baker by trade and after a short stay with his brother Christof in Tanga he, with his wife and children, set off to the interior to establish a farm near Lushoto (Wilhelmstal) in the Usambara Mountains. This venture was an arduous one and his returns during the early years were poor. This led Ulrich Reinhardt to participate in gold exploration in the Uluguru Mountains in 1899 and

10. The school in Tanga where Christof Reinhardt taught and became principal

1900. However, before his endeavours became profitable, he contracted malaria and, despite ongoing quinine treatment, soon started suffering from blackwater fever, a manifestation of malaria. Severely ill he returned to Palestine in 1902. In March of that year he died at Jaffa and was buried in the Jaffa-Sarona cemetery.[14] After Ulrich Reinhardt's death his wife Caroline married Karl Friedrich Kaiser in 1904, who took over the Reinhardt bakery in Jaffa.

Johannes Reinhardt, the pioneer, probably died at about that time and nothing is known of him after 1900. He was buried in the Dar-es-Salaam cemetery.[15]

THE TEMPLER COUNCIL DID NOT TAKE UP THE OFFER AND NO NEW SETTLEMENT PLANS OUTSIDE PALESTINE WERE PURSUED

In 1896, the Chief Clerk of the German East Africa administration visited the Templers in Palestine to discuss possibilities of establishing settlements in German East Africa. He pointed out that the Templers would readily adapt to the climate in Africa and that the new colony was within easy reach of Palestine. The Templer Council did not take up the offer and no new settlement plans outside Palestine were pursued. As Sauer writes in 'The Holy Land Called': *"The leading men of the Temple Society could not overcome their grave doubts regarding settlement in Africa, because their thoughts and actions were still guided by the religious objective to build the spiritual temple in Palestine".[16]* This was despite the fact that the Temple Society had been negotiating with the British authorities since 1894 about purchasing land in Cyprus for the purpose of establishing further Templer settlements.[17]

The Templer leaders were also aware of the impending visit to the Holy Land by the German Kaiser, Wilhelm II and his wife, Kaiserin Augusta Victoria, in October 1898. They were hoping that this visit would result in new opportunities for settlement in the Holy Land.[18]

At the turn of the century, the Kopp family from Sarona emigrated to German East Africa: Johannes Christian Kopp, his wife Margarethe 'Luise' (née Edelmaier) and their children Johannes, Luise Katharina, Wilhelmine Karoline, Friedericke Christine, Martha Selma and Karl Gottlob. It is not known where they settled in the new colony. Karl Gottlob died of malaria in German East Africa in 1904.[19]

FACTORS INFLUENCING THE ESTABLISHMENT OF NEW SETTLEMENTS IN GERMAN EAST AFRICA

Despite the indifference displayed by the Templer Council, the vision of a Templer settlement in German East Africa remained alive among a group of young settlers in Sarona. From 1900 to 1908 this group, who had been born in Palestine during the 1880s, seriously began to consider a German East Africa venture.

The major factors in the deliberations of this group were the economic conditions in Sarona and the concerns about the future of younger settlers starting families of their own.[20]

The Sarona farmers owning land that had been acquired in earlier times were relatively well off in the early 20th century. However, the younger generation had little opportunity to buy land. In some cases, original family holdings had been split, often due to inheritance, into small allotments that were no longer economically viable. Farmers with enough land were able to generate good incomes, particularly when the orange groves became productive, but they were being burdened with constantly rising costs over which they had no control. For example, 25 farmers in Sarona, owning approximately 300 hectares of land between them, had to pay 40,000 *francs* in rates and taxes. These rates and taxes were subject to annual increases. Furthermore in 1908, the Turkish authorities had increased the tax on primary produce from 12.5% to 14%; only potatoes were exempt from this tax.[21]

Due to the mass immigration of Jews, particularly from Russia, as well as an increase in the Arab population, land prices had increased dramatically and strong competition was forthcoming from newly established Arab and Jewish agricultural ventures. In some cases, land prices around Sarona doubled within a few years (from 3,500 *francs* per hectare to 7,000 *francs*).[22] The increase in land values was not only confined to the Jaffa/Sarona region but occurred throughout Palestine. For example, near the Haifa settlement, land prices had increased fifteen to twenty-fold in the 25 years since the early 1880s.[23]

To overcome these difficulties, some of the settlers formed companies and raised capital to develop orange groves. The future of these companies was at risk because they were totally dependent on strong overseas markets and good orange prices.[24]

The Sarona settlement itself had limited freehold land and the Turkish authorities had prohibited the sale of land to Europeans. Because of land prices escalating dramatically, mainly due to the large-scale orange groves being started by Arabs and Jews, leasing or renting land for agricultural ventures close to Sarona had become uneconomical. There was some outlying land but it was of poor quality and yields were low. In addition, these outlying areas were expensive to run and were exposed to crop theft.[25]

LAND PRICES AROUND SARONA DOUBLED WITHIN A FEW YEARS

36

CHAPTER THREE

In the late 19th century land ownership in Palestine had been subjected to close scrutiny by the Turkish authorities. This had caused considerable unrest and uncertainty amongst the Templers as it raised doubts about the ownership of many land holdings. Finally in 1898, the Turkish Sultan issued an irade [decree] for title deeds to be granted to clarify land ownership.[26] Despite this irade many settlers were still uneasy about land ownership. The settlers believed that in Africa, with German authorities in charge, greater certainty of land ownership and protection of German citizens would prevail.

Another factor that had a strong bearing on the thoughts of the prospective Africa settlers was the feeling of personal insecurity affecting many Templers in Palestine at that time. This was most apparent in the newly established settlements of Wilhelma and Betlehem. In addition to a high level of theft, the settlers there had to cope with open hostility from Arab youths under the banner of the "Young Turk Movement".[27]

Templers and other Germans in the Holy Land were lobbying the German government for protection because their "nationality status" was unclear. However, due to the delicate political situation between the German and Turkish governments, little progress was made. It was not until 1913/14 that laws relating to German citizenship were enacted to clarify nationality issues for many Templers in the Holy Land.[28]

ARGUMENTS AGAINST SETTLEMENT IN GERMAN EAST AFRICA

The notion of new Templer settlements in German East Africa was at first not taken seriously by many settlers and by the Templer Council. However, as more and more people, especially in Jaffa and Sarona, showed interest in such a venture, countervailing views were expressed and published in the *Warte*. These 'anti-East Africa' views were of a religious, historical and economic nature.

Although the economic difficulties and uncertain future facing many young settlers was acknowledged, it was felt the situation was not as bad as first thought, especially with orange production likely to increase and wine production also likely to continue without any immediate local competition. It was argued that wherever agricultural enterprises were started capital was needed and the returns were not always guaranteed because prices would be influenced by many factors. Also, there were indications that some of the ownership

THE SETTLERS BELIEVED THAT IN AFRICA, WITH GERMAN AUTHORITIES IN CHARGE, GREATER CERTAINTY OF LAND OWNERSHIP AND PROTECTION OF GERMAN CITIZENS WOULD PREVAIL

THESE 'ANTI-EAST AFRICA' VIEWS WERE OF A RELIGIOUS, HISTORICAL AND ECONOMIC NATURE

restrictions imposed by the Turkish authorities on the property of Europeans might be eased.[29]

The uncertain future in German East Africa was raised as an issue. This arose after comments made by the Colonial Secretary of the German government, Bernhard Dernburg, in February 1908, before an Economic Estimates Committee of the German Parliament, which was debating the budget for the German East Africa colony. During the hearing, Dernburg said that he was looking forward to economic development as well as cultural advancement in German East Africa. Dernburg indicated that he regarded it as important that many fit and diligent Germans come to German East Africa, but he was unsure about whether they would be able to live and progress there; therefore, in the government's view, he was unable to recommend immigration. Such an admission showed, or so the opponents of the German East Africa venture claimed, that settlement in East Africa would be very difficult, if not impossible for Germans.[30]

THE OPPONENTS OF THE GERMAN EAST AFRICA VENTURE CLAIMED, THAT SETTLEMENT IN EAST AFRICA WOULD BE VERY DIFFICULT, IF NOT IMPOSSIBLE FOR GERMANS

In addition to the uncertainty aspect a number of other matters were put to the prospective settlers. These included that the success of the new ventures would rely heavily on the goodwill of the German Government and that the settlers should consider the cultural standard of the general population in Palestine, which was of a far higher order than whatever they would find in Africa. Furthermore, in Palestine there already existed orderly and respectable property and production conditions; suitable transport facilities; cheap labour and ready markets for agricultural products such as milk, oil, potatoes, vegetables, wine etc. Another advantage Palestine offered was that it did not have a *tsetse* fly problem and animals such as horses, mules and donkeys could be used for heavy work, whereas in Africa this would have to be done by human effort or with expensive imported machinery.[31]

On the historical side, some rather tenuous arguments were raised as reference was made to the 'unsuccessful' Germanic migrations [*Völkerwanderung*] to the South during the 4th, 5th and 6th centuries, including those to Italy, Spain and northern Africa. These Germanic tribes, it was alleged, were not defeated by the climatic conditions encountered, but by the unfamiliar cultures and customs of the host nations amongst whom they had to live as minorities. A comparison was also made with the Crusaders who, it was claimed, failed because they became 'infected' by and succumbed to the "corrupt and depraved oriental way of life".[32]

CHAPTER THREE

The most vocal opposition came from religious opinions. Religious arguments were raised to play on the minds of the prospective settlers and to create feelings of guilt. They virtually portrayed the pro-East Africa settlers as traitors and their attitude as deviant from the ideals of the Templers.[33] The question was posed: is the work of the Temple Society in Palestine of so little value (importance) that it may be abandoned in good conscience for imaginary benefits? Several articles in the *Warte* entitled *Palästina oder Deutsch Ostafrika?* [Palestine or German East Africa?] and *Palästina, nicht Deutsch Ostafrika* [Palestine, *not* German East Africa] clearly indicated that there was no alternative; there could be only one place – Palestine![34]

Dr Jonathan Hoffmann wrote in the *Warte* that: *"[...]the founders of the Temple Society did not have a migration goal for a surplus of Germans, but they searched for a place where it would be possible to be the guardians of and build the Kingdom of God [...], undisturbed by State or Church, in the form of community life. [...] This could only be achieved by a strong belief in God and a presumption that, despite all well intended or dire warnings, the experiment (venture) has proven itself. The reason, however, why Jerusalem and Palestine were chosen as the starting point for this success, lies partly in the known history of this city and this country, and on the other hand on past established hope and future significance for the development of mankind. No other place on earth, least of all German East Africa, can be compared to the history of Jerusalem and Palestine. [...] There is no other place on earth where the fulfilment of this venture of founding a community and "Volksleben" on pure original Christianity can be achieved, than in the well known circumstances of Jerusalem. Therefore, anyone who wishes to hold fast to the original ideals of the Templer movement would never leave this place and swap it for another, regardless of whether the real or perceived prospects are better.[...] Any thought of resettling from Palestine to German East Africa now, shows total disregard of the thoughts and beliefs that inspired the founding members of our settlements in this country. Any resettlement of Templer members from Palestine to German East Africa is therefore difficult to reconcile with the views of the Temple Society and the establishment of the Kingdom of God."* [35]

He indicated that his comments were not directed at, or applied to non-Templer Germans.

Further support was added to the religious argument by Paul Aberle in Jerusalem, who also appealed to the conscience of the prospective settlers. He quoted extracts from *Occident und Orient* as to the

---

RELIGIOUS ARGUMENTS WERE RAISED TO PLAY ON THE MINDS OF THE PROSPECTIVE SETTLERS AND TO CREATE FEELINGS OF GUILT

directions the Templer movement should take in the settlement of the Holy Land including *"[...] for the settlers in the Orient, the indispensable conviction must be that the work they are fulfilling for the highest interests of mankind is willed by God".[36]*

He outlined the difficult times and conditions the first settlers had to endure. The successful outcome that had been achieved through their unshakeable faith and because they were called by God to complete this work. The reasons now presented by representatives from German East Africa to go there were threadbare and showed little regard for the progress achieved in creating the Kingdom of God. The biggest danger Aberle foresaw was not the external difficulties being encountered, but rather that the next generations would lose their belief in God and the benefit of the good work done by the Templers. He appealed to the young men of the second and third Templer generations to continue the work of their forefathers and not be distracted from the ordained task of the Templers in the Holy Land.[37]

ARGUMENTS IN FAVOUR OF SETTLEMENT IN GERMAN EAST AFRICA

Undeterred by the anti-settlement views of many senior Templer figures the young pro-Africa settlers continued to present their case. Their arguments were built around a number of key factors of an economic, nationalistic and religious nature.

The prevailing economic issues are outlined above. The young settlers were desperate to secure a sound future for their families and saw very few – virtually none – opportunities in Palestine to do so. German East Africa, on the other hand, offered an opportunity to improve their economic well-being as well as securing a future for their families. Since the Templer Council and the local community could not offer much, they felt that they had little option but to leave and try their luck elsewhere. They had observed other settlers doing this before.

The pro-Africa settlers were German patriots at heart. No doubt the pride in the new German Reich having colonies and the satisfaction of being given a chance to participate in the development of such a colony had certain attractions. The prospective settlers from Palestine provided the German East Africa authorities with a number of advantages over settlers who came direct from Germany or Russia.

THE BIGGEST DANGER ABERLE FORESAW WAS NOT THE EXTERNAL DIFFICULTIES BEING ENCOUNTERED, BUT RATHER THAT THE NEXT GENERATIONS WOULD LOSE THEIR BELIEF IN GOD AND THE BENEFIT OF THE GOOD WORK DONE BY THE TEMPLERS

THE YOUNG SETTLERS WERE DESPERATE TO SECURE A SOUND FUTURE FOR THEIR FAMILIES AND SAW VERY FEW – VIRTUALLY NONE – OPPORTUNITIES IN PALESTINE TO DO SO

Firstly, they were educated and *kerndeutsch* [German to the core].

Secondly, they would adapt very quickly to the tropical climate as they had grown up in sub-tropical conditions.

Thirdly, they were used to hard work and had shown their capacity to do it.

Fourthly, they were familiar with workers who came from other cultures and spoke different languages.

Fifthly, many would be financially independent.

Sixthly, many would come with families, which would help to establish white (European) settlements, where inter-marriage with natives was most unlikely to occur.[38]

The prospective East Africa settlers did not envisage departure en masse from the Temple Society in Palestine, but rather that German East Africa would provide opportunities for 'surplus' settlers. It was thought that the departure of some 10 to 20 persons would not weaken the Templers' role in Palestine and that any such loss would be quickly and easily made up by other Templers from Russia or Germany.[39] It was acknowledged that the highlands of German East Africa were suitable for large-scale farming which was not possible within the small intensive farming communities of Palestine. The establishment of compact Templer settlements along the lines of the 'Palestine model' might therefore be more difficult to achieve.[40]

THE PRO-EAST AFRICA SETTLERS EXPRESSED THE OPINION THAT THE KINGDOM OF GOD COULD BE ESTABLISHED ANYWHERE IN THE WORLD, NOT ONLY IN THE HOLY LAND

Concerning the religious aspects, it was pointed out that the Temple Society *already* had communities outside of Palestine. Templer communities existed in the United States and in southern Russia, so why should German East Africa be such a problem for practising and spreading the Templer ideas? The pro-East Africa settlers expressed the opinion that the Kingdom of God could be established anywhere in the world, not only in the Holy Land. It was the *spirit* of the Templer ideals that was important, not the *location*. They did not regard emigration to German East Africa as opposing the Templer ideals but regarded it as an opportunity to expand the movement and had no intention of giving up their Templer belief.[41] They considered emigrating as a group as a way of preserving their Templer way of life. They had previously witnessed situations where individuals had left Palestine and usually were lost to the Temple Society. As early as 1908, the Templers debated how to cope with Jewish mass immigration and its impact on the Society's future in Palestine. There were fears of hard times ahead for the Temple Society. Articles written by Fritz Lorch (published in *Warte* No 8, 1908) and by a German cleric, Pastor Wilhelm Zeller, head of the Jaffa Protestant community, warned that the Jews were serious about settling in the Holy Land and predicted that the Germans would not be able to expand their activities in Palestine and that there was a real danger that they would eventually be driven out.[42]

In an article in the *Warte,* titled *Palästina und Deutsch-Ostafrika* [Palestine and German East Africa], Pastor L. Reinhardt reasoned that Templer settlements could exist in both Palestine and German East Africa. He argued that the move to German East Africa and the establishment of a Templer settlement there might well enhance the influence of the Templers on the German government. Reinhardt concedes that the loss of young families from the settlements in Palestine would cause some initial pain, however *"[...]this loss will be richly replaced when the German people are awakened out of their present indifference* [to the Temple Society – author]. *Nothing appears to me to be more appropriate than the establishment of a Templer Community in a German colony. As long as the work of the Templers is restricted to Palestine and non-German countries, it will stay outside the main interests of the German people.[...] A far more significant view of the Templer movement would emerge if it were to participate in a colonial venture."* Reinhardt concludes that not only would the German East African colonial authorities recognise and probably promote the Templer cause, but the German Parliament and the German People would also be more likely to become aware of the Templers' achievements. Furthermore, the difficult beginning and hard work in Palestine would become far better known and more recognised than the Templer founders could ever have imagined.[43]

THE YOUNG SETTLERS PURSUE THEIR GOAL

Undaunted by the ongoing debate and the pressures applied by the opponents of the German East Africa venture to stop the emigration, the young Templers of Jaffa and Sarona went about their goal of founding a settlement in German East Africa.

Karl Knoll from Sarona, a young settler who was born in 1876, became the leading advocate for the group that planned to emigrate to German East Africa. To avoid starting in unfavourable conditions, the group decided to send a representative to German East Africa to assess various locations for the best and most appropriate areas

THE MOVE TO GERMAN EAST AFRICA AND THE ESTABLISHMENT OF A TEMPLER SETTLEMENT THERE MIGHT WELL ENHANCE THE INFLUENCE OF THE TEMPLERS ON THE GERMAN GOVERNMENT

CHAPTER THREE

for settlement. The group contacted and negotiated with the German Consul, Walter Helmut Roessler, in Jaffa. Roessler had previously served in Zanzibar and Mombassa and was familiar with the conditions there. He supported the group of settlers and the concept of sending representatives to explore the settlement options in German East Africa. He arranged for a grant of 1,000 *marks* for this purpose through the German government's Settlement Commission in Berlin. He was also able to arrange, through the German Foreign Office in Berlin, for the German East Africa Line to provide a 50% reduction in travel costs for a representative from Palestine to visit German East Africa.[44]

Before sending a representative to German East Africa, the group of prospective settlers arranged for a meeting with the Consul. The group invited the leaders of the Temple Society to attend this meeting. The Temple Society President, Christoph Hoffmann II, and Gottlob Paulus from Wilhelma attended, but advised that they would do so only as observers. This was another clear indication that the Temple Society did not wish to participate in, or give support to this venture. At a meeting in early 1907, Karl Knoll and Paul Ernst Egger were elected as representatives of the pro-Africa settlers to go on an exploratory fact-finding tour to German East Africa.[45]

CHAPTER FOUR

THE 1907 FACT-FINDING TOUR TO GERMAN EAST AFRICA

THE KNOLL AND EGGER TOUR

This tour was crucial as to whether any settlements were possible, not only for the Templers, but also for other Germans living in Palestine. The aim of the tour was to establish what type of land was available, what crop types could be cultivated, what animal husbandry could be undertaken, what returns could be expected and what living conditions would be like. More importantly, if settlement was attractive, in which region or district of this vast colony should the settlers go to start their new lives. In other words, the tour was to provide a comprehensive report on settlement prospects in German East Africa.

On 16 July 1907, Karl Knoll left Jaffa by ship to commence the exploratory tour. Paul Ernst Egger, due to work commitments, was unable to leave on that date, but followed a short time later. On 19 July 1907 Knoll boarded the German Africa Line Steamship *Feldmarschall* in Port Said for German East Africa. The route went via the Suez Canal to Suez, through the Red Sea with temperatures as high as 48°C , to Aden, then on to Mombassa (which was in the British Colony of East Africa, or Kenya), before finally arriving in Tanga, one of the main ports of German East Africa, on 2 August 1907 – a voyage of 18 days.[1]

1. Karl Knoll

Knoll was fortunate, because Colonial Secretary Bernhard Dernburg from the German Government and his staff were on board, as well as 150 relief troops for the Protection Force in German East Africa. Knoll was able to arrange a meeting with Dernburg and was well received and treated in a friendly manner. Dernburg was aware of the difficulties with the Turkish authorities in Palestine and was particularly interested in the economic circumstances of the Templers, that is, in their agricultural work and in how they marketed their produce. He gave Knoll his opinion and promised that he would speak to the Governor of German East Africa, His Excellency Baron Georg Albrecht von Rechenberg, about the venture. He indicated that they would meet again. Von Rechenberg was the first civilian Governor of German East Africa (1906-1912).[2]

On board ship Knoll met five Russian-German families, who were planning to settle in the Moshi district of the Usambara Region, not far from Arusha. Other southern 'Russian' families had already settled in that region. This group had been organised by Admiral Strauch, leader of the Colonial Society's Settlement Committee in Berlin. What surprised Knoll was that this group's travel costs were paid for by the Committee; they were provided with all the agricultural equipment, clothes, footwear and household utensils at no cost to themselves. They were to be met by an agent in Tanga, who would provide free travel by railway and ox-drawn wagons to their final destination. In addition, the Committee paid for temporary housing, as well as for six months of living expenses and a year's wages for up to ten workers.[3]

2. Christof Reinhardt's house in Tanga circa 1905

On arrival in Tanga, Knoll visited Christof Reinhardt who had migrated from Jaffa to German East Africa in 1896. Reinhardt was pleased to meet someone from Palestine and welcomed Knoll as his guest.[4]

REINHARDT WAS PLEASED TO MEET SOMEONE FROM PALESTINE AND WELCOMED KNOLL AS HIS GUEST

During his few days in Tanga, Knoll met with the Tanga District Commissioner Noessel to arrange for a personal guide for his planned visit to the German agricultural research station at Oramani in the Usambara high country. Knoll left Tanga for the interior on 5 August 1907.[5]

By this time in the colony's development the German Government had started to build railway lines from the coast to the inland. One line was to be over 1,000 km long, from Dar-es-Salaam to Uniamwesi, and another line was planned from Tanga through the Usambara region to the Mt Meru and Mt Kilimanjaro districts and on to the eastern shores of Lake Victoria.[6]

The latter line, although still under construction, extended inland for approximately 120 kilometres as far as Mombo and was used by Knoll to travel to Kiuhui, where he picked up his guide. Knoll described the extent of land clearing and cultivation, which had already occurred along the railway line in the coastal plains west of Tanga. Large commercial sisal and rubber plantations had been established, although vast areas where still uncleared.[7]

THE EAST USAMBARA REGION

In Kiuhui, Knoll met Mr Feilke the head of the Prince Albrecht Plantation. During discussions with him, it was agreed that Knoll should continue his journey by rail to Niussi, from where the journey to Oramani would be less strenuous, because the ascent into the high country would not be as steep. Whilst in Niussi, the guide assigned to Knoll disappeared, and Knoll had to organise new assistants to help him with his further travels. He managed to get two porters with the help of the local officials. His problem was that he could not speak Swahili. Despite this, he set off on foot from Niussi to Oramani with his two porters. They finally reached Oramani after five and a half hours of strenuous walking, which took them up steep paths into the magnificent country of the East Usambara Mountains, and past a sawmill, where timber was being cut into planks.[8]

At the Oramani research station Knoll met with a senior scientist, Professor Albrecht Wilhelm Philipp Zimmermann (1860-1931). The professor was most hospitable and showed Knoll various research

3. Albrecht Wilhelm Philipp Zimmermann - a leading German botanist in German East Africa

47

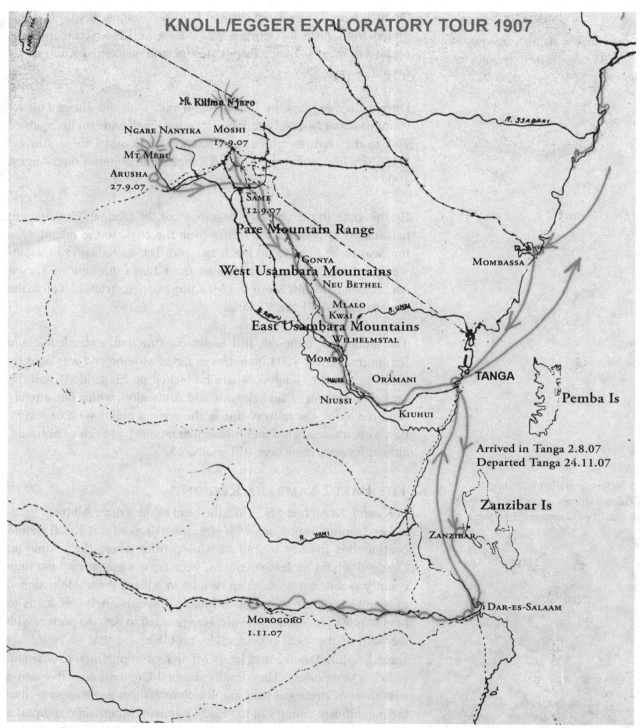

KNOLL/EGGER EXPLORATORY TOUR 1907

Mt. Kilima Njaro

NGARE NANYIKA   MOSHI
                 17.9.07

MT MERU

ARUSHA
27.9.07

SAME
12.9.07

Pare Mountain Range

GONYA

West Usambara Mountains
        NEU BETHEL

MLALO
KWAI
East Usambara Mountains
    WILHELMSTAL

MOMBO

MAURA   ORAMANI

NIUSSI

KIUHUI

R. SSABARI

MOMBASSA

TANGA

Pemba Is

Arrived in Tanga 2.8.07
Departed Tanga 24.11.07

Zanzibar Is

ZANZIBAR

MOROGORO
1.11.07

DAR-ES-SALAAM

4. Map –showing the route of the Knoll/Egger fact-finding tour projects, including latex extraction and the utilisation of banana leaf fibre. Knoll was introduced to the head of the research station, Councillor Franz Ludwig Stuhlmann (1863-1928), who warmly welcomed him and inquired about his background and intentions. He also indicated that he would help Knoll to meet other officials in the colony's interior. He was unable to give Knoll any relevant advice as to the likely return of agricultural production, because the research was still in its infancy. It was suggested to Knoll that rubber, sisal, coffee and cotton should be considered as possible commercial crops, as well as sesame, maize, wheat and tobacco. He met with several other researchers and was shown the station's plantations of coffee, tea, rubber and sisal as well as its research with indigenous plants used to extract medicinal compounds and poisons. Research was also being carried out on a variety of trees planted – conifers, casuarinas, cypress, camphor and good timber producing trees – including a variety of local and European fruit trees.[9]

THE WEST USAMBARA REGION

After spending several days at Oramani, Knoll returned to Nuissi where he caught the train to Mombo, the end of the railway line. Mombo is situated at the foot of the West Usambara Ranges, where several German families had settled and the German government had established yet another research station.[10]

5. Typical native porter

From Mombo, Knoll and his porters proceeded on foot to Wilhelmstal (known as Roschodo to the natives). Wilhelmstal was in the high country of the mountain range. Although a road had been constructed, Knoll followed the trails crisscrossing the country. They were very steep at times. The country, studded with granite outcrops, was lightly timbered. Dense forest was found at higher altitudes. The mountain range rose steeply from the surrounding plains. On the way to Wilhelmstal, Knoll met and stayed with a German settler, Mr Hedde, who had started growing vegetables, as well as establishing a coffee plantation. Later, Hedde helped Knoll to devise a travel plan for his further exploration of the West Usambara region.[11]

Wilhelmstal was a small town with government administration facilities and a military depot, situated in a narrow river valley. The water from the river was used to irrigate the farms in the area. Brickworks had been established there, and all the European houses, as well as the barracks, the administration centre and the hotel were built of brick with painted corrugated tin roofs. Knoll met with the District Administrator von Gross and discussed settlement opportunities in the western Usambara region and the possibility of joining

6. View of Usambara Mountain Range

an exploratory fact-finding tour that Colonial Secretary Dernburg was undertaking in the region. From Wilhelmstal, Knoll visited several religious missions to gain a better understanding of agricultural production in the area. He did all his travelling on foot, often walking for five hours a day. The mountainous country with its steep valleys and numerous rivers had few roads.[12]

He continued his journey into the West Usambara region, stopping and discussing settlement prospects with plantation owners as he went. Near Bumbuli, he stayed on a large coffee plantation owned by Captain Peter von Prince and his wife, and managed by a Mr Richards. Captain von Prince had established several other coffee plantations in German East Africa and was employing up to 8,000 workers on his properties. He had established all the plantations from virgin country. The plantation Knoll visited was beautifully laid out in the high country, surrounded by dense forest.[13]

Knoll continued to Konkeital where he met more settlers who grew coffee as well as vegetables and grain crops (rye). He was impressed that vegetables could be grown in this valley all year round.[14] On he went, through Gare to Kwamkusse, where he viewed cattle farms, market gardens and a sawmill that cut boards to make cases (boxes), which were used to transport the vegetables from Kwamkusse to Wilhelmstal, and from there to the railhead at Mombo.[15]

HE DID ALL HIS TRAVELLING ON FOOT, OFTEN WALKING FOR FIVE HOURS A DAY

7. Dense forest at higher altitudes in the mountains

From Kwamkusse he went to Kwai, which is 1,400 metres above sea level, where he wanted to meet a Bavarian settler, Mr Ellich. Ellich was not only a farmer and leaseholder in this area but was also an astute businessman with a number of other interests. He had been in Africa for nearly twenty years and had served as an officer with the Protection Force of German East Africa for a number of years. On Ellich's farm Knoll was shown a horse stud (at this altitude there was no tsetse fly problem); the rearing and fattening of pigs (the piggery contained between 200 to 300 pigs) and the production of ham and other smoked smallgoods, which were sold throughout the colony (Ellich smoked and tinned his own products on site). He had started a dairy cow breeding program by crossing European bulls with Barmah (zebu) cows (this program had resulted in a substantial increase in milk production) and some poultry was also kept. In order to protect his beef cattle and dairy herd from disease, a sharpshooter was employed to immediately kill feral animals or stray cattle entering Ellich's property. In horticulture, Knoll was provided with details of potato growing and yields: 300 to 400 *zentner* [a *zentner* is similar to a hundredweight, or 50 kilograms] of potatoes per hectare were not uncommon. In good seasons two crops per year were possible. Rye, barley, *Runkelrüben* [mangel-wurzels] and Egyptian clover were successfully grown; many European vegetables, including peas and beans were grown the whole year round if irrigation was available. Ellich advised Knoll that, in his view, people from southern Germany with a farming background were the most suitable settlers for the development of the colony. Furthermore, he considered that the Kilimanjaro/Meru region would be the most appropriate area to start new enterprises. He was critical of the government's slow progress in extending the railway, because he believed the railway was vital to further development.[16]

On leaving Kwai, Knoll continued on foot to Mlalo, through the so-called Kwangbuguland. This area was undulating open country, good for cattle grazing, but also very dry. Knoll regarded this area as unsuitable for settlement, because of the lack of water; it was too far from the planned railway line and, because of the cool climate at high altitude, the possibilities for plantations would be limited. At Hohenfriedberg near Mlalo, the Leipziger Missionaries had established several mission stations. Knoll was made to feel welcome there and stayed several days with Pastor Wohlrab and Pastor Bove. The view from this high area in the West Usambara Mountains is said to stretch into the savannah as far as the Kenyan border.[17]

ELLICH ADVISED KNOLL THAT, IN HIS VIEW, PEOPLE FROM SOUTHERN GERMANY WITH A FARMING BACKGROUND WERE THE MOST SUITABLE SETTLERS FOR THE DEVELOPMENT OF THE COLONY

8. Rugged terrain in the Usambara Mountains

Pastor Bove lent Knoll his donkey for him to ride to an outlying farm that had only recently been started by a German farmer from Natal in South Africa. En route, Knoll saw banana, sugar cane, bean and rubber plantations. Corn was grown mainly by the natives. Beekeeping and honey production was another small industry. After riding many hours, he finally arrived at the farm of the Reiches. This family had left South Africa after the Boer War because of the poor economic conditions prevailing in Natal. Reiche had started planting *Gerber* [tanning] acacias. These trees grew to a height of ten metres and were usually cut down after six years. The bark of the tree contains 30% tanning resin, which sold for high prices in Europe. The timber was hard and durable, ideally suitable for making wheel-spokes and axe handles. Reiche told Knoll that he had planted these trees in South Africa and that he had made good money from them. The Reiches were also experimenting by growing various South African fruit varieties, and had brought some angora goats with them for breeding. Reiche explained to Knoll that because of the economic hardships the Boers were experiencing, many of them were now migrating to German East Africa and settling near Mt Meru to breed merino sheep and horses.[18]

When Knoll returned to Hohenfriedberg, he was informed that Colonial Secretary Dernburg had changed his travel plans and would not be going to the Kilimanjaro area via Wilhelmstal. Knoll decided to return to Wilhelmstal and from there plan his journey westwards to the Kilimanjaro region.

On returning to Wilhelmstal, he received news from Paul Egger (the other representative from the Jaffa settlement in Palestine), who had now arrived in German East Africa and was in Tanga. Egger suggested that they should continue their fact-finding tour in the Kilimanjaro/Meru area and enquired what supplies were needed for this purpose. In addition to general provisions, a tent and two camp beds were acquired and transported to Mombo with the assistance of Christof Reinhardt. Egger was able to arrange transport – on ox-drawn wagons – with several Boer families, who were trekking to the Kilimanjaro region.[19]

The observations of the West Usambara ranges in Knoll's summary are interesting. He noted the rugged terrain, with steep valleys, fast flowing rivers, rocky outcrops and few level areas; the temperatures were quite cool and no malaria existed at the higher altitudes. He noted that the natives were not used to work and were generally lazy, because they lived in an environment with an adequate food supply. He refered to the natives as *"[...] accomplishing relatively little themselves, however, with proper encouragement and supervision they could be made to work [...] but a view amongst the European settlers was that they (the Europeans) lose their authority and status if they do too much of the work themselves [...].* To overcome this work difficulty, the German authorities introduced measures whereby every able-bodied native male had to work at least ten days a month (for which they were paid) and that the time worked would be recorded on a 'work card'. If he did not work voluntarily, he would be forced by the authorities to do compulsory work. The missionaries in the area supported this work requirement and started training the natives in various trades and skills. Another problem encountered by settlers in this region was the damage caused to crops by birds, monkeys and wild pigs.[20]

THE KILIMANJARO AND MERU REGION

Knoll went from Wilhelmstal back to Mombo, where he met up with Egger. In Mombo they joined several Boer families (some of whom

9. Typical native huts and banana plantation

had trekked from South Africa), who were going further inland. A German officer was also there on his way to the Kilimanjaro/Meru area, as well as Ulrich and Maragete Trappe who would later be neighbours of the Blaich family.

On 4 September 1907 they started their journey to the Kilimanjaro/Meru region. Their belongings had been packed onto the heavily laden Boer wagons, each of which was pulled by eight oxen. Progress

10. Traditional method of crushing corn

was very slow as these cumbersome wagons were extremely difficult to manoeuvre over the unmade tracks and across country - there just were no roads! The wagons had to be propped up several times to prevent them from toppling over. Sometimes they became bogged when streams and rivers had to be crossed. Knoll and Egger often walked next to the wagons as riding on them was an uncomfortable experience: not only because the ride was bumpy, but also because the oxen stirred up all the dust. The trip took them along the base of the West Usambara Ranges and then they turned west and continued between the Pare Ranges and the Pangani River. As lions abounded in this open plains country, the oxen had to be tethered to the wagons every night. Due to the very slow progress, the food supplies Knoll and Egger had brought with them from Mombo began to dwindle and they were fortunate to get some food – chickens, eggs, goat's milk, cornflour and bananas – in the native villages. The food was often in short supply because the workers building the new roads and telegraph line were buying it as well.[21]

On 12 September they reached Same, the border town between the districts of Wilhelmstal and Moshi. The climate at Same was pleasant and large wheat fields were observed by Knoll and Egger. Knoll considered Same as a possible settlement area, especially because the railway line was to pass there.[22]

They travelled further to the west on foot, coming across a German who was shipping wildlife in crates and cages to Germany. For the last part of their journey they travelled on the wagon of a German settler who was going in the same direction. From the western side of the Pare Ranges, they could clearly see Mt Meru and snow-capped

AS LIONS ABOUNDED IN THIS OPEN PLAINS COUNTRY, THE OXEN HAD TO BE TETHERED TO THE WAGONS EVERY NIGHT

11. Mt Kilimanjaro

Mt Kilimanjaro, the highest mountain in Africa. On 17 September 1907 they reached Moshi which was a district centre with a police station. Knoll describes Moshi as a neatly set out town with good wide streets and an impressive *Boma* [fort or district office] at the end of the main road.[23]

On arrival they went to the District Office and were welcomed by District Officer Metner. He provided Knoll and Egger with detailed maps of the region and told them he was very interested and would support a Templer settlement in the Mt Meru district and suggested the Maji-Tschai River area as being suitable. His reason for suggesting the Mt Meru district was that the foothills of Kilimanjaro had already attracted many European settlers, including Italians and Greeks, who had started coffee plantations, and most of the good land was already being farmed.[24] Metner was critical of the lack of facilities to transport agricultural products from the interior to the coast and, vice versa, for bringing supplies inland. Transporting goods by porters to the rail head at Mombo had become expensive and was inefficient. The settlers in the region were lobbying the German authorities hard to speed up the extension of the railway to Arusha and to the shores of Lake Victoria. Although construction work had commenced for a road it would be twelve months before this would be completed. Another suggestion put forward by the local settlers was for the construction of a narrow gauge railway for freight.[25]

Whilst in Moshi, Metner wrote to the District Officer in Arusha requesting him to arrange for ten porters and an *askari* (native soldier serving with the German Protection Troops) to meet Knoll and Egger in Ngare-Nanyika, which was the destination of the Boers with whom Knoll and Egger were travelling.[26]

On their journey to Ngare-Nanyika, they passed many coffee plantations mainly owned by Greeks. There were very few German settlers in this district. Knoll noted the abundance of wildlife in the area: rhinoceros, elephants, herds with hundreds of springboks (described by Knoll as being like large flocks of sheep), many other types of antelopes, herds of zebras, as well as ostriches. Finally, after 19 days travel with the Boers, they arrived at Ngare-Nanyika where a Boer settlement had been established. Ngare-Nanyika was on the northern slopes of Mt Meru. Here the Boers had established cattle farms, ran horse studs and breeding programs with imported merino sheep. The cattle were allowed to graze during the day but at night were kept in corrals with three-metre high walls made from very thorny

TRANSPORTING GOODS BY PORTERS TO THE RAIL HEAD AT MOMBO HAD BECOME EXPENSIVE AND WAS INEFFICIENT

12. Countryside near Ngare Nanyika

acacia branches to protect them from attacks by lions. The Boers had planted wheat, corn, vegetables and fruit trees for their own consumption. For meat the Boers hunted antelopes. A few farmers were experimenting with ostrich farming.[27]

Shortly after Knoll and Egger's arrival in Ngare-Nanyika, the porters and the askari arrived from Arusha. On 25 September 1907 they set off on foot for the Arusha district, which is on the south side of Mt Meru. Mt Meru, similar to Mt Kilimanjaro, is a freestanding mountain and an extinct volcano. Mt Meru is approximately 5,000 metres high with good rainfall on the southern and eastern slopes and jungle-like vegetation in the higher regions. At altitudes of 1,200 – 1,400 metres above sea level the land was partly covered with scrub interspersed by grassy plains. After two days of solid walking they reached Arusha, a small town with a military garrison and a district administration office. They were met and welcomed by District Officer Zenke who was most helpful. He discussed with them the district and suggested the area around the Maji-Tschai River as a possible

13. Mt Meru

settlement area. Zenke provided a soldier and porters and his own hunting boy to help them with orientation.[28]

Again, on foot, they set off from Arusha on an unmade road in an easterly direction. The country through which they trudged alternated between grassy savannah and plain type country with bushy vegetation. They noted several mountain streams which they had to cross before they turned north approximately 20 kilometres from Arusha. Here they came upon a small Russian-German settlement where they met up with Captain August Leue[29], one of the German officials in Arusha, and Lieutenant Trappe and his wife, who were already known to them from Mombo. There they set up their camp and next morning Knoll and Egger, a few porters and the boy went to explore the surrounding countryside and the headwaters of the Maji-Tschai River. For this trip they armed themselves with rifles, pistols and axes against possible attacks by wildlife, rhinoceros in particular. They climbed the eastern slopes through jungle vegetation and thickets looking for the source of the river. The going was very difficult and often they had to use the tracks made by elephants or rhinoceros. Streams were flowing in the gullies but their banks were usually swampy and covered with reeds. They were concerned about

14. Undulating country near Mt Meru

15. Open plains east of Arusha

attacks by rhinoceros, because they found fresh tracks and droppings more than once. Several elephants were encountered but these turned away from the human intruders. Finally they came to the Maji-Tschai River. The name of the river literally means 'tea water' (Maji = water Tshai = tea), because the colour of the water is similar to that of milky tea. The water derives its colour from the 'tanning acacias' that grew in the area. The water was drinkable but had a distinct plant flavour. They observed the area from several small rises before returning to their camp late that night.[30]

Next day they explored an area traversed by the Usa River to the west of their campsite. The Usa flowed throughout the year with crystal-clear, fast running water. The land between the Usa and Maji-Tschai rivers was relatively flat and was covered with bush and the

16. Native children

60

occasional thorny acacia tree. Knoll and Egger noted that the soil was of a volcanic nature and of a dark grey colour; they considered that it should not be too difficult to plough and cultivate. They were impressed by the land between these two rivers just east of Arusha. Several Russian-Germans had settled in the region, but during discussions with German officials they were told that these settlers, who had come from the Caucasus Region in southern Russia, were largely illiterate, and the only thing German about them was that they still spoke German. They were said to be slow learners, unable to adapt to the area and constantly complaining about anything and everything. The Russian settlers had planted small areas of wheat – with encouraging yields – as well as potatoes, vegetables and melons.[31]

Before leaving Arusha, Captain Leue told Knoll and Egger that he strongly supported their settlement plans in the area. He indicated that he would arrange for tents from the Settlement Committee, build temporary houses for the new settlers and plough some land for them. Furthermore, he would be an advocate for the settlers and recommend their plans to the Settlement Committee and ask the German authorities to advise the German Consul in Jaffa of developments. He would also recommend that the land between the two rivers be made available for settlement and held on a temporary basis for the Templers from Palestine.[32]

RETURN TO TANGA

Knoll and Egger left Arusha for Moshi which they reached after two days of steady walking. In this region they observed much wildlife and shot several antelopes for meat for their porters and the accompanying askaris and boy servant. At Moshi they were given new porters and an askari to accompany them to Same, which was on the boundary of the local district. From Same they headed back into the Usambara Mountains. They went through several native villages and met some village elders from whom they were able to get fresh food. In Gonia (a small native settlement), they changed their porters, but only after Knoll showed the local chief the official travel permit he had received from the German authorities in Wilhelmstal. They continued along the slopes of the mountains meeting several missionaries at Kiuhui and at the *Neu-Bethel* Leipziger Mission. They ascended into the higher reaches of the mountains to meet with Pastor Doering and his wife who were both very interested in Palestine. They stayed and rested with the Doerings for a short while. Doering lent them his donkey to explore the surrounding forested country where many cedars had been felled for timber. Two Germans had built a cable train to get the timber out. The German authorities had granted permits for timber cutting on condition that the cleared areas be replanted.[33]

THE JOURNEY FROM MOSHI TO TANGA TOOK THEM TWELVE DAYS, INCLUDING THEIR REST DAY

On 18 October 1907 they reached Wilhelmstal again and from there they walked most of the night to catch the morning train from Mombo back to Tanga. The journey from Moshi to Tanga took them twelve days, including their rest day. The distance from Arusha to Tanga is 350 kilometres.

On 22 October 1907 they watched the celebrations of 'Her Imperial Majesty's [*Kaiserin*] Birthday in Tanga. These celebrations included native dancing, brass bands playing, speeches and various games. The entire population – natives, Indians, Arabs and Europeans – all participated in the festivities. Both Knoll and Egger were pleased to receive some mail, which had been sent to Christof Reinhardt, with news from Palestine – they had been away for three months![34]

DAR-ES-SALAAM AND THE MOROGORO REGION

After three days in Tanga, Knoll and Egger set off once more to explore the Morogoro area inland from Dar-es-Salaam. They went by steamship to Dar-es-Salaam, after having stopped briefly at Zanzibar.

They were most impressed by the harbour at Dar-es-Salaam with its sandy beaches, palm tree lined boulevards and two German warships,

17. A herd of giraffes

Seeadler and *Bussard*, lying at anchor. The ships were used to patrol and protect the coast of German East Africa. In Dar-es-Salaam, Knoll and Egger met with the Governor of German East Africa, His Excellency Georg Albrecht von Rechenberg who, after lengthy discussion, approved their plans and suggested that the northern district of German East Africa would be the most suitable area for settlement. Von Rechenberg gave an assurance that he would discuss the matter with the Commissioner of the Northern District, Baron von Palmen.[35]

From Dar-es-Salaam, they took the train for the 210-kilometre trip to Morogoro. The trip took them through coconut plantations and, further inland, through savannah and timbered country. Near the Rufu River the area was suitable for cotton and rice cultivation. The railway line was good until they reached Girengeri, but from there to Morogoro, the track had only recently been laid and was still unstable. Knoll describes this part of the train trip like being rocked about in a yacht![36]

AFTER A STRENUOUS CLIMB THEY REACHED THE SITE WHERE A GERMAN COMPANY WAS QUARRYING MICA

In Morogoro, Knoll and Egger met an acquaintance from Jaffa (only referred to as Mr B. in Knoll's report) who had established a company here with a Mr Stollofsky. Stollofsky was Acting District Officer at the time. Mr B. took Knoll and Egger into the mountains near Morogoro. After a strenuous climb they reached the site where a German company was quarrying mica. The next day they inspected a rubber plantation, which was owned by Traun, Stuerken and Devers, a German company where Mr B. was employed as a supervisor. A small number of other settlers had also started rubber plantations in the dark red fertile soil of this area.[37]

RETURNING TO PALESTINE

After two days in Morogoro Knoll and Egger returned to Tanga, where Knoll and Egger were unable to get berths on the regular passenger ship because all places had been booked. They had to wait three weeks before they were able to secure a place on the German steamer *Feldmarschall* for their return trip to Port Said. During their three weeks in Tanga, Egger spent some time in Amani.

After leaving Tanga on 24 November 1907 they arrived in Port Said on 6 December 1907. Unfortunately, their return to Palestine was further delayed as they were advised that due to quarantine restrictions, ships were bypassing Jaffa and passengers had to disembark in Beirut. The ship they wanted to go on for the next leg of their homeward journey was delayed by twelve days, so they could not leave Port Said until 18 December. Although, in the meantime, the quarantine restrictions for Jaffa had been lifted a severe storm now prevented their landing at Jaffa, and they had to go on to Haifa before they could set foot in Palestine again. From there they went by horse-drawn wagon to Sarona to meet their loved ones again on 21 December 1907.

The Knoll/Egger exploratory tour had taken over five months.[38]

SUMMARY AND CONCLUSIONS OF KNOLL'S REPORT

The report written by Karl Knoll is a very detailed description of what he and Egger observed and encountered. The report and its findings were crucial to the settlers in Palestine who were contemplating to go to German East Africa to start a new life there. In order to provide proper details, the paragraphs below are a full translation of the summary of Knoll's findings.

"Overall Impressions and Prospects for Settlement

Of the various districts we journeyed through, I believe the Meru district is the most suitable for a settlement. The Meru district is approximately 250 kilometres from Mombo which is the railhead at present. When the railway is extended through to the Meru area, travel time from there to the coast will be one day. Without the railway, the area is at present rather remote and somewhat difficult for settlement. However, we were assured that the railway would be extended. The German parliament is expected to give its approval for this work. When the railway line to the southern side of Mt Kilimanjaro is constructed across the Pangani River and on to Arusha, the whole area will benefit. In the event of the railway line not being fully extended, the establishment costs and transport expenses will be higher but, on the other hand, other advantages prevail to offset these costs. I am aware of the high prices charged in Tanga for vegetables – carrots, eggs, poultry, meat, flour, tinned food and alcoholic liquor. Possibilities also exist for rubber, coffee, sisal, sesame production.

A scheme (plan) for the commencement of a settlement is not included as no large scale model settlement has been established for agricultural purposes [In the areas they visited – author], *however, I will attempt to describe the conditions and possibilities there.*

The climate is attractive because the area under consideration is 1200-1400 metres above sea level – the temperature does not fall below 0°C or exceed 27°C. The health situation, according to the

Russian-German settlers and a German Army Medical Officer I spoke to, is described as good and virtually malaria free. The Russian-Germans, who have been living in the area for nearly a year, reported no sickness, whereas many of those that returned to Tanga suffered from high fever.

The rainy season is from March to June and another short rainy period occurs in November. The best time for prospective settlers to arrive in the Meru district would be July or August so that the necessary preparatory work (building and soil preparation) is completed before the wet season.

The soil in the district between the Usa and Maji-Tschai rivers, approximately three to eight kilometres east of the Russian-German settlement, is dark grey and volcanic, with prolific grass and bush vegetation. This area is currently being reserved for us by Captain Leue. The two rivers are approximately four to five kilometres apart and water from these could be used to irrigate large areas. The water flow could also be harnessed for flourmills, sawmills and possibly for the generation of electricity for power and lighting. Towards Arusha, the soil is a reddish brown colour and of good quality.

18. Typical native mud hut

Buildings can be constructed from stone or from kiln-fired or air-dried bricks. Suitable clay for this can be found and there is plenty of timber for burning. Lime (stone) is found in the steppe. The timber would have to be logged and cut in the nearby forests and, when the railway line is built, it could be brought in by rail. Although the forests are owned by the government, the local forester in Arusha informed us that trees were allowed to be logged for building purposes. The job of felling and cutting beams and planks is done by natives with handsaws. I see no need to comment on the suitability and quality of African timbers. There is a shortage of roof covering material, the grass thatched roofs are good but need replacing every few years. Once the railway line is built, corrugated iron decking will come into use.

Each native worker is paid three rupees (5 francs) per month and the native Meru people, if treated and guided properly, work well.

The land, some of which has been assigned to the Settlement Committee for settlement purposes, will be made available to settlers on the same conditions as Government land. In order to prevent speculation, the land is initially leased at a very low rate of one-fifth rupee per year per hectare, and once the land is productive, the amount of land a settler will then be allowed to purchase is doubled. For example, if 10 hectares are made productive, a settler can purchase 20 hectares, or if 50 hectares are made productive, another 100 hectares may be purchased. This applies not only to cultivated land but also to grazing land. The purchase price is two to five rupees per hectare and a settler can initially have a purchase right for up to 200 hectares. If a settler can demonstrate that he is able to manage more land, he qualifies for the purchase of additional land.[39]

The European vegetable and grain varieties do well there, but I believe the grains from Palestine would do even better, because they have shorter growing periods and the climatic conditions of Palestine are similar to those of the higher country of German East Africa. The hot sirocco winds of Palestine, which often adversely affect crops, do not occur there. Clover and other stockfeed plants, as far as they may be necessary, should do very well there, besides there is sufficient grazing fodder available all year round for the stock. What garden vegetables one needs for ones own personal use should readily be able to be grown after the initial six months. Settlers should cultivate crops or rear animals that can readily be sold to provide them with a cash income to cover their expenses. The crops should also be able to withstand lengthy transport times. Flour, poultry, eggs, etc will find a ready market, and potatoes which can nearly be planted all year round should also sell well. These products are sold at the coast at exceptionally high prices. Furthermore, plantation owners, whose workers often come from far away districts, are obliged to give their workers either rice or corn. The owners prefer to buy corn, which is far cheaper than rice. At the same time, settlers should experiment with growing sesame, tobacco, cotton, rubber, sisal and acacias. Coffee, wherever it can be planted, cultivated and irrigated, will produce a very high return. Maybe vineyards could also be established. A German in Arusha had a very good crop of grapes last year. A distillery may also be viable as bananas, sugar cane, corn and potatoes are easy to obtain and any spirits produced would readily be bought by the Europeans. Alcohol is not permitted to be sold to the natives. Many European as well as tropical fruit varieties can be planted there.

Cattle and pigs may be reared, especially with the abundant grazing conditions. One would have to be on the lookout for cattle plague and protect the stock with the assistance of the local district authorities. The tsetse fly is not found at these altitudes. The tsetse fly's bite (sting) is deadly for horses, donkeys and cattle. Fortunately, it will only fly short distances and is only found in certain places such as in Mombo and in parts of the Kilimanjaro foothills. The Boers know exactly where these areas are and will only travel through them at night. As soon as the railway line to Meru is completed, the exposure of cattle and horses to tsetse fly attack during transit will be eliminated. Sheep, horse, donkey and poultry husbandry should also be profitable. Horses, in particular, as well as oxen are necessary for intensive agriculture; imported breeding bulls are necessary to improve the local herds.

An individual can see from the above that a large settlement is needed, so that the community can assist each other and have the means to jointly purchase equipment and machinery. A general store is required from where the settlers can buy what they need so that the profits from sales remain within the community. The necessary tradesmen should also be in the community. The government will provide a teacher. To cover the resettlement costs, capital in the order of 5 - 10 thousand franks is required. Settlers will have no government expenses other than a house tax, which ranges from 10 – 30 rupees depending on the size of the house.

Anyone who wishes to obtain more details should contact the Government offices in Dar-es-Salaam or the Information Office for Emigrants, Berlin, W9, Schellingstr. 4, for the brochure "Information for settlers in the Moshi District".

Initially, some damage by wildlife should be expected. Some wildlife is attracted by cultivated farming areas, however, some animal species are protected and details which wildlife may be shot should be checked out with the authorities. Food for wildlife is naturally plentiful and therefore damage to farms should be minimal.

The natives of northern German East Africa are peaceful and cowardly. I travelled unarmed and never felt threatened. A large closed community would be a deterrent against any unlikely uprising. As mentioned before, the natives are cowardly and have become accustomed to the strict rule of the German authorities.

No-one is able to give a guarantee as to the success or otherwise of a new settlement. I will leave that to each individual to decide. I am, however, of the view that our people from Palestine would be the best suited pioneers for that area, the climatic conditions are similar to

what we are already used to, our people have experience with different forms of agriculture and will therefore farm much more intensely than the Boers or the Russian-Germans.
Karl Knoll''[40]

This report was published in the *Warte* in early 1908. Individual Templers could now consider their resettlement opportunities in German East Africa in more detail and make a reasoned judgement of the conditions there.

19. Passport issued in Jaffa, Palestine to Johann Albert Blankertz, his wife Dorothea and daughter Hulda in order to allow them to travel to German East Africa

THE SETTLEMENT YEARS
1908 TO 1914

THE IMPACT OF THE FACT-FINDING TOUR

The findings of the Knoll/Egger exploratory trip created considerable interest amongst many settlers in Sarona and Jaffa and confirmed that resettlement to German East Africa offered opportunities for themselves and their families. Several settlers prepared to sell their properties to go to German East Africa.

As it became apparent that some families were going to emigrate, the anti-East Africa voices in the Temple Society, although still not condoning such a new settlement, began to be more conciliatory. For example, in a *Sprechsaal* [open forum] in mid 1908, which focussed on German East Africa and the settlement history of the Templers in the Holy Land, A. Fast concludes, *"We would do well by giving Karl Knoll, the so-called emissary of German East Africa, our blessing for a settlement there. He, and those who go with him, will remain united with us in spirit and spread the word of the Templers to the wider world without having to disown the belief of his forefathers or sever his ties to the settlements here. We hope that he maintains his belief and faith in God's might and guidance, and above all, his love to others, which he will need to cope with the difficulties that will surely have to be faced on resettlement."* [1]

Dr Jonathan Hoffmann also tempered his vitriolic attacks on the pro-German East Africa settlers. Following the *Sprechsaal* referred to above he wrote, *"No matter what finally befalls Mr Knoll and his thoughts for a settlement in German East Africa, I want to be the last to oppose such a venture. I would be very happy if the settlement succeeded. For me, however, the founding of the Kingdom of God in such a settlement has no more meaning than a settlement in Brazil or Kansas. I believe that it is far more significant to establish God's Kingdom in Palestine if we believe at all in the establishment of his Kingdom on earth."* [2]

THE SETTLERS DEPART FOR GERMAN EAST AFRICA

In 1909, the first settlers since the Knoll/Egger fact-finding tour left Sarona and Jaffa for German East Africa. The settlers' journey took them from Jaffa to Suez, from where they would take a ship of the *Deutsch-Ostafrika Linie* to either Mombassa in British East Africa (Kenya), or Tanga in German East Africa. This first part of the journey took approximately two weeks. From Mombassa they would take a train, on the Mombassa to Nairobi railway line, to Voi; or alternatively from Tanga to as far as the northern railway line extended in German East Africa. The last part of the journey was on ox-drawn wagons or by walking next to the wagon. General Maland (who had been a General with the Boers in South Africa) and Georg Korntheuer, a German living in Moshi, arranged for ox-drawn wagons for new settlers arriving in Voi or at the German railhead and transporting them to the districts around Mt Kilimanjaro and Mt Meru, where they wanted to settle. The time from disembarking at Tanga until they reached the area for settlement would take another 10 to 14 days

THE LAST PART OF THE JOURNEY WAS ON OX-DRAWN WAGONS OR BY WALKING NEXT TO THE WAGON

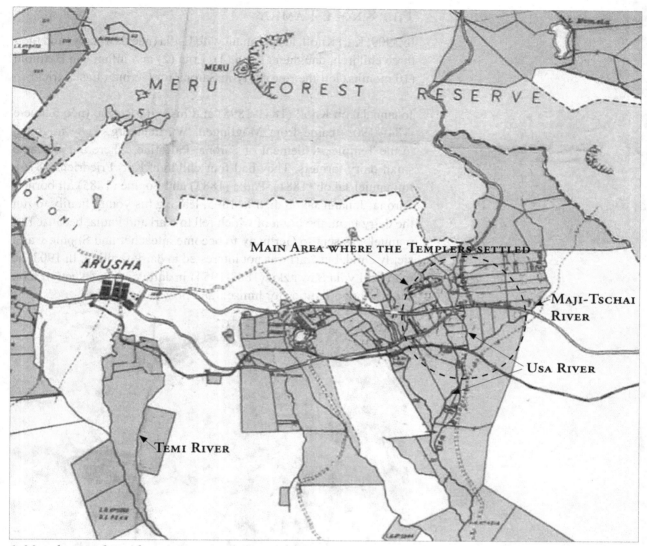

*1. Map showing the settlement area
east of Arusha*

– a total travel time of approximately four weeks. Korntheuer was able to arrange supplies for the settlers as well.[3]

During 1909 several prospective settlers went from Sarona to see for themselves what German East Africa had to offer. For example, Gottlieb Glenk and young Gotthilf Blaich both went and returned in the same year.[4]

Emigration to East Africa started in earnest in 1909/10. During the research for this book, reports from individual families and of their journey to German East Africa were found. These reports give insight into the experiences and conditions encountered by these settlers as they travelled to their new destination. Below are descriptions of the travel experiences of several families.

The Knoll Family

In 1909, Karl Knoll, his pregnant wife Lydia (née Sawatzky) and their three children, daughters Rosa (4), Erna (2) and infant son Berthold (10 months) left their property in Sarona for German East Africa.

Johann Jakob Knoll (1841-1895) and his wife Rosine (née Schuele -1845-1903) came from Möglingen, Württemberg. They migrated to the Templer settlement of Sarona, Palestine, where they became small dairy farmers. They had four children, Karl Friedrich (1876), Immanuel Jakob (1881), Paula (1883) and Sophie (1885) all born in Sarona. Johann Jakob died in 1895, leaving his young family to run the dairy farm, the brunt of which fell to Karl and Paula, because Immanuel was sent to Germany to become a teacher and Sophie was a sickly child, but Karl was not interested in dairy farming. In 1903, he married Lydia Sawatzky (1883-1954) in Jaffa and was keen to look for new opportunities for himself and his young family.[5]

2. Karl and Lydia Knoll with daughters Rosa and Erna and son Berthold circa 1908

3. A primitive wooden bridge on the track to the settlement area

THE KNOLLS WERE THE FIRST TEMPLER FAMILY TO SETTLE IN THE MT MERU/ARUSHA AREA AND A NUMBER OF FAMILIES STAYED WITH THE KNOLLS WHEN THEY FIRST ARRIVED IN THE REGION

The family travelled to the Arusha/Meru area where Knoll had previously met Captain Leue. Knoll's intention was to establish a coffee plantation there. The Knolls were the first Templer family to settle in the Mt Meru/Arusha area and a number of families stayed with the Knolls when they first arrived in the region. Whilst in Africa, Lydia suffered badly from malaria, which eventually forced the family's return to Palestine. The Knolls went through the joy of having two sons, Kurt (1909) and Erich (1911) born in German East Africa, but they also went through the heartbreak of losing a son, Berthold, in 1910.[6] The loss of a child is an ordeal for parents at any time, but in their remote location without any support services – no doctor was available to pronounce the child dead – they were totally dependent on themselves. In order to determine that their son had died, Karl Knoll, in the presence of and much to the anguish of his wife, made an incision on their son's cheek to see what fluid would flow from the cut. As the fluid was not red, but pale yellow, he knew that the plasma serum had separated from the blood and their son was dead.[7]

THE BLAICH FAMILY

Young Gotthilf Blaich was so impressed with what he had seen that he convinced his parents to go to German East Africa.[8]

THE BLAICHS ORIGINALLY LIVED IN A GRASS AND MUD HUT LIKE THE NATIVES UNTIL KARL BLAICH, A BUILDER AND A NEPHEW OF JAKOB BLAICH, CAME AND BUILT A STONE HOUSE

In 1870, Johann Georg Blaich, of Neuweiler in the Black Forest, Württemberg, and his family were the first Blaichs to come to the Haifa Templer settlement. In 1872, his brother, Sebastian Blaich (1822-1874), his wife Margaretha (née Seeger – 1831-1913), and sons Jakob (1859-1943), Sebastian (junior) (1857-1937) and Johann Georg (1851-1910), also migrated to the Holy Land. Sebastian (senior) died in 1874, and his son Jakob went to the Templer settlement of Sarona, where he found work in the winery. In 1887, he married Maria Rosine Glenk (1864-1947) and they had seven children, Frieda (1888), Margarethe (1890), Gotthilf (1892), Bernhard (1895), Paula (1897), Fritz (1900) and Otto (1904).[9]

In early 1910 the Blaich family, Jakob, his wife Marie and their children left Palestine. The family packed all their possessions into large wooden boxes and went from Jaffa to Suez, then by ship to Mombassa in Kenya. From there they caught the train to Voi and then continued their journey by ox-drawn wagon to the Usa River near Arusha. In order to help start their farm, they had brought with them farming equipment and seeds, like maize, wheat and various vegetable seeds. Coffee seeds were bought in Kenya. The Blaichs originally lived in a grass and mud hut like the natives until Karl Blaich, a builder and a nephew of Jakob Blaich, came and built a stone house.[10]

4. The Blaich Family –
(back row l to r) Frieda, Paula , Fritz,,
Bernhard, Margarethe (front row)
Marie, Otto, Jakob

CHAPTER FIVE

THE GLENK FAMILY

Gottlieb Glenk also came back impressed with what he had seen and with the potential of the Mt Meru area.

Johann Bernhard Glenk (1834-1901) and his wife Barbara (née Meiser) (1844-1917) migrated from Standorf, Württemberg to Sarona in 1875. They came with five children from Johann's first marriage and Friedrich (1874) from his second marriage. Another four children were born in Sarona, Ernst (1876), Pauline (1880), Karl (1881) and Gottlieb (1885). Johann was a cooper by trade and worked initially for the winery at Sarona before buying some land and starting an orange plantation. Gottlieb worked with his father in Sarona. In 1907 he married Pauline (Paula) Katherina Knoll, who was born in 1883 and had lived all her life in Sarona.[11]

In November 1909, Gottlieb and Paula and their infant son Ewald (nine months) emigrated to German East Africa. They sold part of their property and leased the remainder. Carl Kuebler, Gottlieb's brother-in-law, went with the Glenks to look at the proposed settlement area in German East Africa. The Glenks travelled by ship to Tanga, where Mr Schmidt, a former teacher in Sarona, welcomed

5 Ewald Glenk (1909) just before leaving for German East Africa

6. Gottlieb and Paula Glenk circa 1908

THE GLENKS TOOK WITH THEM FARMING IMPLE-
MENTS, SEEDS AND A MARE IN FOAL

them. He worked in a business that printed items in Swahili. They also visited Mrs Margarethe Reinhardt, who was now widowed and ran a small business in Tanga. The Glenks took with them farming implements, seeds and a mare in foal. The mare, for which a special hood had been made to protect her from tsetse flies, was taken immediately from Mombassa to Arusha so that the time spent in the tsetse fly infested area was kept to an absolute minimum. Karl Knoll and Hans Groezinger, who had come to German East Africa the year before, had ridden on horseback from the Meru area to Tanga especially to meet the Glenks. After welcoming the new arrivals they took the mare and quickly rode back to their homes and out of the tsetse fly-infested areas.[12]

The Glenks took the train to Same, where the 'official' railway line ended. The line did in fact continue for another 25 kilometres, but the track could only be used by the construction crews or by passengers with special permission, and even then only if the passengers signed an indemnity in case of an accident. The Glenks had originally planned to travel the last part of their journey from Same to the Meru district by bullock-drawn Boer wagon. Unfortunately no wagon was available, so the only alternative was to walk. The Same District Officer, Mr Eschenberger helped to arrange for one askari and fifteen porters to escort the Glenks and carry their possessions to the Mt Meru district. The Glenks had brought with them a small one-horse buggy which they assembled and greased. The next day

7. Mt Meru near Arusha

it was loaded with most of their possessions and, after a permit was issued to continue the journey by train, the buggy with all its freight was loaded onto the train. The porters and the askari travelled on the same railway carriage as the buggy. The Glenks, Carl Kuebler and several others – a few young men from Germany, a Mr Trapper from the USA and an elderly gentleman, Mr Boss, sat on another open railway carriage. After a very bumpy two-hour trip, the train stopped and everybody had to get off – the end of the line had been reached. Everything had to be unloaded and the journey continued on foot. The porters were placed along the shafts of the buggy so that they could pull it. Paula Glenk, nursing her infant son, Ewald, rode on the buggy and everyone else walked. They travelled as a group. Travel was slow and the daytime temperatures were high. By 10 o'clock in the morning, the porters were exhausted, particularly in the hilly country near the Pare Ranges. They usually rested until three o'clock in the afternoon and travelled again until nightfall. After another rest, they started again at midnight to walk in the cool of the night. The journey was not without danger; lions were seen several times and a cheetah was shot. During the night one adult male always kept watch by a campfire.[13]

After several days they reached the small town of Bujuni, where they rested for a day and replenished some of their supplies. The snow-covered peak of Mt Kilimanjaro was clearly visible from here. After another long day's walk, during which they met several Boer

TRAVEL WAS SLOW AND THE DAYTIME TEM-PERATURES WERE HIGH. BY 10 O'CLOCK IN THE MORNING, THE PORTERS WERE EXHAUSTED

farmers with their wagons, delivering farm produce to the railhead, they finally reached the vicinity of Moshi. Several members of the group wanted to go to Moshi, whilst others, including the Glenks, continued westwards towards Arusha. The road took them over some very narrow, primitive bridges. The group was very pleased when a horseman approached whom they recognised as a good friend from Palestine, Samuel Sickinger. He was employed by a large plantation owner in the district. The next day, as they slowly left Kilimanjaro behind them, they could see Mt Meru beckoning. They saw an ox-drawn wagon approaching and were over-joyed when this turned out to be driven by Karl and Gotthilf Blaich, who had come out to meet them. Gladly they loaded everything onto the Boer wagon and were able to 'enjoy' the last ten kilometres of their journey riding on a wagon instead of walking. Tired, but happy, they finally reached their destination and, after 28 days, were among friends and relatives again.[14]

THE ROAD TOOK THEM OVER SOME VERY NAR-ROW, PRIMITIVE BRIDGES

8. Postcard sent from Tanga by Carl Kuebler to Jon Weller in Sarona, 1909

CHAPTER FIVE

THE BAUER FAMILY[15]

The Bauers of Jaffa emigrated to German East Africa in the late summer of 1910.

Gottlieb Immanuel Bauer (1881-1927) was the son of Gottlieb Bauer of Höfen near Winnenden, who had come to Palestine in 1869 and settled in Bethlehem where he started a shoemaking business. His father had served at a young age as a missionary for the *Basel Mission* in Nubia and the *Bahr al-Ghazel* of the southern Sudan. There he had campaigned against the Arab slave trade and promoted the Christian faith amongst freed slaves. After his early death due to malaria in 1881, his son, Gottlieb Immanuel, was raised in the Syrian Orphanage at Jerusalem. When he was 16, his stepfather and guardian, G. Strecker, enabled him to return to his father's native Württemberg to serve an apprenticeship as a mechanic in Stuttgart-Feuerbach. After its completion and a further two years as a designer with Daimler Motor Works in Bad Cannstatt, and as a mechanic with Bosch in Stuttgart, Gottlieb returned to Palestine in 1902. In Jaffa he took up employment as a master mechanic in the Wagner Bros. engineering and foundry works and, as a trained well-driller, dug numerous wells in the coastal plain between Gaza, Sarona and Ramleh. His ability to find water by divining rod was a gift that would prove quite beneficial later on in East Africa.

His ability to find water by divining rod was a gift that would prove quite beneficial later on in East Africa

In 1906 he married Pauline Elise Blankertz (born 1886) - daughter of the well-to-do Jaffa brewer Johann Albert Blankertz. The marriage had been planned by the young couple as early as 1904, but Pauline Elise's parents would not hear of it until she had proved herself ready for marriage by gaining sufficient housekeeping skills. Therefore in 1905, she was sent to Alexandria in Egypt, where she worked for a year as housekeeper in the family of the merchant Fritz Hess, a business partner of her father. Here she cared for the merchant's elderly mother and for his eleven-year-old son Rudolf, who later became Hitler's deputy.[16]

Due to the continuing unrest in Palestine at the beginning of the 20th century and concern about their own security and future, Bauer decided to settle in German East Africa together with Philipp Albert Blankertz, his brother-in-law and fellow mechanic at the Wagner foundry. They were encouraged by the reports from their uncle Christof Reinhardt, who had settled in Tanga in 1896, and from the German Consul in Jaffa, who told them of the availability of vast tracts of land at very reasonable prices.[17]

9. Gottlieb Bauer and Elise Blankertz in Jaffa 1906

THE SETTLEMENT YEARS 1908 TO 1914

CHAPTER FIVE

The Bauers were the first to leave and the Blankertz family planned to follow a year later, when Gottlieb had successfully established himself.

The time of departure was chosen to coincide with the end of the African rainy season. In late August 1910, Gottlieb Bauer boarded a small coastal steamer in Jaffa and, accompanied by his wife Elise, his widowed mother Friedericke Ehmann (born 1844 in Grunbach, Württemberg), and their children Gertrud (3), Theodor (2) and Helmut (6 months), departed for Africa. They took with them 37,000 *francs* as start-up capital. After a short stopover in Port Said, they travelled through the Canal to Suez on board the steamer *R.P.D. Prinzregent* of the German East Africa Line, on to Aden, and then down the African east coast towards Mombassa and Tanga.

DURING THE VOYAGE, THEIR INFANT SON HELMUT, BECAME SEVERELY ILL. THE ILLNESS OF THEIR SON FORCED THE BAUERS TO CHANGE THEIR PLANS

During the voyage, their infant son Helmut, became severely ill. He had yellow fever and his parents were given little hope of his recovery by the ship's physician. He survived however and reached Tanga alive, but in an extremely feeble and dehydrated state. The illness of their son forced the Bauers to change their plans; they had to postpone their trip to the African interior. They stayed with their widowed aunt Margarethe Reinhardt at her small trading post in Tanga for ten days until Helmut was well enough to travel.

This unforeseen and costly delay was not without benefit. It gave Gottlieb Bauer the time and opportunity to gather more information about the interior from German farmers visiting the town for supplies; to thoroughly organize their trip from the end of the railway line to Mt Meru; and to complete his supplies and equipment by buying the appropriate vegetable and grain seeds, two guns, a revolver and sufficient ammunition. He also purchased a white Maskat-mule and a large dog, which later proved to be of great value in defending their farm at night against lions and hyenas and against marauding Massai warriors during the war years.

In mid September 1910, after Helmut's recovery, the family set out on the Usambara railroad for the interior. From the railhead at Mombo, they continued towards Mt Kilimanjaro with two Boer wagons that carried their belongings. Each wagon was pulled by 10 pairs of oxen. One wagon carried the small children, clothing, and some furniture brought from Palestine, as well as food and the family's water supply. The other wagon carried Gottlieb Bauer's heavy tools, mechanical equipment, farm gear, a steam engine and the seeds he had bought in Tanga.

10. The Bauer family trekking to the Meru region 1910 with their belongings loaded on a wagon being pulled by ten pairs of oxen

While Elise walked alongside the wagon for most of the way, Gottlieb accompanied the trek on his newly acquired mule, always on the lookout for beasts of prey that might approach. He added meat to the daily diet by hunting game along the way.

During the hottest hours of the day, the family would rest under an acacia tree with its wide umbrella-like branches and the children would sleep in the shade under the wagons.

AFTER TRAVELLING FOR 12 DAYS BY WAGON AND ON FOOT, THE BAUERS FINALLY REACHED MOSHI AND, AFTER THREE MORE DAYS, LEGANGA

On day nine of their trek, Mt Kilimanjaro and snow-covered Kibo emerged from the haze of the African savannah, and from then on this majestic mountain served as a beacon guiding their way. After travelling for 12 days by wagon and on foot, the Bauers finally reached Moshi and, after three more days, Leganga on the southern foothills of Mt Meru. Here the family had leased 1,200 hectares of land from the German Colonization Society for the price of 3,600 *rupees*, equivalent to about 5,800 *francs*.[18] This vast area would have been worth an incredible sum in Palestine, probably such that no one could ever have afforded to buy it, because a comparable tract of land there would have cost 4-8 million *francs*.[19]

11. Map showing location of the three Bauer farms (1910-1930)

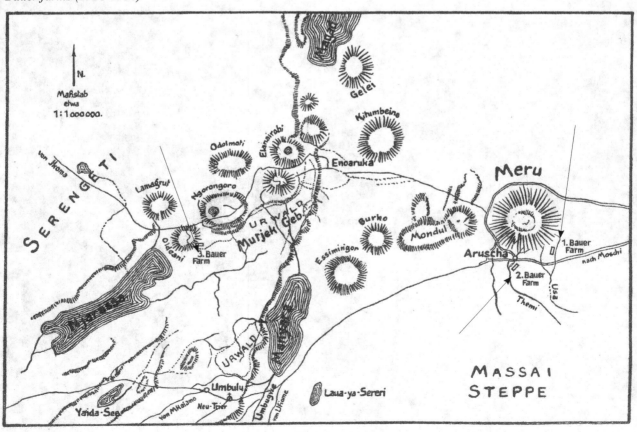

THE SETTLEMENT YEARS 1908 TO 1914

CHAPTER FIVE

The Bauers' delay in Tanga had reduced the time available to become established before the 'little rains' of November and December. Time was of the essence to build a provisional shelter for the family, to clear land for a vegetable garden and to plant some corn and wheat for subsistence, because not much would grow during the long dry season after the rains.

After arriving at Leganga in September 1910, the Bauers lived in an old army tent for a few days while building, with the help of locally hired labourers, a round African-style mud-hut with a thatched roof of banana leaves. By the end of the month, 20 hectares of bush had been cleared, and four hectares were freed from weeds and stumps and prepared for cultivation.

12. View of Leganga (known as Leudorf) in 1910

The 1,200 hectare property was located on the Maji-Tschai River that earned its name from the swampy brown tea-coloured water it carried. Gottlieb Bauer dug a small channel from this waterway to bring water to the house and farm but, as there was some doubt about the water quality, a well was dug close to the farmhouse. Whilst digging his well, Bauer hit bedrock and was unable to reach water. During the following weeks, he went prospecting with pick and divining rod, testing several sites in order to find water. He soon came to realize that under most of his property there was a massive layer of rock at depths of 1-3 meters that could neither be dug nor drilled though. His hopes of growing coffee here were shattered, as coffee plants require deep soil for their long taproots.[20]

Furthermore, the community life and social environment in Leganga was not to Bauer's liking. He had hoped to find peace of mind for himself and his family in Africa's vastness. Instead, the family found itself in a settlement smouldering with unrest and intrigue.[21] The village, also called *Leudorf,* had been founded in 1906 by the retired *Schutztruppe*-Captain August Leue at the behest of the German Colonization Society. Leganga was the first colonial "village" in East Africa and was meant to be a model settlement. It was hoped that its success could be replicated in other areas of the colony. Unfortunately, the Colonization Society made a mistake in the type of settlers it chose for this settlement. With the best of intentions, they selected Germans from the Caucasus region in Russia, generally regarded as hardworking, pious and honest people.

13. Gottlieb and Elise Bauer arriving at their Temi River mill site with their caravan of porters (note newly dug mill channel)

As an incentive, these lucky settlers received full passage and equipment, free land, provisional housing, and supplies for half a year. They were also allocated ten paid labourers to cultivate their land during their first years. Once these early support measures came to an end, they made little progress and became a heavy liability for the Colonization Society. The individuals chosen were soon "branded" lazy; they proved to be quarrelsome, prone to drink, and possessed of an attitude that expected to get everything for free.[22] They had been unwisely chosen, poorly prepared, and were hardly suited for farming in East Africa or to the quirks of its climate. Bitter disputes erupted between Leue, the settlers, and the Colonization Society's Settlement Committee, culminating in an official investigation of Leue's role in the failure of the venture. Many of the 'Russian settlers' left before the end of the second year, some died of disease, and most of those who stayed lived in poverty.[23]

14. Painting of the Bauer's house and mill at the Temi River. Note the separate kitchen building in the foreground. Kitchens were usually built away from the main house as a safety precaution in case of fire (painting by Lore Bauer based on a lost photograph)

After some initial success in vegetable growing and the planting of cereals, and with the knowledge that their land at Mount Meru was unsuitable for coffee cultivation, the Bauers made arrangements to move to the Temi River. During the dry season of 1911, Gottlieb

15. Gottlieb Bauer with his mother Friedricke Ehmann and his sister-in-law Hulda Blankertz celebrating New Year in 1912 at their first home in Leganga

Bauer explored the terrain on the southern Meru slopes and around the town of Arusha for a better spot to raise his family. He soon found suitable land in the beautiful forest area on the Temi River in the territory of the Wa-Dshagga tribe. The land was within sight of Arusha, and a half hour ride from Leganga, located between the villages of the chiefs Angarashi, Toronge, and Mekogi.[24] The river had year round water and enough flow to power a mill. The Bauers bought a further

16. The Bauer family on their plantation near Arusha circa 1914

17. The Bauer family at the Temi River at the site where the waterwheel was later installed

GOTTLIEB BUILT A PERMANENT HOUSE ON THE TEMI RIVER WITH SEVERAL LARGE SHEDS FOR ALL HIS TOOLS AND EQUIPMENT

400 hectares of land there, intending to farm coffee and vegetables, but Gottlieb's focus was on building a flourmill, a sawmill and an oil-press. During 1911 Elise, his wife, and his mother, Friedericke, remained with the children in Leganga (where in December 1911 Rudolf was born), and continued with the vegetable and grain farming, while Gottlieb built a permanent house on the Temi River with several large sheds for all his tools and equipment, which included his workbench and lathe, as well as a blacksmith's shop.[25]

In the autumn of 1913, Friedericke Bauer died at the Temi, aged 69. She, and her mother Jakobina Ehmann (née Ilg), had joined the Templers in 1864 only after the death of her father, the stonemason Immanuel Ehmann (1805-1870), who had opposed the Templer movement all his life. Following her father's death, Friedericke left her native Grunbach for Palestine in the mid 1870s where she met and married Gottlieb Bauer (sen.) in Bethlehem.[26]

CHAPTER FIVE

THE BLANKERTZ FAMILY[27]

In 1911 the Blankertz family joined the Bauers at Mount Meru. Initially, only the oldest son Philipp Albert (born 1887 in Jaffa), with his wife Margarethe (née Klotz born 1887 in Zwerenberg) were going to leave Sarona in Palestine. But after receiving enthusiastic reports from their sister, Elise and brother-in-law Gottlieb Bauer, the other siblings, Friedrich Philipp and Hulda Luise Blankertz, also decided to participate in the harsh pioneering life in the interior of the new German colony. They went despite all the pleas and warnings of their parents who had come to Palestine at a young age as pioneer settlers and who knew only too well about the hardships and sufferings likely to be encountered in a strange and hostile environment. Their mother, Dorothea Pauline Blankertz (née Reinhardt) in particular, could not comprehend the idea of a Templer settlement in Africa. She had come to Palestine with the first Templers in 1869 and was amongst the founding group of the Haifa settlement. She was of the view that to attempt building 'God's Kingdom' and to return to the true pure Christian faith was a mission that could not be accomplished at 'some Meru mountain' deep in darkest Africa, but was only achievable in the Holy Land. Furthermore their other daughter, Johanna Marie, had married in 1906 and moved to Cairo, Egypt. So as not to be left alone in Palestine, Johann Albert and Dorothea Blankertz, both in

18. Johann Albert Blankertz and wife Dorothea Pauline née Reinhardt in Jaffa about 1890

their fifties, reluctantly decided to go along with their sons. Dorothea left Jaffa with a heavy heart in the late summer of 1911, believing she was betraying her ideals and those of her parents with whom she had come to the Holy Land.[28]

Wilhelm Blankertz (born 1821 in Hückelhoven) and his wife, Johanna née Lehnemann (born 1824), had come from the Rhineland to Palestine in 1858 and settled in Jerusalem with their four children. Together with his brother-in-law Peter Lentholdt, Wilhelm founded Jerusalem's first brewery. Only two of the Blankertz children survived to adult age. Wilhelm (junior) (1851-1929) became the head of the Hospice of the Order of St John in Jerusalem and married Henriette Roggenbauch (1858-1916), a Templer from Nagold. Johann Albert Blankertz (1854-1930), Wilhelm's younger brother, learned his father's trade and became a brewer in the family's business in Jerusalem.

Johann Albert was not a Templer and only joined the Temple Society after his marriage to Dorothea Pauline Reinhardt of Oberkollwangen, daughter of Philipp Reinhardt (1814-1872), a Templer elder of the Black Forest area.[29]

19. Philipp Albert Blankertz

After his father's death and disagreements with his uncle Lentholdt, Johann Albert Blankertz moved to Jaffa and opened his own brewery there in the early 1880s. In the first years, while establishing his brewery business, he also worked as a tourist guide during the pilgrimage season to earn some additional income.[30] However, the brewery soon became a prosperous venture and, by 1890, Johann Albert Blankertz was selling beer to Jerusalem, Amman, Beirut and Alexandria. In 1898 he became a partner in the renowned Cairo *Bierhalle* which, from 1906, was run by his son-in-law .... König of Haifa.

Blankertz had initially hoped that his son Friedrich Philipp would take over the family business in Jaffa (the other son, Philipp Albert, was employed as a master mechanic at the Wagner Bros. foundry, working alongside his brother-in-law Gottlieb Bauer). When it became apparent that both his grown-up sons would leave for Africa, he sold the brewery and joined them. Having already gained some experience with tobacco cultivation in Palestine, he planned to grow tobacco at Mount Meru.[31]

The Blankertz's journey to Mount Meru in 1911 was an arduous and perilous one. After their arrival and brief stay with their sister-in-law, Margarethe Reinhardt, in Tanga, the family travelled by train to the railhead. From there, the family continued on foot and by wagon

CHAPTER FIVE

THE BLANKERTZ'S JOURNEY TO MOUNT MERU
IN 1911 WAS AN ARDUOUS AND PERILOUS ONE

along the ridges of the Usambara and Pare Mountains and through the Massai Steppe. Dorothea Pauline Blankertz, 56, who had lost a leg in Palestine a few years earlier due to infection, was unable to walk or ride alongside the ox-wagons. Even riding on a wagon was only possible for short periods because, after a few hours of bumpy road, her bones would be so sore that she could neither stand nor walk. For two weeks, porters carried her in a hammock that was tied to a long pole.

One night some Massai warriors attacked their camp, intending to steal the oxen. During the attack, a number of porters deserted in fear and were never seen again. A few nights later lions raided the camp, killing two oxen and a porter, as well as wounding several others who had come to his rescue. Due to their injuries, the porters had to be left behind in a nearby village. However, no new porters could be found and the Blankertzs had no choice but to carry part of their loads on their own backs. When they finally reached Moshi, they were in a state of exhaustion and despair.[32]

NO NEW PORTERS COULD BE FOUND AND THE
BLANKERTZS HAD NO CHOICE BUT TO CARRY
PART OF THEIR LOADS ON THEIR OWN BACKS.
WHEN THEY FINALLY REACHED MOSHI, THEY
WERE IN A STATE OF EXHAUSTION AND DESPAIR

After a few days of rest in Leganga with their daughter Elise Bauer, Johann Albert Blankertz and his wife set out for the Tengeru area on the western slopes of Mount Meru. Here their son-in-law Gottlieb Bauer had acquired land that was suitable for tobacco farming. He had already hired many labourers for clearing the bush and for preparing the soil.

20. The Blankertz mansion on their tobacco estate at Tengeru (note the leopard skin on display)

In 1912, after a house had been built and the fields had been planted with tobacco, Blankertz built an enormous structure with several storeys for tobacco drying. It was built of local materials, had a thatched roof of banana and palm leaves, and was said to be the largest structure ever built in the Meru-Kilimanjaro region. During the heavy summer downpours of the 1914 rainy season, the roof of the building collapsed and was replaced on the eve of the World War I by a similar, but much stronger structure, with sheets of corrugated iron. The building material had to be brought to the interior by train from Tanga, and then by some 90 carts – each pulled by 24 oxen – from Moshi to Meru. Since that many ox-teams could not be found at the one time, all the oxen had to do the trip several times.[33]

The eldest son, Philipp Albert Blankertz decided to stay on in Leganga with his wife Margarethe, and established himself there as a mechanic and fitter after taking over the land and house of his brother-in-law Gottlieb Bauer, who had resettled to a property on the Temi River in early 1912.

IT WAS BUILT OF LOCAL MATERIALS, HAD A THATCHED ROOF OF BANANA AND PALM LEAVES, AND WAS SAID TO BE THE LARGEST STRUCTURE EVER BUILT IN THE MERU-KILIMANJARO REGION

22. The rebuilt tobacco drying shed at Tengeru

23. Hulda Blankertz on her plantation at Tuilani at Mt Meru

24. Hulda Blankertz

The second son, Friedrich Philipp stayed at Tengeru with his parents for a year before obtaining employment in Tabora, in central German East Africa, on a large coffee plantation owned by Captain Maier.[34]

The daughter, Hulda Luise Blankertz, joined her brother in Tabora and looked after his household for a while. In 1915 she married Rudolf Berger, a first aid attendant of the *Schutztruppe*, and settled with him at Tuilani near Mt Meru and established a small farm there despite the start of the war.

THE BÄUERLE FAMILY

The Bäuerle family lived in Jaffa before they – Wilhelm Gottlob Bäuerle, his wife Rosalie, née Meier, and their two daughters Luise and Rösle – emigrated to German East Africa. Luise Kopp (née Bäuerle) recalls: *"Upon our arrival [in German East Africa], we travelled north towards our future home. The wagons were canvas-*

25. Wilhelm Bäuerle swimming in the Usa River

MOST OF THE SETTLERS WHO WENT FROM PAL-ESTINE TO GERMAN EAST AFRICA LEFT BE-TWEEN 1909 AND 1912

covered, drawn by ten to twelve pairs of oxen. It was one wagon per family, with all the family's bags and baggage. We were with other families from Jaffa, and they became our neighbours. After travelling for many days, Papa came and told us that he had to stay behind with Mother, as we had a little sister, so we travelled with other families.

After a fortnight, we arrived at the Knolls, a family who had settled there prior to our arrival. A bath was prepared for Rösle and myself. I can remember only too well [...] a tub of warm water on a low stool in the middle of the farmyard, and Frau Knoll scrubbing us down in it. After the long, dusty trek, we must have been really grubby.

Soon after, our parents arrived with our new sister."[35]

When the little girl, Magdelena, was born on the move between Tanga and Arusha, the women travelling with the Bäuerles did not want to act as midwives for fear of something going wrong during the birth, so a German army officer stepped in and acted as midwife to deliver the baby.[36]

THE EGGER FAMILY

Paul Egger (born 1882) returned to Palestine with Karl Knoll in December 1907 after their exploratory tour of German East Africa. In 1909, he married Katherine Magdalene Kappus in Jaffa and, in 1912, set off again for Africa with his wife and young family to settle in the Arusha/Mt Meru region with the other German settlers from Palestine.[37]

*　　*　　*　　*　　*

Most of the settlers who went from Palestine to German East Africa left between 1909 and 1912. Below is a list of persons who are known to have migrated as part of this settlement venture. The list may not be complete but includes the names obtained during the research for this book. (See also Appendix 2-Family Trees)

Gottlieb Immanuel **Bauer** with his wife Pauline Elise, their children, Gertrud, Theodor and Helmut, and his mother Friedericke Bauer (nee **Ehmann**)
Wilhelm Gottlob **Bäuerle** with his wife Rosalie and daughters Luise and Rösle

CHAPTER FIVE

Jakob **Blaich** with his wife Marie and children Frieda, Gotthilf, Margaretha, Paula, Bernhard, Fritz (Friedrich) and Otto

Karl **Blaich**

Philipp Albert **Blankertz** with his wife Margarete

Johann Albert **Blankertz** with his wife Dorothea Pauline

Friedrich Philipp **Blankertz**

Hulda Luise **Blankertz**

Paul **Egger** with his wife Katherine Magdalene and family

Gottlieb **Glenk** with his wife Paula and son Ewald

Hans **Groezinger**

Christian **Groezinger**

Samuel **Kappus**

Karl **Knoll** with his wife Lydia and children Rosa, Erna and Berthold

Johann Christian **Kopp** with his wife Margarethe (Luise) and children Johannes, Luise, Wilhelmine, Friedricke, Martha and Karl

Carl **Oldorf** with his wife Marie and family

Johannes **Reinhardt**

Christof **Reinhardt** with his wife Margarete and daughter Anna

Ulrich **Reinhardt** with his wife Caroline and children Gottlieb, Lydia and Anna

Fritz **Schlichenmeier** of Wilhelma (who was engaged to Margaretha **Blaich**)

Samuel **Sickinger**[38]

SETTLEMENT BEGINS NEAR ARUSHA AND IN THE USA RIVER DISTRICT

Newly arrived settlers usually lived for a short period with an already established family. A house was then built as soon as possible – usually with walls from clay or mud, reinforced by straw (wickerwork) and with a thatched roof. The inside floor was of clay. These homes served as temporary dwellings until permanent stone houses were built. In those days, it was customary to build the kitchen away from the main residence because of the danger from fire.[39]

IT WAS CUSTOMARY TO BUILD THE KITCHEN AWAY FROM THE MAIN RESIDENCE BECAUSE OF THE DANGER FROM FIRE

In early 1912, the Bauers left Leganga and resettled in their new house on the Temi River. Rudolf Bauer's memoirs provide a good description of a typical settler family home and its surroundings:
"It had a solid foundation and was built up to the raised ground floor with cement and then with bricks, which my father had manufactured with the help of native employees. In a mud pit, the clay was pounded with the feet, filled into wooden moulds and dried in the sun. In this

way two large rooms emerged. In the front was the living and dining room, and behind it the parents' bedroom. A wide staircase led upstairs. To the right of these stairs was the bedroom for us children. The left side served as a provision room. There non-perishable foodstuffs were stored, such as two sacks of raw coffee, one or two sacks of rice, as well as a large sugarloaf. The roof of the house was covered with corrugated iron. In front of the residence was a porch [...] Behind the building a beautiful flower garden had been created of which our gardener Lempoto was in charge [...] The living quarters and the kitchen building were about 20 meters from the mill-stream. On the right hand side a path lined by lemon trees led to the brick oven. To the left of the garden was an avenue of cypress trees. Opposite of the residential building was a big poultry yard, in the middle of which was a large pond for geese and ducks. Many chickens, guinea fowls, and turkeys were kept in the chicken shed, which was raised very high off the ground to provide safety from predators. Next to it was also a pigsty".[40]

MOST PROPERTIES HAD WATER FRONTAGES TO THE USA RIVER AND SOME TO THE TEMI RIVER

The land where the new arrivals settled was leasehold land; it had been surveyed and was hilly. Some areas were timbered with large trees and other growth, whilst other areas had only scrub type vegetation. There were numerous small creeks and other waterways and most properties had water frontages to the Usa River and some to the Temi River. Water was channelled to the fields to irrigate the crops. The snow-capped peak of Mt Kilimanjaro was clearly visible as was Mt Meru, which sometimes also had snow in December. As the land was virtually on the equator, there was no twilight as the sun rose and set around six o'clock mornings and evenings all year round.[41]

THE SETTLERS EXPERIMENTED WITH GROWING AND GRAFTING A VARIETY OF PLANTS AND TREES

The soil was rich and did not need to be fertilised initially. The settlers used compost in areas where vegetables were grown. Oxen were used to clear and plough the land. Vegetables, also needed for the settlers' own consumption, provided a quick return and source of income because they could readily be sold to the German military stationed in the area. Coffee beans were sown and the seedlings were planted out to form coffee plantations. It took three to five years for the first crop of coffee beans to be harvested. The settlers experimented with growing and grafting a variety of plants and trees. For example, Jakob Blaich planted nut trees, papaya, melons, cantaloupes, custard apples, peanuts, pineapples, sweet potatoes, cotton and bananas; Gottlob Bäuerle experimented with fruit trees such as peaches, apricots, figs and almonds; and Johann Albert Blankertz planted numerous tobacco varieties and tried his luck with cotton and sisal. The tropical climate and watering were ongoing problems for many of the introduced plants and trees.[42]

26. Using oxen for transport

All the settlers employed natives to help with clearing the land, preparing it for farming and with actual farmwork. Native women and boys were employed as domestics in the household and around the homesteads. All the native workers had to be paid. The German authorities levied taxes against the tribal chiefs as an incentive for the chief to send workers to the farms to earn money so that they (the chiefs) were able to pay the taxes. The settlers preferred to employ

27. Ploughing with oxen

Wameru natives as they were better workers than the Warusha (cousins of the Massai). The latter were more nomadic and not used to farming. The Marshai usually had cows and goats and were often resentful that they had been forced off their grazing land. The spoken language of the natives was Swahili; and the new settlers quickly had to learn to communicate in Swahili. Most settlers from Palestine who stayed in German East Africa became quite fluent in this language, which was relatively easy for them to learn because Swahili contained many Arabic words very familiar to them. [43]

The settlers bought most of their supplies from Arusha. Arusha was a small town with a *boma* (district office and military depot). A South African, Goodall Bloom was a hotelier and merchant there through whom the settlers bought their supplies. Rudolf Bauer provides a good description of Arusha: *"[...] on entering the town, from the Bauer farm direction, the Post Office was on the left and the cemetery on the right, then came the large crossing. To the left the road went to the mission post of Missionary Blumert. To the right was the*

28 Massai shepherd with his cattle herd

road to Moshi over the Temi River, which flowed through Arusha. The road also passed the Hotel Schmiedhuber, where later Miss Ludmer taught us some reading and writing. In earlier times, my three older siblings went to Missionary Blumert for their education. Now returning to the crossing near the Post Office the road straight ahead continued to the boma – a fortified town hall which was surrounded by a deep moat. Before reaching the boma there was the Hotel Blum, and a number of shops, mostly run by Indians. The Nashornapotheke *[Rhinoceros Pharmacy], owned by Mr Schmidtgen – a very good and long-time friend of my father's. [...] the boma was surrounded by homes built of concrete - no doubt for the officials, and a hospital was also built there...*"[44]

29. Native women in traditional dress

30. The courtyard of the Boma in Arusha

The very small nearby village of Usa had a general store, where some basic provisions such as flour, sugar, salt and kerosene could be purchased. Some local native 'beer' was also sold there and the natives would gather to meet and sometimes 'dance'.[45]

In the early days, all meat was obtained from hunting. Various antelopes and bucks were shot to provide meat for both the settlers and the native workers. Occasionally a guinea fowl was shot. Later, as the farms became established, the settlers would slaughter cattle, pigs and poultry for meat.[46]

31. Bringing home the meat – natives after a hunting expedition

In the first years of settlement, wildlife was prolific in the area – lions, hyenas, cheetahs, elephants, rhinoceros, leopards, various antelopes, springboks and monkeys. Monkeys caused much damage to crops,

103

(Left:) 32. The Bauer family with their large waterwheel

especially to corn, where they would rip the cobs off the stalks. Later, when the coffee bushes came into bearing, the monkeys would eat the beans until they were intoxicated by caffeine. Guards were employed to protect the crops and shoot the monkeys. Dogs owned by the settlers had to be protected, because leopards killed and ate dogs. Elephants once caused much damage when a settler had unwittingly started a plantation on an elephant migratory track between Mt Meru and Mt Kilimanjaro. When the elephant herd moved through, they trampled everything and pulled out all plants in their way.[47]

In addition to the agricultural enterprises described above, Gottlieb Bauer's flourmill and workshop soon became a well-known and respected business.

After the house, workshop and mill buildings had been completed, Bauer constructed the mill fittings, including the waterwheel, and dug a two to three-meter-wide channel from the Temi River to the

33. Gottlieb Bauer building his waterwheel

mill for the water to drive the wheel. Over 100 native workers were employed to dig out the channel, which was partly lined with concrete. A small weir was also constructed for water storage. The weir attracted crocodiles, which had to be killed for the sake of persons' and especially children's safety.[48]

The workshop and mill built by the Bauers were the first in the Arusha region and soon became a well-known stopping point for Boer families who had trekked with their oxen and wagons from South Africa before settling in German East Africa. The mill was a successful venture; many nearby farmers had their flour milled there and native women carrying bowls of cereals on their heads would arrive from the surrounding villages each morning to have their produce ground.[49]

Despite its scenic beauty, life in the Mt Meru region was not without its dangers. In 1912, for example, while Gottlieb Bauer was in Moshi to collect millstones and axles for his mill, a band of marauding Massai attacked the farm. The tribesmen had roamed the Mt Meru region and had killed a number of African villagers and white settlers burning several farmhouses in the process – acts the German

34. Construction of the waterwheel and mill. Gottlieb Bauer on the right

colonial authorities had proved powerless to prevent. When a servant warned Elise Bauer of the Massai tribesmen's approach, the family barricaded themselves in the homestead, sent the children to the upper floor and prepared themselves to defend their lives and property. A heavy cupboard was pushed against the door to block the entrance. While Elise guarded the front with a hunting rifle, old Friedericke Bauer positioned herself at the back door, armed with a large brass pestle and an old muzzle-loader. She shouted to the attackers that she was going to kill them all with her *Bundike*, (the gun) and, to enforce her words, she hit the heavy pestle against the cupboard with all her force. The shot-like noise had the desired effect and sent the Massai running, but they soon returned. The assailants tried in vain to break down the heavy doors and window shutters, and when they eventually prepared to set fire to the building, help literally arrived at the last minute. Elise's mother, Dorothea Blankertz, had come from her farm in Tengeru with a group of porters, and when she became aware of the situation, she quickly rushed to her daughter's rescue. The one-legged old lady leapt out of her sedan-chair and hobbled towards the assailants, shouting at them in her Swabian dialect, ferociously swinging her crutches, and piously cursing *O heiliges Korntal* [Oh holy Korntal].[50] The marauders were puzzled by this peculiar apparition and, uncertain how to react, watched the old woman's approach with wide-open eyes. When the nearest of them was hit on the head by Dorothea's crutch and fell to the ground stunned, the others fled in panic, leaving their wounded comrade behind. He was tied up by the determined ladies and delivered to the Boma in Arusha where he was interrogated, and the whereabouts of his gang soon established. They were hunted down by the *Schutztruppe* and hanged after a short trial, with their bodies left on display for several days at the gallows outside the Arusha mission.[51]

THE TRAPPE FAMILY

The Trappe family from Silesia in Germany became neighbours and good friends with many of the German settlers from Palestine. They helped some of the new arrivals and provided advice when needed.

Ulrich Trappe married Margarete Zehe in 1907 and the young newly wed couple migrated to German East Africa shortly after. They had been advised by a Mr Lewinsky, who had already settled in the Usambara region, to come as settlers rather than for Ulrich to volunteer for service with the *Schutztruppe*.[52]

After arriving in Tanga, they travelled by train to Mombo, the end of the line and joined a group of Germans from the Caucasus region in

THE ASSAILANTS TRIED IN VAIN TO BREAK DOWN THE HEAVY DOORS AND WINDOW SHUTTERS

THE TRAPPE FAMILY BECAME NEIGHBOURS AND GOOD FRIENDS WITH MANY OF THE GERMAN SETTLERS FROM PALESTINE southern Russia, who were planning to start a new settlement near Leganga. This group was under the protection and guidance of Captain Leue of the German Protection Force. They trekked for two weeks until they reached Leganga, but the Trappe family and their porters kept going higher up into the mountains. After resting on a rise and enjoying the grand views of the eastern slopes of Mt Meru (native *Oldonyo Orok* – the sinister mountain) they decided this would be the place for their home.[53]

The Trappe's first farm of 6,000 hectares was known as Ngongonare. After 12 months, they acquired another property of 2,200 hectares, known as Momella. Their first home was a quite primitive native hut before temporary buildings of corrugated iron were built. A substantial stone house with a corrugated roof was then constructed. The Trappes fenced off a large part of their property and built large corrals from thorn bushes to protect their livestock not only from predators but also, and more importantly, from native cattle thieves. The stock had to be guarded day and night to prevent losses through theft.[54]

35. Ngongonare, the Trappe homestead

The Trappes developed a large herd of stock of beef cattle and dairy cows and became major milk producers in the area. To safeguard the herd, they built a huge stock *boma* [fort] with stonewalls 2.5 meters high and one meter thick, which could accommodate up to 1,500 head of livestock.[55]

36. Cattle Boma at Ngongonare

At the high altitude of their farms the Trappes could safely breed horses because their land was beyond the reach of the scourge of the tsetse fly. The Momella farm was at 1,800 meters above sea level and Ngongonare between 1,650 and 1,700 meters with a temperature range from 2-28 degrees C.[56]

The Trappes also developed and improved pastures for their stock; they started a piggery; raised poultry; and planted corn, lucerne, potatoes and a variety of vegetables. Pineapples were grown as well as grapes, and beehives were kept for honey, which was produced for sale. Apart from a vegetable garden, Ulrich Trappe laid out a beautiful rose garden with more than one hundred varieties.[57]

THE TRAPPE FARMS, WHICH AT ONE STAGE COMPRISED NEARLY 18,000 HECTARES, BECAME RENOWNED AS MODEL FARMS THROUGHOUT GERMAN EAST AFRICA

The Trappe farms, which at one stage comprised nearly 18,000 hectares, became renowned as model farms throughout German East Africa and attracted many visitors who came to view these vast properties and their developments.[58]

COMMUNITY LIFE

ON SUNDAYS THE FAMILIES WOULD SOCIALISE BY VISITING EACH OTHER FOR MEALS OR AFTERNOON COFFEE

New arrivals were always made welcome by the already established settlers. The large farms did not allow for much day-to-day contact between the settlers. On Sundays, however, the families would socialise by visiting each other for meals or afternoon coffee. Sometimes several families would meet at one location.[59]

The settlers had quite a number of visitors from Palestine, especially from relatives. These visits were pleasant times for the settlers, seeing their relatives and catching up on news from Palestine. The visitors would usually bring a range of things with them – often items previously requested by the settlers. For example, in 1912, when Sebastian Blaich came to visit his brothers Jakob and Karl, he brought with him a donkey and many plants and plant cuttings – figs, pomegranates, almonds, peaches, apricots and prickly pears (which later became a noxious weed).[60]

37. Native women and children

Most of the settlers from Palestine were devout Templers but, unfortunately, the Temple Society's Central Council did not support the African venture. The settlers had no spiritual or religious leaders. The lack of religious guidance and pastoral care created problems for this small like-minded community. They, therefore, turned to the local mission posts for their religious and spiritual needs. The missionaries, however, were sometimes reluctant to help because the Templers were of a different faith. They, for example, would not conduct a marriage service unless the couple were baptised, which was not customary amongst the Templers.[61]

38. Market scene in Arusha

Schooling for the children was provided at Leganga, a small village where many Russian-Germans had settled. Leganga was approximately an hour's ride from most of the Templer settlers. The schoolchildren had to ride on donkeys through some dense bush and across watercourses to get there. At school, the donkeys were unsaddled and tethered for the day. During the wet season, the streams were full and flowing and the donkeys had to swim across with the children on

39. A school building in the Kilimanjaro region

their backs. The children went barefoot and carried their school bags on their back. Young children were usually accompanied by a native boy to guide and protect them. Another safeguard was for the children to travel as a group to and from school. At the school there were two German teachers Mr Henke and Mr Wittrich. The six-day school week was broken down into certain subjects being taught on particular days – religion and geography on Mondays; dictation, essay writing and history on Tuesdays; arithmetic and literature (poetry) on Wednesdays; revision on Thursdays and Fridays; and singing on Saturdays. The school hours were from seven in the morning to twelve noon. Homework was set and had to be completed on a regular basis. The main school holidays were six weeks with a few other holidays during the year.[62]

Unfortunately, many of the new settlers had selected their land at the foot of Mt Meru, which was swampy in parts, especially near the watercourses. These swampy areas filled with water during the wet season and became prolific breeding grounds for mosquitos. Malaria and other tropical diseases transmitted by mosquitos caused illness and death amongst the settlers, strikingly similar to the beginnings of Sarona in 1871. After a few years, most of the surviving settlers started moving to higher ground to avoid these pests. Disease also was one of the main reasons why many settlers left [63]

DISEASE WAS ONE OF THE MAIN REASONS WHY MANY SETTLERS LEFT

There was a German cemetery in Arusha and most deceased German settlers from that region were buried there. In 1910, Berthold Philipp Knoll and in 1913, Friedericke Bauer died and were laid to rest there.[64]

A number of children were born to the settler families. The birthplace for these children was often recorded as *am Ussa bei Aruscha* [on the Usa near Arusha] or simply *in Deutschostafrika*. There were instances where prospective mothers experiencing problems or expecting a difficult birth would be sent to Germany where better medical facilities were available. One such case was the family of Christof and Margarete Reinhardt, who had several children born in Africa – Frieda in 1897, Martha in 1900 – but when Margarete was pregnant again, she was advised for medical reasons to go to Germany for the birth of her next child, Maria. Friends in Germany cared for baby Maria when Margarete returned to Africa after the birth.[65]

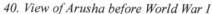

40. View of Arusha before World War I

OBSERVATIONS BY VISITORS FROM PALESTINE

By the end of the first decade of the 20th century the Wieland Tile and Cement Products factory, which had been established in Jaffa in the 1890s, had grown into a substantial enterprise with six or more members of the Wieland family directly involved in the daily running and management of the business. The younger members of the family realised that, although the business in Palestine was still growing, their future opportunities in Palestine might well be limited and they therefore sought to explore business opportunities elsewhere. The family decided that there might be opportunities for development in German East Africa where a number of Germans from Palestine had settled in recent times.[66]

The family chose brothers, Rudolf and Carl Wieland, to go to German East Africa to see first hand what potential there was to develop a cement and tile business. They went to Tanga (the German port city) and then hoped to travel to Moshi and the Kilimanjaro region to visit their friends from Palestine. The following is a description of their journey to Moshi. *"...As we could not get any porters, we caught the train to Mombo railway station and from there we walked to Wilhelmstal in the Usambara Mountains. We found a good hotel there and were well cared for. On our first day we visited District Commissioner* [Koestlin von Murrhardt] *and were invited to join him and his wife for a meal on Sunday. The good Swabian meal* [Spätzle (noodles), Sauerkraut and pickled pork] *tasted just wonderful. The mealtime discussion amongst us Swabians, although a long way from home,* [Swabia is a region in southern Germany] *was most entertaining.*

41. Members of the Wieland family (l to r) Hugo (sen), Rudolf, Karl, Hugo (jun)

*From Mombo we caught the train again and travelled to where the line finished and set up our tent next to a small creek. We had requested that two bicycles be sent to the railhead as we wanted to continue our journey on bicycles. After a most difficult and tedious trip on the wildest of paths we finally reached Moshi, at the end of our endurance. I thanked my Creator, after recovering, as my brother Carl (who had a heart problem) could not have continued any further. We checked into a guesthouse run by Mr and Mrs Jaeger and were well cared for. We stayed and enjoyed several days in Moshi as we recovered from our exhaustion. We then returned to Tanga without having visited our friends." *[67]

42. *Postal Services at the German Post Office in Moshi*

The Wieland brothers then travelled on to Dar-es-Salaam and inspected a limestone quarry that would have been suitable for supplying the raw materials for a cement products business. After considering the prospects, the brothers became quite enthusiastic about such a venture in Africa. During the planning stage, however, they received a letter from their father urging one of his sons to return to Palestine, as soon as possible, with the prospect of a position in the family business. The brothers decided that the development of their planned African venture could not proceed with only one person and, therefore, they both returned to Palestine. Before departing German East Africa they went to Zanzibar and had a meeting with the Governor, Dr Schnee.[68]

Georg Kappus, who went with Sebastian Blaich to visit his relatives in German East Africa in October 1912, wrote a report on his experiences and observations of this trip.

Kappus was impressed with what the settlers had achieved with very little means in just three years. The Governor of German East Africa, Dr Albert Heinrich Schnee, had expressed similar views when he visited the Mt Meru/Usa River area.

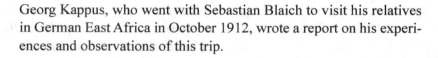

KAPPUS WAS IMPRESSED WITH WHAT THE SETTLERS HAD ACHIEVED WITH VERY LITTLE MEANS IN JUST THREE YEARS

Kappus noted the large areas that were under cultivation, many with coffee plantations. Some of these young plantations were just beginning to show a return. Rubber tree plantations had also been started and some of the trees had grown to a height of 1.2 meters in the deep volcanic soil. Other crops being successfully grown included rye, oats, barley, corn, potatoes and beans. Beef cattle and dairy cows were thriving on this splendid grazing country. Plenty of milk and butter was produced and the manure from the animals was used by the farmers to fertilise their coffee plantations. The settlers in the more open, flatter country could use animals and ploughs for breaking up the soil for crop cultivation; but the settlers in the higher and

115

43. A coffee bush in full bloom

steeper regions had to employ labour to hoe the areas where they wished to plant crops by hand. The mountain forest soil, however, was very rich in humus.[69]

Kappus describes his visit to the area: *"During my stay at Meru, I had the opportunity to see many of the German plantations and all the owners were optimistic about the future. Practically all have started coffee plantations, sometimes amid magnificent forests. I often feel sorrow about how the beautiful forest has been cleared and the most magnificent trees cut down and burnt on the spot. German government authorities have now placed the forests into reserves so that they will be preserved. With deep inner joy I observed the German women, who with diligent hands and a sense of orderliness had established beautiful flower and vegetable gardens around their homes. Some of these garden or park settings are worthy of comparison with the gardens of the nobility in Germany. When the German women work so faithfully with their menfolk, then of course progress is made. I saw much beautiful vacant land still available for settlement. However, the authorities have now temporarily stopped further land allocations for settlement. This beautiful land is presently reserved for the natives, who only sparsely cultivate it because they have few needs. I can understand the concerns of the government in relation to the natives[...]*

The increase in property values due to the settlement process is remarkable. The amount of capital required to start may discourage some new settlers. I estimate that between 20,000 to 30,000 franks minimum are required to start, despite the government up to now only charging four rupees per hectare and this does not have to be paid in cash. With application and diligence it is possible to achieve a good income in a few years, especially if (when) the northern railway line is extended to Arusha[...]

I could write a whole chapter about the hospitality that was extended to me. Everywhere I was looked after and made to feel welcome. The land surely has a great future, and if asked whether I would recommend it then I would like to answer with the quote of our respected Consul Dr Brode. When he was recently asked to promote German East Africa he replied 'I do not have to recommend the land because it recommends itself!' – And he is right!"[70]

Some families from Palestine, who did not go to German East Africa, nevertheless invested money there for future purposes. For example, Eugen Neef, from Sarona, bought land near the Usa River in 1911 for his son, Walter, for the future development of a coffee plantation.[71]

WORLD WAR I
1914 TO 1918

THE APPOINTMENT OF PAUL ERICH VON LETTOW-VORBECK

In early 1914 the German government appointed Lieutenant Colonel Paul von Lettow-Vorbeck (1870-1964) as commander of the *Schutztruppe* [Protection Force] in German East Africa. Von Lettow-Vorbeck had seen active service with the German contingent in China during the Boxer Rebellion in 1900 and in German South West Africa [now Namibia] from 1904 to 1906. In South West Africa he experienced bush warfare first hand during the fighting and eventual suppression of the Hottentot and Herero uprisings. He was wounded in that campaign and spent some time recuperating in South Africa where he befriended General Jan Smuts [later to be his adversary] and had an opportunity to gain insights into the nature of the Anglo-Boer conflict. He returned to Germany where he commanded the Second *Seebataillon* [marines] in Wilhelmshaven before being posted to Africa.[1]

*1. Lieutenant Colonel
Paul Erich von Lettow-Vorbeck*

He had been the commanding officer in German East Africa for barely eight months when war broke out in Europe. Within that short time he had toured and inspected the entire colony, including the Mt Meru and Mt Kilimanjaro regions, where he found "prosperous German settlers who were keen to help if war came". Many of these settlers belonged to sporting and gun clubs and were familiar with the country and the terrain.[2] In the event of war, he developed a military strategy for the deployment of well-disciplined, highly mobile units each comprising 16 Europeans, 160 askaris and 250 porters. These small units later gave von Lettow-Vorbeck a distinct advantage over his British and other opponents, whose cumbersome motorised transport was handicapped by the poor road conditions. The British often had to rely on horses and mules, many of which perished in the tsetse fly-infested areas.[3]

WAR

When World War I started in Europe in August 1914, the hostilities also extended to the colonies of the European powers. German East Africa, cut off from Germany, found itself at war with Great Britain and its worldwide Empire. The German East Africa Command was unable to communicate with Germany, and knew that it could expect no reinforcements or supplies.[4]

One advantage for the Germans in East Africa was that their colony was surrounded by natural geographic barriers: an almost impenetrable string of lakes and mountains extended along the western border with the Belgian Congo. On the border with Portuguese Mozambique in the south, only the upper reaches of the Rovuma River were fordable. Along the Indian Ocean there were few places considered suitable for a landing, and an unhealthy swampy belt ran parallel to much of the coastal strip. In the north, the border with British East Africa (Kenya) was extremely difficult to breach and relatively easy to defend as only one trafficable pass, just five miles wide, existed between the Pare Mountains and Mount Kilimanjaro.[5]

At the outbreak of hostilities in August 1914, there were approximately 7,000 Germans, with 3,500 male adults (exclusive of garrisons), eight million natives and an unknown number of Indians, Boers, Greeks, Italians and others – as well as some Britons – living in German East Africa. Von Lettow-Vorbeck's command included 200 European officers with 2,500 askari soldiers and 45 European police officers with an additional 2,000 police askari, who could be trained as soldiers. The German East Africa *Schutztruppe* had, as its name implies, always been regarded as a protection force to uphold

2. Bernhard Blaich's miltary pass

law and order, not as a defence force against external enemies. Most of the askaris, although trained by the Germans, were poorly armed, with obsolete firearms from the 1870s. The maximum number of soldiers, askaris, and porters the German forces had during the war was approximately 14,000.[6]

Von Lettow-Vorbeck implemented his strategy of using small mobile units for 'hit and run' type missions aimed at tying down Allied forces, which would then not be deployed in the European theatres of war. By 1915, Lettow-Vorbeck had created 60 such companies throughout German East Africa.[7]

These companies included Boer males of military age, who either volunteered or were conscripted to serve with the German forces. The call-up order usually stated: *You are required to report to the xx Field Company. You should bring your rifle* [privately owned, sic], *ammunition, a riding animal and supplies for eight days.*[8] There were some disputes between civilian and military authorities regarding the

3. Extract from Bernhard Blaich's military pass

4. Extract from Bernhard Blaich's military pass, part 2

conscription of civilians. Many settlers believed that they were needed for military service, whilst others thought it would serve a better purpose if they maintained their farms and plantations. However, the military authorities had their way and the male settlers were enlisted.[9] The Boers who had settled in German East Africa fought alongside the Germans. Many of them had previously experienced fighting the British during the Boer War. The first Boers to join the German units did so on 6 January 1915.[10]

Amongst this group called up or volunteering for military service were settlers who had come from Palestine before the war – including Gotthilf, Bernhard and Karl Blaich, Gottlob Reinhardt, Wilhelm Bäuerle, Gottlieb Bauer, and Hans and Christian Groezinger, Friedrich Philipp and Philipp Albert Blankertz and their father Johann Albert Blankertz. Bernhard Blaich, one of the youngest ones to enlist, was 18 years old when he joined the military as a volunteer. Several other men of the same age also volunteered. The men went to Arusha to be fitted out with a uniform and then assembled at Oldonyo Sambu near Mt Meru, where an officer addressed them about conduct in the military. The officers, all members of the *Schutztruppe,* had been trained in Germany.[11]

THE VOLUNTEER AND CONSCRIPTED SETTLERS PLAYED A VITAL ROLE IN THE GERMAN CAMPAIGN

The volunteer and conscripted settlers played a vital role in the German campaign. They had years of experience of living in Africa; they were fluent in Swahili; in many cases they were hunters and knew the terrain and what signs to look for in observing humans and wild animals; they could live off the land; they knew the location of waterholes and springs; they were good horsemen and knew how to shoot. Their bushcraft and other skills were invaluable in finding the water holes during the dry season, in planning ambushes and being part of raiding parties to capture horses and equipment from the British. They were frequently used as scouts and observers of enemy positions and were involved in armed skirmishes with Allied troops. On one occasion Albert Blankertz and his raiding party ambushed some Indian supply merchants of the British army and took all their stores. Gottlieb Bauer, Karl Blaich and Bernhard Blaich were awarded the Iron Cross Second Class for their bravery and service during the East Africa campaign.[12]

Another element of the German strategy was to make use of the homesteads and plantations to support the fighting troops. Women, children and the elderly stayed on the plantations, looked after the animals and tended the farms as best they could. Jakob Blaich, who was too old for military service, regularly visited the wives and children on the farms in his area to ensure that everything was in order. The women cooked meals for serving soldiers who, if time allowed, rested and slept at the farms. The women also helped by washing and mending clothes. The farms provided fresh fruit and vegetables as well as milk and butter for the troops. Basic repairs to equipment was done at the farms and sick and injured horses were treated.[13]

THE FARMS PROVIDED FRESH FRUIT AND VEGETABLES AS WELL AS MILK AND BUTTER FOR THE TROOPS

Ulrich Trappe, a neighbour of the Blaich family, served with the military and his wife Margarete was left with her three small children to look after the farms. In the biography of Margarete Trappe, von Lettow-Vorbeck recalls the considerable problems encountered by white settlers in protecting and guarding their properties after the men had been called up, especially their stock (beef and dairy cattle) from being stolen by the natives. The Massai, in particular, were quick to leave their reservations and seize every opportunity to steal livestock, but even the otherwise reliable workers from the Warusha tribe had become involved in thefts.[14]

5. German 'cavalry', the Kilimanjaro/Meru Farmer Volunteer Group riding during the war
- second from right Johann Albert Blankertz, he was 2nd in command of the Meruschützen (Meru Riflemen),
4th from right Philipp Albert Blankertz,
5th Karl Blaich, 6th Gottlieb Bauer and 10th Sergeant-Major of the Reserve Karl Conrad
Note the Maskat mule in the front row

The War Years 1914 and 1915

At the beginning of the war, the British sent a naval taskforce to Dar-es-Salaam to demand surrender from the German Governor, Dr Albert Heinrich Schnee. The Governor was inclined to discussing surrender but was overruled by von Lettow-Vorbeck.[15]

The Germans planned their first raid into British territory [Kenya] to destroy the Mombassa-Nairobi railway line

The German Command expected an early British attack in northern German East Africa near the Mt Kilimanjaro region and set up basic defensive positions in the area. However, there was no attack. In the meantime, the Germans planned their first raid into British territory [Kenya] to destroy the Mombassa-Nairobi railway line, which was the main link between the coast and the inland. This was during the dry season and the exploratory party ventured far into enemy territory without a map. It soon became evident that lack of water would curtail this operation. The need to know the location of springs and waterholes would be crucial to military success. Bernhard Blaich's first patrol assignment was to reconnoitre the Mt Longido area to find a reliable water supply. The mission was successful; he found water by observing wildlife. This led to the establishment of a base at this strategic location with imposing views over the surrounding countryside. The British positions at Mt Erok could also be observed from a lookout at Longido.[16]

During the first months of the war, the military units formed in northern German East Africa undertook numerous patrols along the Mombassa-Nairobi railway line in British East Africa (Kenya), just north of Mt Kilimanjaro. In one of these exploratory patrols for water in the rugged western mountains in October 1914, the group leader's mule was injured. De Haas writes, *"Karl Blaich, the German from Palestine, took over the leadership. He and his two cousins Bernhard and Gotthilf had developed into outstanding field soldiers, who knew the wilderness like few others"*. He also refers to them as the three brave Blaichs.[17] Several clashes with British forces resulted, and casualties occurred on both sides. During one of these raids near Mt Erok, northwest of Mt Meru, Hans Groezinger was shot in the stomach. Unfortunately, no medical assistance was available and he died a few days later from his wounds. He had only been enlisted for a very short time.[18]

Probably the most significant battle of the early war years was the Battle of Tanga. On November 2, 1914 the British approached Tanga with several large warships and transports. Tanga was the main German port in the north and the start of the main northern railway link to the interior. After landing a small force the British demanded surrender from the local commander. In the meantime, von Lettow-Vorbeck was able to bring in various companies by train from the inland. Von Lettow-Vorbeck was reluctant to become involved in a battle where he could be defeated but, on the other hand, he was determined to hold Tanga which was critical to the Germans' operations in northern German East Africa. When the British landed more troops on 3 November, von Lettow-Vorbeck decided to attack. Although outnumbered eight to one, the Germans won a decisive victory – there were over 800 British casualties against the loss of 15 Germans and 54 askaris; vast quantities of equipment and supplies were left behind by the British. These supplies included stores, half a million rounds of ammunition and sixteen machine guns, as well as telephone systems – all of which were badly needed by the Germans in order to continue their war effort.[19]

Flushed with success, von Lettow-Vorbeck returned to his troops in the Mt Kilimanjaro region on 11 November 1914. A few days later, on 14 November, he received more good news: victories at Mt Longido and Mt Erok, which had previously been taken by the British,

6. The Neunte Kavallerie *regiment from the Kilimanjaro region*

7. Karl Blaich's Iron Cross

had now been regained by the Germans. It was decided to strengthen the defence of these strategic outposts.[20]

Following the Battle of Tanga, a lull occurred and this enabled von Lettow-Vorbeck to prepare his troops for a long campaign. He continued his hit and run raids and attacks against the Mombassa-Nairobi railway line and stole horses and equipment from the enemy whenever possible. The raiding parties, which involved the young Germans from Palestine, usually comprised only ten men. In one such raid Karl Blaich captured an elephant gun as the enemy retreated. Although Karl was pleased with his 'trophy', the use of such a weapon caused concern among the German forces. The donkeys brought to German East Africa from Palestine by the settlers also proved to be most useful animals for riding and carrying goods in the dry, rugged terrain. In the two years from 1914 to 1916, some 20 trains, as well as many miles of track and bridges were destroyed.[21]

In 1915 the British mounted another major attack near Jassin just north of Tanga. The Germans again inflicted heavy casualties estimated at over 700. After four days of fighting the British forces (Indian companies with British officers) surrendered. The German losses were also heavy and included six officers. After this, von Lettow-Vorbeck realised that he could not continue fighting head-on battles and that guerrilla warfare was his only option.[22]

In 1915 the British mounted several attacks on German shipping on Lake Victoria and sank a German gunboat, the only armed vessel on the lake. The British were then able to take the town of Bukoba on the western shore of Lake Victoria, causing the Germans to withdraw from that region.[23]

8. Karl Blaich's citation

CHAPTER SIX

In October 1915, the Farmer Volunteer Corps No.16 carried out a successful raid deep into British Territory and blew up the Uganda Railway line between Mbuyuni (Ndi, north of Voi) and Tsavo derailing and destroying a supply train. The commando raiding party comprised Sergeant-Major of the Reserve Karl Conrad, Lance Corporal Gottlieb Bauer, eight askaris and ten porters. Bauer was wounded but made it back to German territory where he was hospitalised for several weeks at Moshi. Bauer received the Iron Cross Second Class and was promoted to Corporal of the Reserve for his part in this operation.[24]

Throughout 1915 the German forces conducted hit and run attacks not only at the border with British East Africa, but also in the south, destroying and damaging forts, bridges and railway tracks in Rhodesian territory. The well trained and disciplined askaris became more and more confident as their fighting experience increased. The askaris were very loyal and von Lettow-Vorbeck and his command respected their loyalty with admiration and fairness.[25]

Concerns and suspicions arose within the German units about the Massai, because the location and movements of the German forces seemed to be known to the British. The artificial border between British and German East Africa had been drawn by officials in Europe without any regard to tribal territories or spheres of influence. The Massai, a largely nomadic group of natives, were divided by this border. Far from being concerned that the Europeans were fighting each other, they saw an opportunity to exploit this situation. The British were quite willing to bribe the Massai with promises of rewards, such as livestock, in exchange for information about the movements and location of the enemy. As the Germans had Massais within their own territory as well, it was most difficult to stop these spying activities.[26]

THE BRITISH OCCUPY NORTHERN GERMAN EAST AFRICA – 1916

There was further sporadic fighting on the western border of the colony. In April and May 1916 the Belgian forces, under the command of Colonel Tombeur, attacked the province of Ruanda in German East Africa from the Belgian Congo by moving through Uganda. Also in May the British, under General Northey, launched a series of attacks in the southwest of German East Africa from Rhodesia and Nyasaland. The large lakes in western German East Africa were under British control.[27]

9. Massai warrior

10. Mt Longido, a strategic vantage point in German East Africa near the Kenyan border

The Allies were not the only 'enemy' the Germans had to face. By being constantly on the move and living in the wild, the forces frequently encountered dangerous wildlife – on several occasions lions had attacked humans; horses, donkeys and mules were spooked whenever they sensed or were stalked by lions. A constant guard had to be maintained to ensure safety. Other incidents involved elephants, rhinoceros, buffalos and crocodiles. The most feared however, were snakes, especially adders, the bite of which meant certain death.[28]

In early 1916 the British amassed thousands of troops near Voi, on the Mombassa-Nairobi railway line, not far from the northern border of German East Africa. These troops were under the command of General (later Field Marshall) Jan Smuts, an experienced officer. During the Boer War Smuts had been a Boer General fighting the British but was now serving with the British military. Smuts hoped to encircle large numbers of German forces and achieve a surrender. When Smuts attacked in February 1916, he had 45,000 troops at

CHAPTER SIX

THE GERMAN FORCES INITIALLY REPULSED THE
ATTACKS AND INFLICTED SUBSTANTIAL CASUAL-
TIES

*11. Friedrich Philipp Blankertz in
army uniform*

his disposal, including 19,000 South Africans, 14,000 Indians, plus troops of a number of other nationalities. The German forces initially repulsed the attacks and inflicted substantial casualties. Tropical diseases, especially malaria, affected many of the Allied forces in the area.[29]

After several weeks of fighting and with more fresh Allied troops arriving, the Germans began a strategic retreat whilst at the same time continuing to harass the enemy. The German forces continued to receive assistance and shelter from the persons still on German farms.[30] The Allies gradually advanced into northern German East Africa. Their thrust was twofold – one group advanced through the valley between Mt Meru and Mt Kilimanjaro to attack Moshi, which was the *Schutztruppe* Commander's headquarters as well as the administrative centre for the Germans. Moshi was taken by the Allies on 12/13 March 1916. The other group advanced south along the western slopes of Mt Meru towards Arusha. The 8th Mounted Unit, which included the "Blaich Boys", was forced to retreat from Mt Longido in February 1916. From the slopes of Mt Meru, they watched in awe and in anger as several thousand Allied cavalry men and 4,000 infantry soldiers from many parts of the British Empire flooded past. The troops moving into German East Africa were all well armed and were backed up by artillery and motorised transport units fully laden with supplies.[31]

Just before the Allies occupied the farms of Templer settlers, Gotthilf Blaich had an opportunity to visit his farm, probably for the last time. Just before he arrived at his home, his cousin's (Karl) unit came across a German farmhouse that had already been looted and ransacked. The members of the unit were unsure what they would find at the Blaich property. De Haas writes, *"It was already dark when they arrived at the Usa River, the area where the Palestine Germans lived. They were mostly Templers, who had come from the Promised Land a few years ago. [...] On arrival they threw small stones at the windows to raise the occupants. Caution was necessary, because one could not know who was inside. Suddenly, a shot rang out from a window as it was opened from the inside. "Don't shoot", the young Blaich called out. His voice was recognised by his sister* (Frieda) *"It's Gotthilf", she said with shock and relief"*. Fortunately, neither strangers nor enemy troops had reached the farm yet. The German farmers feared the unruly bands of marauding Massai the most. Sitting down and having a meal in a German farmhouse had become a rare event for Gotthilf Blaich; it may well have been the last time before he was taken prisoner.[32]

12. Gottlieb Bauer's war decorations. He was awarded the Iron Cross 2nd Class for bravery, the Colonial Medal also known as the 'Elephant Medal' and the Wounded Medal (in black). His belt buckle is shown as well as the ornamented bullet that wounded him in 1915

Rudolf Bauer gives a moving account of his father Gottlieb leaving his family in early 1916. Gottlieb and Elise had five children, and Elise was pregnant with their sixth and all doctors were gone, *"My father volunteered even though he, due to a heart complaint, had been found unfit for military service when still in Palestine. There was hardly a man left in the whole district. Even the hospital had been closed. My father, with his gun over his back, mounted his mule and, followed by our only dog 'Schnapps', just disappeared.[...] I can still remember my mother weeping [...] we children and all our native workers were also crying. I did not see my father again until 1920."[33]*

Arusha was taken by the British on 20/21 March 1916. Shortly after the Arusha/Mt Meru region was occupied by British forces, all German women and children were ordered into a homestead for their own safety and protection, because armed, unruly Massai were following the British into the occupied areas and plundering the German properties. Irmgard Schoer (née Bauer) provides a graphic account of the situation her mother and children found themselves in, *"[...] It was the rainy season and Elise Bauer was heavily pregnant with her sixth child. The rain was teeming down and it was night when Elise started to have contractions. She was placed on a hammock and had to be carried to the plantation to which they had been*

CHAPTER SIX

13. Gottlieb Bauer in uniform

14. Hulda Blankertz at her plantation at Tuiliani/Meru circa 1915

ordered to go. Her old mother, Dorothea, who only had one leg, also had to be carried as did the two youngest children. When this small caravan train finally arrived at the plantation, they could hardly find any space. The house was already filled with stricken mothers and crying children. This is where Elise Bauer gave birth to a son, whom she named Willi."[34]

After the fall of Arusha, the British forces pushed on towards the coast along the Pangani River valley – Same was occupied on 25 May, Mombo on 9 June, Wilhelmstal on 12 June and Tanga was finally captured by the British on 7 July 1916. With the capture of Tanga, the British controlled the northern part of German East Africa and the Usambara railway. Importantly, it also gave the British a port in German East Africa and allowed military provisions and personnel to be brought directly into German East Africa to support the British campaign.[35]

The Allied forces took the large German plantations during the first half of 1916, including the farms of the Templers. Once the situation became stabilised, the German women, children and elderly men were allowed to return to their farms. They saw scenes of total devastation – their homes had been broken into and everything was stolen, pillows and mattresses were slit open with the contents strewn about and the lovingly tended gardens were overgrown with weeds. A Major Brown was the commanding officer in the Mt Meru region and he was described as a very understanding person. The farms were

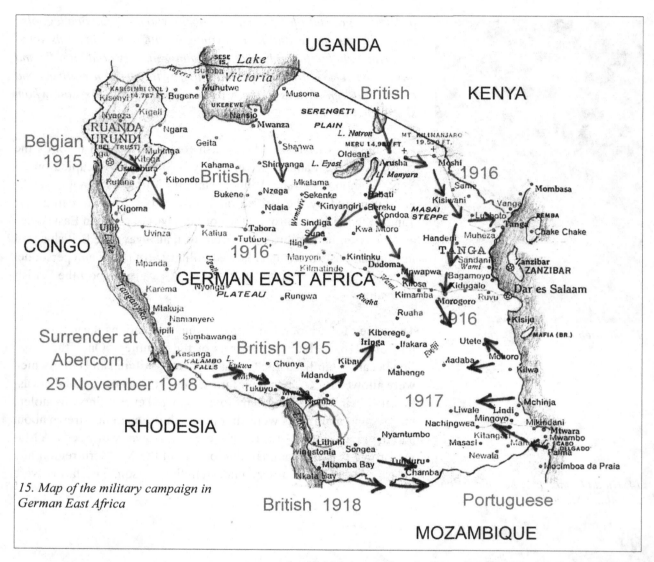

15. *Map of the military campaign in German East Africa*

now under British control and all produce had to be given up to the British authorities. Jakob Blaich was allowed to travel to Arusha as required.[36]

Once the situation became stabilised, the German women, children and elderly men were allowed to return to their farms

Elise Bauer and her six children returned to their mill and the British authorities requested her to mill flour for the British forces. She was told that if she declined, the mill would be confiscated. As she had nine persons to feed and clothe and was in dire straits, she agreed to the request. Although the British had promised her some payment, she never received a thing.[37]

After overrunning the Tanga-Moshi railway line the British commenced their advance to Tanga.[38] Once the northern half of German

132

CHAPTER SIX

East Africa was firmly in Allied control, the British appointed Mr (later Sir) Horace Byatt as administrator. Byatt introduced some new administrative concepts into the civilian sector, which were based on his wide colonial experience in Kenya and Uganda.[39]

The younger men left with the Lettow-Vorbeck troops to continue fighting the British as they advanced further into German East Africa. Most of the German settlers in the army were eventually taken prisoner. During the campaign, Gottlieb Bauer became very ill with malaria and black-water fever and had to be left behind with an askari to protect him from wild animals until the British would find him. He was taken to a British field hospital, then transported to Egypt via Dar-es-Salaam and interned in the Sidi Bishr prisoner-of-war camp. In the early phase of the war, a number of captured German soldiers were taken to India and interned, including Friedrich Philipp Blankertz and Ulrich Trappe, the latter who had been wounded and taken prisoner in a battle near Longido. Later in the war, as the Allied forces conquered more and more German East African territory, they established prison camps in the occupied areas. At the end of the war, many prisoners were taken to the Sidi Bishr, Rafa, Tura and Maadi camps in Egypt and interned.[40] The Germans captured in Palestine were also interned in these camps.[41]

The Allies also attacked towns and installations along the coastline and Dar-es-Salaam fell on 4 September 1916.[42]

Before withdrawing most of his forces to the south and the interior, von Lettow-Vorbeck ordered that the farmers' livestock be herded and driven south to provide food for the German troops and to prevent it from falling into enemy hands. During the withdrawal to the south, the Germans kept units in the field and continued to harass, ambush and delay the advance of the allied forces. Von Lettow-Vorbeck continued to avoid committing large numbers of troops to any one decisive battle.[43]

During the rainy season in 1916, the allied forces with their heavy transport vehicles became bogged on impassable roads, whereas the Germans retained their mobility by using porters. As they moved further south, away from the high mountains in the north of German East Africa, the Allies lost many men through illness, and their horses died in their thousands as they fell sick from tsetse fly-inflicted diseases. The German troops and their horses were also adversely affected by the changed climatic conditions.[44]

MOST OF THE GERMAN SETTLERS IN THE ARMY WERE EVENTUALLY TAKEN PRISONER

133

.... *entwischte uns inzwischen da es dunkel geworden ist.*
... got away since it had meanwhile become too dark.

1. [August] 11 Uhr nachts marschierten wir südl. vom Grabenrand bis Yumbe Magumu.
11 o'clock at night we marched southward from the ridge of the rift Valley to Yumbe Magumu.

2. [August] 6 Uhr morgens Ankunft beim Yumben, da waren die Engländer des Abends schon durchgekommen, fanden noch eines ihrer zurückgelassenen Pferde vor, und konnten von Eingeborenen erfahren, dass der Feind gleich nebenan die Wasserstelle besetzt habe, auf das hin ging eine Patrollie hin um näheres festzustellen. Patr. fand den Feind auch dort, und beschoß ihn in aller Ruhe, wir hatten ein sehr schönes Ziel, zirka 300 Pferde und Mannschaften, welche auf einen Klumpen liefen, wir zogen uns danach zurück bis Yumben Muanga von da bis Igne wo wir im Busch übernachteten
6 o'clock in the morning arrival at Yumben, there the enemy had already passed through the evening before. We still found one of their horses that they had left behind and were able to get the information from the natives that the enemy had occupied the water hole nearby. A patrol was sent out to obtain more information. The patrol did indeed find the enemy there and in all calm took him under fire. We had a nice target, some 300 horses and troops, who all ran in one heap/lump. After this we pulled back to Yumben Muanga, from there to Igne where we spent the night in the bush

3. [August] Igne über Madschongo bis Munja (schöne Wasserst.)
Inge via Madschongo to Munja (nice water hole)

4. [August] Munja Richtung Sekenke bis Yumben Baga, von da bis Yumben Masemaki.
Munja in direction of Sekenke up to Yumben Baga, from there until Yumben Masemaki.

5. [August] Masemaki bis zur Mission Everth
Masemaki to the Everth Mission

6. [August] Mission bis Sekenke.
Mission to Sekenke.

16. Extracts of Johann Albert Blankertz' war diary. Translation by Peer Gatter

6. [Dezember] 6 Uhr weiter in Richtung des Linderuto Berges, 3 Uhr am Murira-Fluß, sehr schönes Wasser

six o'clock moved onwards in direction of the Linderuto mountain, at 3 o'clock at the Murira River, very nice water.

7. [Dezember] Ruhetag

Day of rest.

8. [Dezember] 6 1/2 Uhr weiter in Richtung des Esimingoro [Kraters], 10 1/2 Uhr am Grabenrand, sehr schlechter Abstieg, unterhalb der Manyara-See, da übernachten.

6 .30 am onwards in direction of the Esimingoro [Crater], 10.30 am at the edge of the rift valley, very difficult descent, below the Manyara Lake, there we spent the night.

9. [Dezember] Erlegte einen großen Büffel 12 Uhr versuchten wir den See zu passieren, mussten aber wieder nach 3 Std. zurück, da uns die Sache zu schlammig wurde, de Haas wurde im See beinahe Ohnmächtig.

I shot a big buffalo, 12 o'clock we tried to pass through the lake but had to turn back after 3 hours since endeavour got too muddy, de Haas nearly lost consciousness in the lake.

10. [Dezember] Weitermarsch dem Nord-Rande des Sees zu, wo wir 1 Büffel, 1 Nashorn erlegten gingen noch bis Mtu ya Umbu.

March onwards towards the northern edge of the lake, there we shot 1 buffalo and 1 rhino. Continued to Mtu ya Umbu

11. [Dezember] 7 Uhr weiter bis an einen Nebenfluss des Mtu ya Umbu, 11 Uhr rasten. 3 Uhr weiter bis an den Fuß des Esimingoro [Krater], da eine Giraffe erlegt.

7 o'clock onwards until a tributary of the Mtu ya Umbu, 11 o'clock making a halt, 3 o'clock onwards to the foot of the Esimingoro [Crater], there killed a giraffe

12. [Dezember] 6 1/2 weiter der Straße Mbugwe zu, 11 1/2 Uhr am Mtuyuni.

6.30 am onwards towards the road of Mbugwe, 11.30 at the Mtuyuni.

13. [Dezember] 9 1/2 Uhr an der Straße Bufimi da legten wir uns in den Busch und haben mal alles abgefangen was vorüber kam, u.a. 5 Aruscha Leute, von denen ich so manches erfahren konnte, von da weiter bis Snakini.....

9.30 am on the Bufimi Road, there we hid in the bush, and captured whoever passed through, among others 5 people from Aruscha, of whom I got quite some information, from there on to Snakini....

At the end of 1916, Smuts was recalled to South Africa. Although he had captured vast areas of northern German East Africa around the Mt Kilimanjaro region as well as the Tanga-Moshi railway line, and had driven the German forces south and into the interior, he had not been able to force a surrender from the Germans.

THE WAR YEARS 1917-1918

During the latter war years more and more allied troops were deployed. Well-trained Ghurkha units and battle-hardened regiments from the Gold Coast (now Ghana) and Nigeria forced the German forces further and further south. When the Germans first encountered the Ghurkhas and observed them from a distance, some thought because of their small stature that they were Japanese and that Japan had entered the war.[45] Although von Lettow-Vorbeck avoided large-scale battles, his losses (especially of experienced officers) through casualties and illness were starting to affect his units' fighting capabilities. The Allies captured part of the southern railway line from Dar-es-Salaam and new forces were advancing northwards from Northern Rhodesia (now Zambia). Furthermore, the Belgians were pressing into the west of the colony from the Congo. Support amongst the native population was beginning to wane as news of the Allied advances became known. The Germans still had a large herd of live-

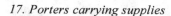
17. Porters carrying supplies

CHAPTER SIX

18. Philipp Albert Blankertz at Sidi Bishr Camp

19. German soldiers in Sidi Bishr prisoner of war camp in Egypt

stock with them as they retreated further south and into the interior of their colony. This stock was gradually being slaughtered or lost. Food and other supplies to sustain a fighting force became a major problem for the Germans as they lost control of the larger towns and farms. Many of the men became ill and treatment for the wounded was difficult because their scant medical supplies had been used up and no facilities (hospitals) were available. Von Lettow-Vorbeck reduced the rations for his troops, game was hunted for meat and the number of porters with the units was reduced. Footwear (boots) was made of leather from English saddles, wild honey replaced sugar, and bandages were made of bark. As the supply of quinine ran low, an alternative medicine made from bark was brewed – it was colloquially known as *Lettow Schnapps*.[46]

Probably the most significant battle of the campaign occurred at Mahiva in October 1917. The Germans had set up strong defensive positions before being confronted by some 5,000 Allied troops. In the ensuing battle that lasted four days, the Germans lost 95 men and the Allies had some 2,700 casualties. The Germans captured numerous badly needed machine guns, rifles and other military supplies. Despite this significant victory, the German supply position was still acute and von Lettow-Vorbeck realised that a large fighting group could no longer be sustained. He therefore reduced his force to 2,000 men including 1,700 askaris.[47]

With this reduced force, the Germans moved further south into Portuguese East Africa territory (now Mozambique). On 25 November

20. Kitchen in Camp A at Sidi Bishr
(See postcard below)

1917, the Germans attacked a Portuguese garrison and captured a vast quantity of supplies – modern rifles, machine guns, horses and equipment and one million rounds of ammunition. This booty was sufficient to equip the entire force.[48]

During 1918, food continued to be a problem for von Lettow-Vorbeck and his small band of fighters. On occasions, hippopotamuses were shot for both meat and fat. The combatants were continuously pursued across vast stretches of Portuguese territory. Several clashes occurred with both sides suffering substantial casualties.[49]

By September 1918 the German forces had moved further south, almost to the Zambezi River, where they feared they could be trapped. Von Lettow-Vorbeck decided to change direction and moved north

The postcard reads:

"Sidi Bishr 7 April 1918
Dear Hertha!
The picture on the other side shows the kitchen of camp A where Mr Doh is kitchen chef. Ours is the same as the kitchens in camp B and D. In camps A, B and D there are only Germans and Austrians, whilst in Camp C there are Turks and Arabs. Altogether it is a huge camp. In the middle of the camp complex is a large exercise - sporting area. We have electric lights on the whole night, everything is brightly lit up. With fond regards your
(Signed R.Lippmann [1204])"
(Translated by Helmut Glenk)

21. Post Card from Sidi Bishr Camp

22. German War Memorial in Tanga

again, hoping to avoid detection by the Allies. However, his moves were detected and the Allied forces regularly attacked his troops. By mid September, the German forces had been reduced to only 170 Europeans and 1,400 loyal askaris. To make matters worse, an influenza outbreak reduced the number of fit men even further.[50]

In October 1918 the German forces re-entered German East African territory, but the Allies were in hot pursuit, so they went west into British Northern Rhodesia where only a few Allied troops were stationed. On 11 November 1918, unaware of the armistice in Europe, the Germans attacked and captured Kasama.[51]

Not long after this, a British dispatch rider under a flag of truce arrived at von Lettow-Vorbeck's headquarters with a message saying that an armistice had been signed in Europe and that the war was over. Von Lettow-Vorbeck refused to believe it, so the British sent more messages, including one for unconditional surrender. Finally, on 23 November 1918, von Lettow-Vorbeck laid down the German East Africa Force's arms at Abercorn, Rhodesia. His final force, undefeated, comprised 30 officers, 125 European soldiers and 1,100 askaris plus some porters. He disbanded his force and handed over 400 machine guns and 1,000 rifles – almost all Portuguese and British. Von Lettow-Vorbeck was taken to Dar-es-Salaam and, on 17 January 1919, he departed Africa to return to Germany.[52]

In four years of war, the small German force that fought in East Africa had been confronted by 137 Allied Generals and 300,000 soldiers. The Allied forces despite their overwhelming superiority had been unable to capture and defeat von Lettow-Vorbeck and his remaining fighters. The German campaign in East Africa had achieved its aim of tying down large numbers of Allied troops which otherwise could have been deployed on the Western Front in Europe.[53]

On 11 November 1918, unaware of the armistice in Europe, the Germans attacked and captured Kasama

THE IMMEDIATE POST WAR PERIOD 1919 TO 1921

THE AFTERMATH OF WORLD WAR I

The defeat of Germany had an immediate and devastating effect on the German settlers in East Africa, including those from Palestine. The colony was now firmly under the control of the British authorities. Horace Byatt, who had been appointed Administrator over the northern part of German East Africa during the war, was now given control over the whole of the colony. In the mid 1920s, Byatt's title was changed to Governor. Major Brown, who had been in the Mt Kilimanjaro area as military commander for several years, was transferred.[1]

At the end of 1918 Spanish influenza, the worldwide pandemic, reached the Mt Meru area. The women, children and old men who had remained on the farms imposed strict quarantine measures on their loved ones. Anyone who had contact with outside persons had to sleep in sheds away from the house. The problem of treating infected persons was made more acute by the lack of medication. The farmers introduced preventative measures such as cold tea with eucalyptus leaves every morning. People became infected anyway. The treatment then was a dose of milk with turpentine drops and frequent cold poultices. Fortunately, none of the settlers covered in this book died from the influenza.[2]

THE PROBLEM OF TREATING INFECTED PERSONS WAS MADE MORE ACUTE BY THE LACK OF MEDICATION

During the war some of the captured German and Boer soldiers had been taken to prisoner-of-war camps in India, whilst others were interned in camps in East Africa. In 1918, after the war was over, the British transferred the prisoners held in former German East Africa, to the Tura, Maadi and Sidi Bishr camps in Egypt. The men were initially taken to Voi in Kenya, by rail to Mombassa and then transferred by ship to Egypt, where they were interned together with many Germans from Palestine. From Egypt, many were repatriated by ship and temporarily accommodated in Bad Mergentheim.[3]

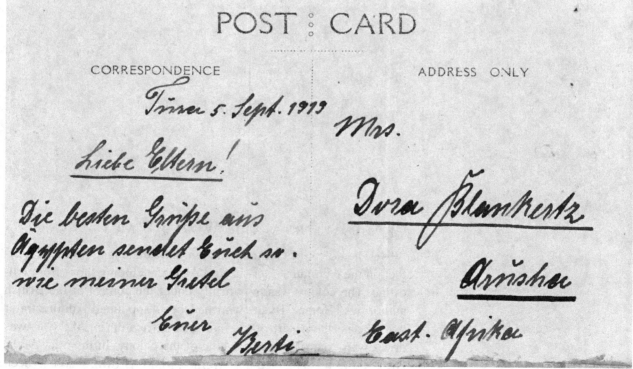

1. *Post card sent by Philipp Albert Blankertz (Berti) during his internment at Tura, Egypt to his mother, Dorothea in Arusha, 1919*

CHAPTER SEVEN

In the meantime, the women, children and old men who had worked tirelessly during the war years to keep their farms going and even started to build up their herds again were hopeful that the men would soon come home. Major Brown, at the request of the remaining settlers, made representation to the High Command for the interned men to be released and allowed to return to their loved ones, but it was not approved.[4] As time passed, and the men did not return, serious concerns arose about the future of the settlers of former German East Africa.[5]

As time passed, and the men did not return, serious concerns arose about the future of the settlers of former German East Africa

Farewell to German East Africa

In mid 1919 the fate of the Germans – women, children and elderly men – in German East Africa was sealed. The settlers' worst fears came true when the British authorities announced that all Germans had to leave the country. The farmers' families were given only a short time to vacate their farms and plantations. They were allowed to pack only clothing and linen (manchester) and take no more cash than 500 rupees per adult and 250 rupees per child. These amounts were regarded as "pauper money". Any livestock that could be sold – which was very difficult under the circumstances – was sold at very

2. Elise Bauer and her six children at their plantation and mill near Arusha just prior to their deportation in 1918/19

low prices. The farm workers – loyal natives – became despondent and despaired at the news of their employers' departure. The few belongings that could be taken were packed into large wooden boxes that were quickly made up for this purpose. All this had to be done in the absence of men except for the elderly.[6]

LEAVING THE PROPERTIES WAS A HEARTBREAK-ING EXPERIENCE

Leaving the properties was a heartbreaking experience. The farms and plantations that had been wrested from the wilderness with so much hard work, hope and sacrifice had to be abandoned. The women had struggled to maintain the properties after the men had gone. Now all would be lost. The loyal native workers – so much part of the daily life – the dogs and horses and the lovingly tended gardens would soon be only memories. It was a time of great sadness and a time the women could not share with their distant loved ones.[7]

The first group of settlers and their luggage were taken by train to the port of Tanga, where it was found that too many persons had arrived and not all could board the ship that was to take them to Germany. When the places were allocated, several families were split, causing additional personal anguish. For example with the Bauer and Blankertz families, Hulda Blankertz and Margarethe (wife of Philipp Albert Blankertz) were ordered to go on board, while their disabled mother Dorothea Blankertz, and their sister Elise and her six children had to stay behind.[8]

3. The harbour at Massawa, Eritrea circa. 1920

Quarantined in Eritrea

Towards the end of 1919 another ship finally arrived to take the next group of German women, children and old men who had been stranded in Tanga to Europe. As soon as the ship had left, there was an outbreak of smallpox in Tanga. Because of this the ship carrying the former German settlers was ordered to berth at Massawa, a small island in the Red Sea just off the coast of Eritrea, which was an Italian colony at the time. Massawa is renowned for its stifling and unbearable heat.[9]

ELISE BAUER, HER CHILDREN AND MOTHER WERE FORCED TO SPEND A WHOLE YEAR ON THIS INHOSPITABLE ISLAND

Elise Bauer, her children and mother were forced to spend a whole year on this inhospitable island. They were accommodated in a grand old colonial building that had been built for the former civilian and military governors when the Italians took possession of Eritrea in January 1890. The island was connected to the mainland by a railway line on an embankment. However, their forced stay was longer than expected because ships from India, on which bubonic plague had been detected, were periodically quarantined there and the whole coast was closed off.[10]

The food rations on Massawa were scant and halfway through the year (1920) the children had been reduced to skin and bones. In an effort to supplement these rations by earning some money, Elise Bauer obtained a permit from the Italian authorities to start a small café. She had no chairs and tables and all her customers had to sit on mats until she had earned enough money to buy the furniture. The café

MASSAUA - Palazzina Orero

4. The quarantine camp in the "Orero Palace" at Massawa, Eritrea

with its fine coffee soon became famous and was even very popular with the Italian officials.[11]

After twelve months the quarantine at Massawa was lifted and Elise Bauer, her children and her mother were finally able to continue their journey. They travelled to Genoa via the Suez Canal on board a small Italian steamer. From there they caught a train to Munich, Germany, to be re-united with their husband and father. Elise Bauer and her family had been separated from him for over four years.[12]

RETURN TO GERMANY

In September 1920, the last group of German settlers left the former East African colony. They were taken to Tanga, where they boarded a small steamer. The captain's instructions were to take the German and Boer women, a few old men and 100 children to Rotterdam, Holland. The journey went around the Cape of Good Hope, South Africa. Nearing the Cape, the ship developed mechanical trouble and had to stop at Cape Town. While it remained anchored there for three weeks for repairs, none of the men, women or children were allowed to go ashore – it was an extremely stressful time for the mothers of young children.[13]

After encountering several storms in the Atlantic Ocean, and a particularly severe one in the Bay of Biscay, the ship finally reached Rotterdam. On disembarking there, the settlers were transported by train to Bad Mergentheim in Germany where, for the first time after a long separation, many of the settlers' families were reunited.[14]

CHAPTER SEVEN

Life in Bad Mergentheim

The settlers from former German East Africa not only met their menfolk again, but also relatives and friends from Palestine, who had been interned at Helouan, near Cairo in Egypt. Many had not seen each other for over ten years. In 1918, these people had been deported from the German Templer Palestine settlements of Jaffa, Sarona, Wilhelma and Jerusalem and interned in the former Al Hayat hotel complex at Helouan. In April 1920, 270 of these internees together with some prisoners-of-war from the Sidi Bishr and Maadi camps where brought to Bad Mergentheim in Germany. A number of young males from Palestine who had served in the German army were now living in Germany. They were able to visit their families in Bad Mergentheim. At that stage, it was unclear whether the Templers would be able to return to their former homes and settlements in Palestine.[15]

IT WAS UNCLEAR WHETHER THE TEMPLERS WOULD BE ABLE TO RETURN TO THEIR FORMER HOMES AND SETTLEMENTS IN PALESTINE

After their arrival in Hamburg on 7 May 1920, and following the completion of formalities assisted by the Red Cross, the former internees travelled by special train, via Würzburg and Königshofen to Bad Mergentheim. On the train, the former internees were accompanied by several nurses, and when the train stopped at several larger stations, they were greeted with music and served sausages and hot coffee. At Bad Mergentheim, a former castle which had been used as a military barracks during the war became their home for the next

5. Bad Mergentheim Castle

seven months. Some basic accommodation facilities had been prepared for their arrival and pieces of furniture from the barracks were also available. Over the entrance gate a sign had been erected which read *Willkommen in der Heimat* [Welcome in your home country]. They read this sign with mixed feelings, because they were hoping to return to their homes in Palestine or East Africa. They no longer regarded Germany as their home country.[16]

A committee had been formed in Bad Mergentheim to plan for the arrival and to provide for the internees. They were supported by the *Verein der Palästinadeutschen* [Association of Germans in Palestine] in Stuttgart. The new arrivals gradually rearranged the accommodation to provide more privacy for the families. Even though they were now free some of the settlers still used a communal kitchen to prepare their meals. Most of the men found some form of employment around Bad Mergentheim – many worked for the railways on track maintenance.[17] A Temple Society teacher from Jerusalem and his assistant provided some schooling for the children in Bad Mergentheim. Schoolrooms were set up in the assembly hall and other rooms of the former German knights.[18]

After they had settled in, the Bad Mergentheim officials suggested that the deportees adopt the name of *Palästinagemeinschaft Mergentheim* [Mergentheim Palestine Community]. A leadership group was elected to replace the previous local committee for running the daily business of ordering provisions, organising the kitchen roster and liaising with officials. The funding for provisions was through the *Institut für Volkshilfe* [Institute for Citizen Assistance], which was run by the State. Bread, meat and milk were received and accounted for in accordance with the rationing regime operative at the time. The Palestine group was also fortunate to receive donations from charities, such as local church groups and school committees, as well as to be supplied from neighbouring villages with vegetables - carrots, sauerkraut, beans, peas, potatoes, - fresh and dried fruits and other gifts of kindness. These were sometimes delivered by children pulling fully laden small handcarts. The Quakers in America sent clothing and tinned milk. The kindness of the donors was much appreciated by the recipients.[19]

THE KINDNESS OF THE DONORS WAS MUCH APPRECIATED BY THE RECIPIENTS

For recreation the settlers went for walks in the castle grounds, nearby parks, nature reserves and mountains; they enjoyed the beautiful scenery on their excursions into the Swabian and Franconian countryside. The experience of seeing snow and ice, or actually skate on ice, was something new for many people from Palestine and East Africa.[20]

CHAPTER SEVEN

On Sundays, the Templers conducted religious services in the main hall with hymn singing and music played on a harmonium. In October 1920 they celebrated *Dankfest* [Thanksgiving] within the confines of the castle.[21]

RETURN TO PALESTINE

Anxious months went by without any firm indication of a return to their former homeland. However, in early August 1920 a letter from the *Wiederaufbaukommission* or WAKO [Reconstruction Commission] clearly indicated a positive outlook for a return. The Reconstruction Commission was set up by the Templers under the auspices of the British authorities to facilitate the return of the settlers to Palestine. When news of their impending departure was confirmed, the town authorities of Bad Mergentheim conducted a special farewell function for the Palestine Germans. Speeches with sincere words of encouragement and best wishes were given by Mr Huber, the District School Inspector and by Mr Klozbuecher, the Mayor.[22]

The patience of the settlers was tested as the formalities for their return were finalised. Weeks went by before they finally departed Bad Mergentheim on 23 December 1920. They travelled by train to Ulm, where another 80 persons, who were also returning to Palestine but who had stayed elsewhere in southern Germany, joined them. Christmas was celebrated in cramped conditions on the train. Their journey took them through Austria on to Trieste in Italy. There they boarded a small steamer of the Lloyd Triestino line, the *Galizia*. Their journey was delayed by several days due to heavy fog in the Venice region. Finally, after steaming along the Dalmatian coast, the ship reached Jaffa on 13 January 1921.[23]

After disembarking, the families from Africa moved in with friends and relatives in the Templer settlements in Palestine. For example, Jakob Blaich's family lived with Sebastian Blaich in the Betlehem settlement; the Bäuerle family found accommodation with the Bachers in Wilhelma, before moving to an old house in Jaffa; Margarete Reinhardt went to Beirut where she found work as a domestic (home help).[24]

The settlers from former German East Africa had to make a totally fresh start in Palestine because they had come back penniless. All they had were the few personal possessions they had been allowed to take with them when they left their homes in Africa.[25]

A NEW LIFE IN GERMANY

A number of former settlers from the Arusha/Mt Meru region did not return to Palestine. They had left Palestine well before the war and had nothing to return to. They chose instead to stay in Germany and tried to make a new start in that country. The families from Africa were generally destitute and had difficulty in adjusting to their new and strange surroundings. For example, when Elise Bauer and her children arrived it was November and very cold – they had come from a tropical climate in Africa and had spent the past year suffering the heat in Massawa, Eritrea. They had no suitable clothing other than felt-lined khaki overcoats, which offered neither protection from the freezing cold nor from ridicule. The children had difficulty being accepted and became known in the local community as the *Afrika-Bäuerles*. The family rented a small apartment in Feuerbach near Stuttgart – a total change from the freedom and space of their lifestyle in East Africa.[26]

As well as having to adapt to a new life in a foreign country, the former African settlers also had to endure, as did all other Germans, the harsh economic conditions of post war Germany, with massive inflation and subsequent revaluation of the currency. The former East Africa settlers received a tiny amount of compensation from the German government for the properties the British had confiscated. For settlers like Johann Albert and Dorothea Blankertz, this money was soon worthless because they received their compensation payout in the early 1920s during the hyperinflation period. Fortunately some, such as their son-in-law, Gottlieb Bauer, received their compensation payment after 1923 when the inflation was over and the currency was reformed, which helped him find his feet in work and business.[27]

6. *Gottlieb Bauer in a sarcastic pose after the lost war in front of the Victory Column in Berlin in 1920. Note his clothes are several sizes too large. These clothes were issued to him by the German government on his repatriation to Germany when he was destitute and had lost absolutely everything.*

7. *The Bauer family in Germany during the 1920s*

THE BRITISH MANDATE PERIOD
1922 TO 1939

GREAT BRITAIN IS GIVEN A MANDATE OVER THE FORMER GERMAN COLONY

After its defeat in World War I and with the signing of the Treaty of Versailles and establishment of the League of Nations, Germany was deprived of all its overseas colonies. The Allies, rather than just taking over the colonies as their own, introduced a mandate system of administration under the auspices of the Supreme Council of the League of Nations. That system still contained a large element of colonialism and only applied to former 'enemy' colonies and territories and not to any pre-war Allied colonies.

Two types of mandates were adopted by the League of Nations – the 'A' type mandate was for the development of full independence; and the 'B' type was where the administering power undertook to "promote the material and moral well-being of the inhabitants as well as advancing the territory's social progress".[1]

Most of the former German colony was renamed Tanganyika Territory and administered by the British. The provinces of Ruanda and Burundi were placed under Belgian administration and an area of 400 square miles around Kianga at the mouth of the Rovuma River was given to Portugal to administer on behalf of the League of Nations.[2]

1. Map of Tanganyika

CHAPTER EIGHT

In 1922, Great Britain was given a 'B' type mandate for Tanganyika. The mandate terms were mainly directed to protect and prevent abuses of the population, such as slavery; provided for labour to be regulated and the sale of liquor to be controlled. An important element was that the sale of land to non-natives was prohibited without the approval of the public authorities. Britain was also required to report annually to the League and any disputes regarding the mandate and its application would be resolved by the Permanent Court of International Justice. Great Britain's last report to the League of Nations was submitted in 1939.[3]

During this period, Germany made representations to the League for the return of its former colonies but these requests were declined. This, together with the need for the authorities' approval to purchase land, restricted the return of many former settlers.[4]

Sir Horace Byatt, subject to the Colonial Office in London, continued to administer Tanganyika without any noticeable change despite the new Mandate. In 1925, he was succeeded by Sir Donald Cameron who introduced a system of indirect rule known as Local Native Administration. This gave some responsibilities to the traditional rulers (chiefs), but the final power of administration remained with the British authorities. In 1926 constitutional effect was given to this form of administration by the proclamation of the Native Authority Ordinance 1926. A number of authorities were established and they dealt with such matters as law and order, collection of poll and hut taxes, and payment of certain salaries. A new judicial system was introduced by the Native Courts Ordinance in 1929. Despite the introduction of a range of administrative measures, difficulties continued in having a cohesive overall uniform system of administration due to tribalism.[5]

In 1929 the northern railway line from Tanga to Arusha, the construction of which was started by the Germans in the early 20th century, was completed. It was officially opened on 5 December 1929 by his Excellency the Governor, Sir Donald Cameron.[6]

Another initiative introduced by Cameron was the establishment of a Legislative Council consisting of the Governor, thirteen official and up to ten unofficial members. The unofficial members were nominated by the Governor "as being particularly fitted to be of assistance to the Governor in the exercise of his responsibilities, having regard to all communities in the territory, both native and non-native

[…]" Initially, Cameron only appointed seven unofficial members - two Asians and five Europeans with expertise in farming, shipping, commerce and banking. The number of unofficial members was increased to ten in 1929. This form of Legislative Council administered Tanganyika until 1939, but no natives were appointed as unofficial members to the Legislative Council during that period.[7]

When the Germans were expelled at the end of the First World War, their farms, plantations, businesses and other estates were confiscated and sold by the authorities to Greeks, Scandinavians, Indians and other individuals, including members of the British military. The former German settlers and property and business owners received none of the proceeds nor any compensation for properties or other possessions they had left behind.[8]

THESE FORMER SETTLERS HAD TO ENDURE THE HARDSHIP OF HAVING ALL THEIR POSSESSIONS IN THE FORMER COLONY AUCTIONED OFF WITHOUT BEING GIVEN AN OPPORTUNITY TO BUY ANYTHING BACK OR CLAIM COMPENSATION

The Temple Society was aware of the plight of its former East Africa settlers who had lost everything they had worked for as a result of the war. Furthermore, these former settlers had to endure the hardship of having all their possessions in the former colony auctioned off without being given an opportunity to buy anything back or claim compensation.

Eventually in 1925, after numerous early unsuccessful attempts, several of the former settlers succeeded in returning, not to their properties, but to Tanganyika. Karl Blaich was the first to return, followed shortly by Georg Korntheuer (the man who had helped the early Templer settlers), Gottlieb Bauer and Samuel Kappus. A land agent had bought several former German holdings and had agreed to sell some of this land.[9]

THE BÄUERLE REPORT ON RESETTLEMENT OPPORTUNITIES

In early 1926 the brothers August, Hans and Hugo Bäuerle visited East Africa and prepared a detailed report on resettlement opportunities in the British East African territories of Kenya and Tanganyika. The Bäuerle brothers had started a chocolate business and a thread-spinning business in Germany after the war. These businesses, although relatively successful, did not bring the results nor the personal satisfaction they had hoped for. None of the three brothers had been in German East Africa before the war. During the trip to East Africa they purchased some property, and after building barrack type accommodation, the Bäuerle brothers returned to Germany to arrange for their families to come to Kenya. The Temple Society became aware of the Bäuerle report and decided, in the interests of the former 'African' settlers, to publish extracts of the report in the *Warte* [Templer Newspaper].[10]

The report was very detailed and provided cost estimates for many aspects of resettlement. Some of the considerations for new or returning settlers were:[11]

1. The trip from Germany with the German East Africa Line took 34 days from Hamburg to Mombassa and cost £Stg38.10s.

2. An entry visa had to be obtained from the British authorities via the Consulate and a £Stg50 deposit paid as a form of security to ensure that an immigrant had some means to support himself. If the immigrants could show officials on arrival that they already had secured employment or prove they had sufficient means of support, the deposit was refunded.

3. No military weapons were permitted to be brought into the territories. Shotguns, hunting rifles and ammunition were permitted but had to be registered with the authorities.

4. Clothing for tropical conditions was essential – either khaki or white suits and a tropical helmet or at least a double felt hat with a wide brim. Clothing could be readily bought on arrival in Mombassa, however, underwear and footwear was better purchased before arrival.

5. A variety of climatic conditions prevail along the coastal and lower areas where it is hot and humid whilst in the higher regions a cooler more temperate climate is found which is far more suitable for Europeans.

6. The railways in Kenya had been well established and extended right through to Uganda and to Lake Victoria. During the war, a railway line had been built between Voi in Kenya and Moshi in Tanganyika. There were regular train services and the trip from Mombassa to Nairobi took approximately 18 hours.

7. Nairobi was the capital of Kenya with a population of approximately 8,000. There the conditions for Europeans were comfortable. Nairobi was a thriving town with many motor cars; the Europeans lived mainly on the outskirts of the town, in a suburb named 'Parklands', in large villas surrounded by cool, shady gardens; everything

needed for daily life was available, as well as luxury items, but these attracted a 20% sales tax; all farming equipment and implements could be purchased and were tax exempt.

8. The areas of land for European settlement had been defined by the British authorities and were available for a 99 year lease. Before this measure, virtually all land had been given away. Much of the land had been acquired in this way by officials and other Europeans. The official land offices in Nairobi and Eldoret were able to offer numerous parcels of land on a leasehold basis at relatively low rates.

9. Getting good workers was a major problem. The settlers had to go to a reservation where, hopefully, some natives would volunteer to come to work on a trial basis. If well treated they would also encourage their family and friends to come and work. If not, they would return to the reservation and the settler would have great difficulty in attracting other workers. Other types of workers were the 'squatters', who bred stock and were prepared to move onto a farm with their family and stock and work for the landlord. The natives had to be paid three shillings and four pence per month on average, as well as two pounds of corn. Normally only males were employed, even as domestic helpers at the homesteads, because they were generally more reliable than the women. Women were mostly employed during the coffee bean harvest. By law, every native over the age of 16 had to have an identity pass and was not allowed to leave the farm or plantation without the permission of the landlord.

2. The villa in "Parklands" where Werner Uhlherr lived in 1929

3. Native women carrying bananas

The report mentioned that *"the price for land varies. For good coffee planting areas near Nairobi the price is £15 to £20* (Author: all currency in pounds Sterling) *per hectare and the further one moves inland the cheaper it becomes, for example near Lake Victoria the price is £8 to £10 per hectare. We found very suitable land on the plateau near Eldoret. It is right on the equator but at an altitude of 2,000 meters; the daily temperature varies between 18-28 °C and during the night 8-15°C. The price of land is £10 to £15 per hectare. Nearly all European and tropical plants grow here. The main crops are wheat – which gives a good return – as well as corn, coffee and pineapples. The land is too valuable for growing sisal, for which an area of 300-400 hectares is needed, [...] requiring an initial capital of at least 40,000 to 50,000 marks; however, if several farmers pool their resources, these establishment costs can be reduced to 25,000 to 30,000 marks. [...] By using joint resources and skills, three per-*

157

sons can work together; for example: one can build the houses and sheds, another obtains the necessary labour, building materials and other supplies and a third one clears the land etc.

After the initial building, 14 to 16 oxen and a sturdy cart have to be purchased so supplies can be brought in. The price for one ox is £10 and a good cart between £80 and £100 [...] to develop a coffee plantation 80,000 to 100,000 marks are needed but the returns are very good."[12]

4. Natives building a hut

*5. A primitive wooden bridge on a
forest road near Moshi*

Cars and motorised transport were becoming more popular and the government was building new roads from which the old heavy Boer wagons were banned.

6. The Nairobi Airport 1929

Bäuerle's report was published in the *Warte* for information purposes only and not as an advertisement to encourage settlement in East Africa. Persons needing more information were encouraged to contact the Bäuerles direct in Eldoret, Kenya.

SOME FORMER SETTLERS RETURN

Not all of the former German East Africa settlers from Palestine returned to Tanganyika after the war. Below are accounts from several families who did.

THE BLAICH FAMILY[13]

Members of the Blaich family yearned to return to the land where they had lived and toiled for over ten years. Palestine was no longer their home!

In 1923, Gotthilf Blaich left his family in Palestine and returned to Germany. He worked in Bremen with a newly formed German-Afghan company. He was asked to establish an office for the company in Kabul and went there via Russia, riding the last leg of the journey on horseback from the Russian border to Kabul. He stayed until 1928, when a revolution overthrew Emir Amanullah and all the Europeans feared they would be massacred and sought refuge in their countries' embassies. The British then flew out all those who wanted to leave, but they had to leave their possessions behind. Gotthilf Blaich met up with his wife and family (who were on a visit from Palestine, but were stranded on the closed Indian-Afghan border) in Rashawar, India, and decided to return to Africa (Tanganyika). They joined other

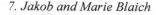

7. Jakob and Marie Blaich

members of the Blaich family who had returned to Tanganyika in 1925 and 1927. Gotthilf and his family managed to purchase some land bordering the Sanya River near Moshi and once again started a coffee plantation.

Fritz and Karl Blaich returned to Africa in 1926. They leased some land near Arusha and lived in a mud brick hut with a thatched roof until they could build something more substantial. Fritz worked the land and Karl, who was a builder, constructed the house and sheds for drying and storing coffee beans. They were joined in 1927 by Frieda, Otto and Heinz Blaich. In 1928 the elderly Jakob and his wife Maria, together with Paula, Trudi, Walter and Herta came just prior to Gotthilf Blaich and family arriving from India. They had to start from scratch, including building a house and outbuildings for their farm. They were not allowed to return to their former properties, now owned by Greeks, and could only watch in despair as the new owners harvested the coffee from the plantations – now fully productive – which they had developed from the wilderness in 1909/10 and nursed through World War I.

8. Map showing the location of the Blaich properties around Arusha

1. 'Usa Farm'
2. 'Gruk Farm'
3. 'Nashorn - Kifaru Farm'
4. 'Fritz & Irene Farm'

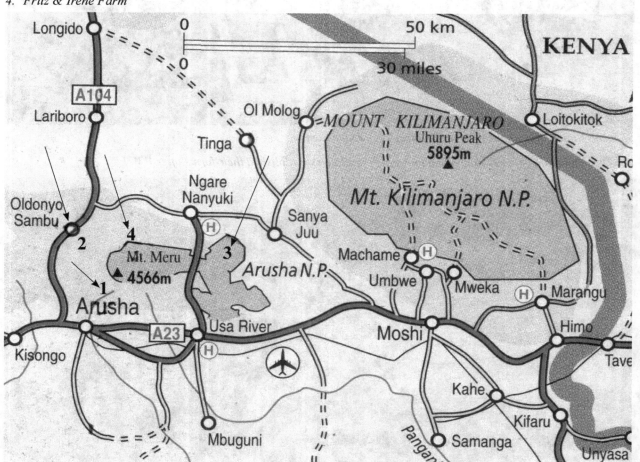

9. Jakob Blaich's farmhouse (front entrance) at Oldonyo Sambu

10. The countryside near Oldonyo Sambu where the Blaich's established their farms after WW I

11. Street scene in Arusha 1938

12. Karl Blaich's house in Arusha

13. Otto Blaich's joinery workshop in Arusha

14. Jakob Blaich in his coffee plantation

The Blaichs had saved enough money to purchase a small property at Sanya, north of Mt Meru in the valley between Mt Meru and Mt Kilimanjaro. It was virgin land and rather stony. They first built a shed and then a house and started to plant coffee. During this early period, Karl and Gotthilf worked as builders and were later joined by Otto who also was a carpenter. This gave them an income until the farm became productive. They saved and were able to buy more farmland west of Sanya.

The coffee plantations gradually produced saleable crops, but the worldwide depression of the 1930s saw the demand for coffee decline which made it hard to sell. Most of the coffee beans the Blaichs produced were bought by the Usagara Trading Company run by a merchant from Stuttgart, Germany, Heinz Bueb, who had established a coffee bean cleaning and drying facility in Moshi and who exported the coffee to Hamburg. The Blaichs purchased most of their supplies through the Usagara Trading Company which had its headquarters in Tanga.

The Blaichs still had some business and financial interests with the family members who had remained in Palestine and they gave them formal Powers of Attorney to conduct their affairs there. Other families made similar arrangements.

15. Power of Attorney given by settlers in Africa to their relatives in Palestine

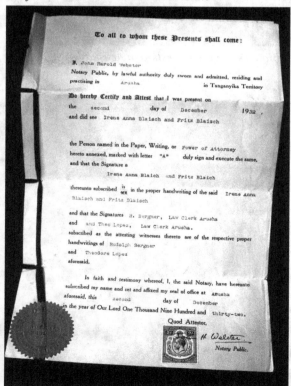

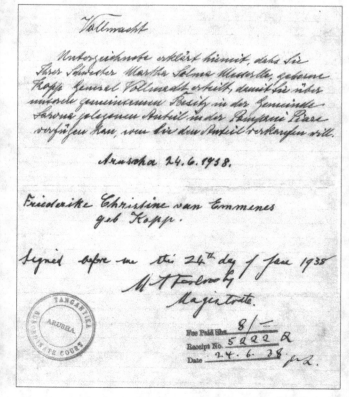

16. Market scene in Arusha

Below: 17. The Blaich and Assmus families in 1930s
(L to R) Karl, Jakob, Marie, Frieda, Heinz, Herta, Gertrude (Trudi), Irene (nee Haering), Ruth-Karin (child sitting), Maria Haering, Eberhard and Paula Assmus, Fritz Blaich

CHAPTER EIGHT

Left: 18. Arusha street scene with the Usagara Trading Store built by Karl Blaich on the right

As life settled down, the families grew and children needed to be educated. The Blaich family children went to the Usambara School which was located not far from their farms. Once "primary" school was completed, any student wishing to continue his or her education had to go to a boarding school in Germany. In 1932, Gerhard Blaich went to a school called the *Friedrich von Bodelschwingh Schulinternat* [boarding school] in the Usambara Mountains and from there he went to Germany in 1935 and attended a small private boarding school in Siecksdorf near Calw. In 1938, Herta Blaich was sent to the *Reichskolonialabteilungsschule* at Rendsburg near Kiel, and Trudi Blaich won a scholarship to a girls high school (Internat) in Germany.

In the 1930s Karl Blaich constructed numerous building, including a power station in Moshi, which generated electricity for the town. In late 1938 he returned to Germany because he could not get enough building work in Tanganyika. He found that most of the work for which he tendered was given to Indians, not only because they worked for very low wages, but also because of his German nationality in a British mandate territory. Furthermore he had become ill with a tropical disease whilst in Tanganyika and had to be treated at the Tropical Diseases Institute at Tübingen in Germany.

19. The New Arusha Hotel built by Karl and Otto Blaich. Note the rhinoceros on the roof-line – it was from the original famous Nashorn Apotheke *(rhinoceros pharmacy) in Arusha before WW I*

THE ASSMUS FAMILY

In 1925 Friedrich (Fritz) Assmus returned to Tanganyika and married Paula Blaich shortly after. He and two German colleagues created a construction company, which was successful until 1933/34 when the effects of the policies of the Third Reich meant that German companies were given no contracts for work. Assmus sold his company and bought 600 hectares of farmland with water frontage on the Usa River. He cultivated 400 hectares with vegetables and corn and 'leased' the remaining 200 hectares to the Massai for grazing, mainly goats. In return for having the use of the land, the Massai looked after Assmus's herd of goats. The farm was at Low Usa near to the farm of Jakob Blaich.[14]

Friedrich Assmus built three water-driven mills along his riverfront. These mills virtually worked non-stop grinding corn for the natives as well as for the European settlers.[15]

20 Water tower built by Friedrich Assmus

21. Paula Assmus with her son Eberhard

22. *The Assmus house during construction in Arusha*

23. *Friedrich Assmus (centre)*

24. *The bridge over the Pangani River in Tanganyika, built by Friedrich Assmus*

THE BLANKERTZ FAMILY[16]

In the mid 1920s Philipp Albert Blankertz and his wife Margarete decided to rebuild their lives in Africa with the help of the meagre compensation they had received for their lost Leganga property. They went to Cameroon in West Africa, where Philipp Albert found employment as manager of a large, formerly German owned, tobacco plantation. The plantation had been confiscated after the war and was now in the hands of an Englishman. Whilst in Cameroon the Blankertz family lived in an old *boma* built by the German *Schutztruppe* before the war. Their stay was however only of a short duration. After three years in Africa, Margarete became seriously ill with malaria leaving her disabled and confined to a wheel chair for the rest of her life. This forced the family to return to Germany where they settled in Kiel, Schleswig-Holstein.

25. Philipp Albert Blankertz (top left) and his wife Margarete Blankertz (lower left) with infant and other passengers on their voyage to Cameroon

26. Margarete Blankertz (far right) and daughter with local workers in Cameroon

27. The former boma where the Blankertzes lived in Cameroon

THE BAUER FAMILY[17]

Gottlieb Bauer had considered buying a small sawmill in Agenbach in the northern Black Forest in Germany with the compensation payment he had received from the German government, but decided against it because of the long cold winters in that region. Instead, he went into partnership and started a mechanical workshop near Stuttgart.

In 1926, when he became aware that Germans were once again allowed to go to East Africa, he decided to sell his business and returned to Arusha with Theo, his eldest son, aged 18. Theo had just completed his training as a toolmaker.

GOTTLIEB BAUER'S INTENTIONS WERE TO BUILD A HOUSE FOR HIS FAMILY AND ESTABLISH A MOTOR CAR REPAIR WORKSHOP

Gottlieb Bauer's intentions were to build a house for his family and establish a motor car repair workshop. He hoped that he would then be able to bring out his family from Germany in a year's time. Gottlieb took with him appropriate tools and equipment to start his new venture in Arusha. His former property now belonged to an Englishman who, after a courtesy call from Gottlieb, threatened to shoot him if he entered the property again.

Living in sight of his former hand-built mill – now in someone else's possession was more than what Gottlieb could endure and he therefore decided not to stay near Arusha. Instead he opted to resettle, together with other returned German settlers, on land near the Oldeani crater, approximately one day's travel to the south-east of Arusha. There he bought a parcel of land on the extinct volcano's eastern slope and lived in a tent at a campsite in the middle of the forest until a small basic house was built.

28. Gottlieb Bauer's camp at the Oldeani Crater in 1926

CHAPTER EIGHT

He started a small coffee plantation and, with the help of his son and local workers, channelled water to his property to service a sawmill. He and his son, Theo, also built a workshop and, because mechanics were few and far between, they soon established a good clientele amongst the farmers.

By mid 1927, with a steady income to support his family, Gottlieb decided it was time to go to Germany and bring home his wife, Elise and their children. He had notified her that he would be in Germany by the end of June 1927, and that she should pack and be ready to return with him. The family, who had been away from their beloved Africa for so long, were excited to go back there again.

Gottlieb Bauer set off for Germany with a shipment of coffee, some cash to buy more machines and equipment, as well money from several other German settlers who wanted him to buy goods for them in Germany. He boarded a German ship of the Woermann Line and, whilst travelling through the Red Sea, he mysteriously disappeared. The shipping line's official version was that he had committed suicide: he had suffered a bout of malaria, had become delirious and was taken to the ship's sickbay; at night, during a moment of inattention by the staff, he left the sickbay and jumped overboard. A steward from the ship later told the family that the crew believed that Gottlieb Bauer was murdered by a member of the crew and his body thrown overboard between Aden and Port Said. The said crewmember disappeared from the ship, probably on a small boat, before the ship berthed in Port Said and Gottlieb Bauer's considerable funds vanished with him.

When the news of Gottlieb Bauer's tragic death reached his wife and children in Germany they were devastated. The family did not have the financial means to pursue the matter through the courts and the shipping line absolved itself from blame by insisting his death was suicide.

Life for Elise and her six children (the Bauers seventh child, a daughter, Irmgard, was born in Germany in 1923) continued in Germany. These were very difficult years for the family, living in a small apartment with very little means. The family depended solely on their son Helmut, who was the only one earning any money.

Theo Bauer stayed in East Africa. He was 19 years old when his father died. Lack of finance soon forced him to sell the property at Oldeani. He then lived for several years as a hunter, a leader of hunting safaris and a gold prospector. In 1935, when his younger brother

29. *Prospecting for Gold*

Herbert found him, he was prospecting for gold on the Lupa River with his friends, Otto and Walter Blaich.

Whilst in Germany, Herbert Bauer had been able to get a one-year contract to work on a tea plantation in Tanganyika. At the end of his work contract, he agreed to build a house for the family with his brother Theo in Africa and with financial support from his other brother Helmut in Germany.

Theo Bauer built the house in Arusha with the help of several skilled native workers. It commanded beautiful views of Mt Meru. Otto Blaich made the furniture and fittings. Otto's workshop was a short distance from the home and Karl and Frieda Blaich lived only 150 meters away. After the house was built, Theo worked as a motor mechanic again.

30. *A Heinz Bueb statement (letterhead) addressed to Helmut Bauer*

KILIMANJARO COFFEE CURING WORKS.
KILIMANJARO MPOSHO MILLS.
AGRICHEMICALS.
KIFUMBU COFFEE ESTATES

STATEMENT.

No. 315

MOSHI, 30/6/ 1939.

Herrn H. Bauer
i. Hause

IN ACCOUNT WITH

HEINZ BUEB

PHONE 17   MOSHI   P. O. BOX 63.

31. Arusha at the foot of Mt Meru (view from the Blaich and Bauer homes)

In December 1937, Elise Bauer and her daughter, Irmgard, arrived in Arusha to move into the new house. A flower and vegetable garden was soon developed around the house and many fruit trees planted.

In 1938, Helmut Bauer came from Germany as he had obtained employment as manager of a coffee plantation named *Kifumbu* , a day's walk north of Moshi on the eastern slopes of Mt Kilimanjaro. He lived at the plantation in a small *boma* that had been built by the former German Protection Force at the turn of the century. Helmut also worked as a sales representative for Heinz Bueb, the manager of the Usagara Trading Company.

The Bauers soon established contact with the former Templer settlers who had returned to Africa. They had regular contact with the Blaichs living in Arusha and they often visited Oldonyo Sambu where

32. Helmut Bauer setting out for Africa again in 1938

33. A freshly felled forest on the Kifumbu Coffee Plantation where Helmut Bauer worked as the administrator

the elderly Jakob and Marie Blaich lived with their son Fritz and his wife Irene and young daughter Ruth-Karin. The Blaichs had two coffee plantations there and the Bauers were always welcome. The Bauers also received visits from "Bob" Egger and his wife with their young son Arwid.

Irmgard, the youngest daughter, went to school in Arusha to learn English. Her parents also planned for her to continue her education at the new German school at Oldeani.

Life was improving for the Bauers after all the personal hardships they had endured since 1916. They had a home again, were working, and the men could go on hunting safaris with their friends.

34. Helmut Bauer on the Kifumbu Coffee Plantation

35. A hunting safari – from left: Otto Blaich, Theo Bauer, Helmut Bauer, and native helpers

The Bäuerle Family[18]

The Bäuerles were another family to return to Africa after WW 1.

Christian Bäuerle, his wife Luise and their children, Rolf, Christian and Bruno migrated to Kenya in 1930. They left just after the tragic death of their youngest son, Herman, who was accidentally shot. In Kenya, Christian and his brother, Herman, tried to start a farm breeding cattle. Unbeknownst to them the area where their farm was had previously been subjected to cattle plague and the venture failed.

Gottlob Bäuerle and his family had been in German East Africa before World War 1 and had returned to Palestine in 1920. There they lived in several locations and he worked for a number of employers. The family also tried its hands at farming at Beisan in the Jordan valley. In 1926 during their time in Palestine, one of their daughters, Luise, married Erwin Kopp. The family worked and saved hard but were unhappy in Palestine.

CHAPTER EIGHT

In the early 1930s Gottlob and Rosalie Bäuerle with their daughter, Rösle, went to Kenya. There they found employment at a goldmine which was managed by Christian, Gottlob's brother. A short time later Erwin and Luise Kopp migrated from Palestine to join her family in Kenya. The family initially lived in a clay hut but later acquired a small farm.

The Bäuerle family also staked out mining claims and dug for gold with little success. In 1939, just before the Second World War started, they established their own mine and built a water-wheel and sluice to wash gold bearing soil. The mine was located near Kagamega, Kenya.

36. Post card from Arusha

THE GOETZE FAMILY[19]

The internment in Egypt in World War 1 at Helouan and the Tura camp had a happy ending for two of the internees. Alfred Goetze from Silesia in Germany, had enlisted in the army and volunteered for and served with the *Schutztruppe* in German East Africa from 1907/08 and during World War I. After being taken prisoner by the Allies, he was interned at the Tura prison camp in Egypt. He was a keen musician and an accomplished violinist. The prisoners-of-war sometimes performed concerts for the civilians from Palestine who were interned at Helouan near Cairo. There he met a young lady internee, Luise Bacher. In 1920, after their release from internment they married in Leipzig, Germany.

37. *Program of the Streich-Orchester (string orchestra) of the German East Africans from the POW camp at Tura, Egypt – August 1919*

CHAPTER EIGHT

Alfred Goetze decided not to stay in Germany. He was able to obtain a Polish passport, because the area of Silesia where he had grown up was now under Polish jurisdiction. This enabled him to return to Tanganyika in 1922. Leaving his wife and baby daughter Erika behind in Germany he went to Tanganyika, where he found work on a sisal plantation in the Usambara region. After saving some money he moved to Mwomsaza, in central Tanganyika, where he met a man who also wanted to start again from scratch. Together, they purchased approximately 200 hectares of land on the west side of Lake Victoria near Muleba, just south of Bukoba (the largest nearby town). The land on the high plateau was open and slightly hilly, the soil was sandy and stony, but several springs provided an ongoing water supply. A house was constructed and Alfred then brought his wife and daughter over from Germany to join him. In 1924 the family welcomed the birth of a son, Friedrich.

The Goetze family farmed the land – coffee was planted on 100 acres and bananas on a smaller area; they established a herd of 100 beef cattle and dairy cows, providing milk and butter; pigs were reared for meat and sausages, and chickens for eggs. The cows were mainly from Zebu stock, which is similar to the Brahman breed in Austra-

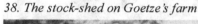

38. The stock-shed on Goetze's farm

lia. The manure from the animals was used to fertilise the plantation as well as their vegetable garden. At times, the Goetzes would exchange dairy products – milk, cheese and butter – for other goods at the nearby mission station. They sold the coffee they grew to Indian merchants as green coffee beans. These merchants shipped the beans by steamboat across Lake Victoria from Bukoba. There were three ships operating on Lake Victoria and up to 1,000 tons of coffee beans could be loaded on each ship. The beans were taken to Mombassa and then shipped overseas. The Goetzes grew most of their own fruit and vegetables. Although they were almost self-sufficient, they purchased their other household needs, such as flour and kerosene, from Kenya. All stock had to be corralled at night to prevent losses from attacks by lions, leopards, hyenas and jackals. They also kept several Alsatians for protection.

39. Erika 2nd from left, Luise, Alfred and Friedrich Goetze

It was mainly the Bahaya natives who came to work on the plantation and they had to be paid. They were handed a timecard on which their hours of work were recorded. The natives lived on the plantation in mud and grass huts and each was given approximately one acre on which they grew maize, beans and vegetables for their own consumption. The Goetzes also grew maize (corn) for the native workers who lived on the property.

CHAPTER EIGHT

Alfred built the Goetze house from natural stone. Natives cut the stones at a nearby quarry and other native workers carried them on their heads to the building site. Alfred taught several natives how to lay the stones. All the walls were of solid stone and the roof was of corrugated iron. The ceiling was constructed from cedar, which was resistant to termites. The house was quite spacious, with four bedrooms, a kitchen, a large dining room and a formal living room. Wide verandas extended along the front and back of the house. The kitchen had a wooden stove and oven for cooking, baking and heating water. They developed a garden around their house and planted cedar and other shade trees. At first, water had to be carried from one of the springs every day, but later a small pump was installed to pump water to a small tank on a stand. Kerosene was used for lighting and for hurricane lanterns. Later on a small generator was purchased for lighting.

The area were the Goetzes lived was quite remote – their nearest neighbour was eight kilometers away and the closest mission station fifteen kilometers. They collected their mail from the mission station. Bukoba, the nearest town was 80 kilometres north of their plantation; approximately 50 Europeans lived there. The shops and businesses in Bukoba were largely run by Indians and Arabs and all monetary transactions were in Pounds Sterling. As the nearest doctor was at Noragi, some 21 kilometres away, it was difficult for anyone

40. Alfred Goetze with his daughter Erika, son Friedrich and a native worker

41. One of the ships used to ferry supplies across Lake Victoria

requiring medical attention. Malaria was always present and, unfortunately, both Erika and Friedrich contracted polio as children. Erika was crippled by the illness and had to be taken to Germany by a missionary Sister for treatment and convalescence.

The education of children was another problem facing the German families in the remote parts of Tanganyika. Initially, Luise Goetze taught her children to read and write and some arithmetic at home. The mission ran a school, but it was only for native children. Friedrich attended the school at Eldoret in Kenya with fourteen other German children. However, when several of the Bäuerle children left, the school became unviable and was closed.

42. The new school built by the German Government in the 1930s in the Kilimanjaro region

43. School children at the new school

During the 1930s, a new school was built at Moshi in the Mt Kilimanjaro area. In 1936 when he was twelve years old Friedrich, accompanied by his father, had to travel for five days to reach the school – first by steamboat across Lake Victoria from Bukoba to Kusumi in Kenya, from there by train to Nairobi and Voi, and from Voi on to Moshi. The school catered for boarders from outlying areas. Approximately 30 pupils, both girls and boys, attended the school, which was supported financially by the German government. The school taught up to the level of the so-called *Einjährige,* which corresponds to 'Intermediate' in the then school terms. Anyone wishing to go on to further studies had to go to Germany.

THE TRAPPE FAMILY[20]

The Trappe family had difficulty in adjusting to the chaotic conditions prevailing in Germany after the war. They yearned to return to their former homes and farms in East Africa. Margarete and Ulrich Trappe left their children with an aunt in Germany and went to South

185

Africa on a temporary basis, hoping that this would make their return easier. Immediately after the war, a return to Tanganyika was only possible for British or Allied nationals. After trying unsuccessfully to repurchase their former principal property at Ngongonare they eventually were able to purchase a small farm, 200 hectares, near Arusha. To return to their 'paradise' in 1925, they travelled the same route they had used 18 years before when they first went to German East Africa. Ngongonare had been "acquired" by a British General named Boyd Moss, and all legal avenues to have the property returned to the Trappes failed. A former friend, a Greek Michael Michaelakis, had bought their other property Momella and was prepared to sell it back to the Trappes. The Trappes, who had lost most of their capital through an unscrupulous businessman in South Africa, managed to raise sufficient funds to pay a deposit on their former Momella property and buy 100 head of cattle.

44. Trappe's Momella farm at the slopes of Mt Meru

They lived in a tent and used another tent for storage. The cooking was done on an open fireplace outdoors. Only two of their former loyal workers were still around and helped. An old friend, Major Brown, who was now Provincial Commander in Arusha, gave them a dog. They bought a horse shortly after and a new start was made. In 1926, they built a house and brought their children back 'home' from Germany. It was a joyful reunion when they picked them up at Moshi after an absence of four years.

CHAPTER EIGHT

The family continued to improve their farm and herd. Loyal natives were employed again. To supplement their income during the 1930s, Margarete Trappe organised and led numerous hunting safaris.

THE NEEF FAMILY[21]

Before World War I, Eugen Neef from Jaffa/Sarona, had purchased land in German East Africa for a future coffee plantation for his second eldest son, Walter. In 1917 the Neef family fled Palestine and went to Germany where they lived until 1923. Whilst in Germany, Walter completed an apprenticeship with an electrical company to install and repair machines and motors. During that time he met his future wife, Anna Margareta Rösch, whom he married in Jaffa in 1925. In 1923 the family had returned to Palestine and Walter worked installing pumps and motors for irrigation. He also became involved with the repair and maintenance of diesel motors.

45. The Neef family and friends
– Anna Neef with daughter Rosemarie, Walter Neef (second from right, in shorts)

He became aware that the German government was offering small loans to former settlers of German East Africa to re-establish themselves. In 1928 Walter and Anna decided to go to Tanganyika to develop a coffee plantation on the land that Eugen Neef had bought in 1911. On arrival he found the land was no longer available and that the loan from the German government was nowhere near enough to start such an enterprise. He therefore declined the loan offer and found work as a maintenance mechanic on a large sisal plantation, the Mikinani Sisal Estates. He worked there for ten years. In 1938

46. The Neef family at their home on the sisal estate

47. Letterhead from Otto Barry

48. On the sisal plantation estate where Walter Neef worked

Walter and Anna moved closer to Tanga where better schooling was available for their daughter Rosemarie. Werner took a position as manager of the Mlingote Sisal Plantation near Tanga, Tanganyika. This plantation was owned by a German, Otto Barry, an importer and merchant. Walter worked there with full responsibility for the factory and the rail network which brought the sisal from the plantation to the factory for processing as well as for the maintenance of all plant and equipment on the plantation. He worked in that capacity until war broke out in 1939 when he was interned.

49. The sisal processing plant on the estate where Walter Neef worked

The MIKINANISISAL ESTATES

Mikimdani,den 18.Mai 1932
(Tanganyika Territory)

Herr Walter Neef ist seit dem 1.Juli 1930 in Mtwara
als Maschinist tätig und wurde ausserdem noch mit Bauarbeiten et
betraut.Ern ist dort der einzige europäische Angestellte und hat
daher eine grössere Verantwotung zu tragen als im allgemeinen üb
ist. Die Hanfproduktion betrug im letzten Jahre nahezu 500 Tonne

Bevor ich meinen Dienst verlasse,bestätige ich Herrn
Walter Neef gern,dass er in all dieser Zeit seine ihm aufgetrage
Arbeiten sachgemäss und pflichtgetreu ausführte und immer willig
und fleissig war.

gez. F.Scheppelmann
General Manager

Vorstehende(n) Abschrift/Auszug beglaubigt
Affaltrach, den 7.3.5o
Ratschreiber: Bürgermeister:

NGOMENI SISAL ESTATE

Zeugnis

Herr Walter Neef war seit Dezember 1928 als Maschinist hier
tätig.Während meiner hiesigen Tätigkeit als Leiter,kann ich nur
Herrn Neef als gewissenhaften,ordentlichen Maschinisten empfehle
der auch gut mit den Leuten umzugehan pflegt versteht.
Die Maschinerie lässt Herr Neef in bester Ordnung zurück.
Meine besten Wünsche begleiten ihn.
Entlassung auf eigenen Wunsch.

Ngomeni,den 26.Mai 1930

Manager
gez. Fritz Koch

Vorstehende(n) Abschrift/Auszug beglaubigt
Affaltrach, den 7.3.5o
Ratschreiber: Bürgermeister:

50. Work references for Walter Neef from Sisal estates

51 Werner Uhlherr in 1933

OTHER IMMIGRANTS FROM PALESTINE IN THE 1930S

In 1929, Werner Uhlherr (17) left the Jaffa Templer settlement in Palestine to go to East Africa. He went with Adolf Knauss and Herbert Faber, who both had visited East Africa previously. At first they lived in Nairobi and worked on a nearby coffee plantation. Faber, a builder, started his own business and built a courthouse and several other public buildings for the British authorities. Knauss, who had an administrative background, worked with a motor garage and hire car company in Nairobi. For a time, the three of them went gold prospecting. Knauss and Werner Uhlherr started a business collecting butterflies and insects for export to teaching institutions all over the world. They also organised and led hunting safaris during the 1930s.[22]

52. Werner Uhlherr prospecting for gold with Herbert Faber

Increased civil unrest was rampant in Palestine during the 1930s as the conflict between Arabs and Jews intensified. The German Templer settlers were caught between the two warring groups. The policies of the Third Reich increased Jewish suspicion and resentment of the German settlers in Palestine. One outcome of this was the boycott of German products and goods in general, and those of the Templers in particular, with adverse effects on German businesses and enterprises in Palestine. Difficulties were also encountered with Arabs. Furthermore, employment opportunities for young German males were very limited in Palestine and resulted in a number of young persons going to Germany for work and education.[23]

It was during this period in the late 1930s, that migration to East Africa became a consideration again for several Templers in Palestine.

Following the general strike in the Arabic part of Jaffa in 1936, Anton Asenstorfer (senior) was forced to close his import business of radios and electronic equipment and look for other opportunities.

53. Anton Asenstorfer (left) on safari

In 1937 he decided to explore opportunities in Kenya, East Africa, accompanied by his son Tony (23). They had to pay a £100 surety to the British authorities before they could immigrate. They caught a ship to Mombassa and the train to Nairobi. Tony (jnr) immediately found work on a sisal plantation owned by an Englishman near Nairobi, looking after the maintenance of the machines in the sisal processing area.[24]

Anton (sen) returned to Palestine to finalise a few personal matters and pack his belongings, before moving to Kenya in 1938. His daughter Waltraud joined him on his move to Kenya and married a German there. In Kenya, Anton (sen) started a mechanical business, repairing and maintaining equipment on farms.[25]

WORLD WAR II - INTERNMENT AND DEPORTATION 1939 TO 1945

W ith war looming, the British authorities made a number of contingency plans, which included appointing 'special constables' to their police force. In many cases, these 'special constables' were non-British nationals from Tanganyika, such as Danes and Greeks. The weapons (shotguns and rifles) and ammunition owned by German nationals and businesses were confiscated; their trucks seized and motor cars thoroughly searched for weapons. Construction of a large compound (an enclosed camp) commenced in Arusha. In the days before the war, large contingents of askaris were mobilised and stationed in the Arusha district. The authorities had also developed a personal dossier on every German in areas under British administration.[1]

AT THE OUTBREAK OF WAR WERNER UHLHERR DECIDED TO ESCAPE FROM BRITISH KENYA TO AVOID INTERNMENT

At the outbreak of war, Werner Uhlherr, Adolf Knauss and Herbert Faber decided to escape from British Kenya to avoid internment. They fled west into the Belgian Congo and travelled through dense jungle until they reached the Atlantic Ocean. After several unsuccessful attempts and avoiding arrest they finally boarded a ship bound for Europe, only to be taken off the ship in international waters by the French Navy and interned at Dakar in French West Africa (now Senegal). When Germany defeated France, they were released and returned to Germany in 1941. A number of other German nationals in East Africa before World War II tried to get back to Germany this way.[2]

Just prior to the commencement of war, Helmut Bauer and his friend the biologist, Dr Bergold, had gone hunting and were not at home when all the German men were arrested in September 1939. Friendly plantation workers warned them that they were 'wanted men'. With a number of porters, they moved into the dense forests on the lower slopes of Mt Kilimanjaro and escaped capture. For several weeks, they lived off the land before they were betrayed, arrested and taken into captivity by the British authorities.[3]

THEY MOVED INTO THE DENSE FORESTS ON THE LOWER SLOPES OF MT KILIMANJARO AND ESCAPED CAPTURE

WAR STARTS - INTERNMENT IN EAST AFRICA

On 3 September 1939 when war was declared, all German nationals, that is German passport holders living in Tanganyika and Kenya, were immediately interned. This included persons who had left Nazi Germany for political reasons as well as some Jews. The German men in Arusha were ordered to pack a few personal effects before being interned in the Hotel Meru in Arusha, which served as a temporary camp. In many cases, the men were given barely an hour to pack and to farewell their wives and children.[4]

In her family history, Irmgard Schoer (née Bauer) provides an eyewitness account of this dramatic event *"[...] The 3rd September was a Sunday. During the morning some friends came to our house in Arusha. Since German forces had crossed into Poland on 1st September we were all nervously waiting for what would happen next. A number of our friends had been contemplating for some time about leaving and going to Abyssinia or Mozambique – now it was too late. For several days now all roads had been blocked with boom gates and guarded by armed askaris. Herbert Bauer had put up a big map of Europe on the wall and had marked with little flags the advance of the German troops according to reports from the German foreign radio broadcasting service. On this Sunday afternoon at about 4.00 o'clock, a large truck pulled up outside the Bauer house. A few Eng-*

lishmen and a number of askaris, all armed, came into the living room where the family had afternoon coffee with friends.

England had declared war on Germany and from one day to the next old, well-known acquaintances suddenly became enemies without having done anything untoward to each other. Everything went very peacefully. The German male visitors who were present were taken back to their own homes and given half an hour to pack their essential belongings. Cameras, torches and typewriters were not allowed to be taken. Any firearms, ammunition, radios and car keys had to be handed in. A brief farewell, and all the men were gone — where to, no-one knew. My mother, Elise and I sat petrified opposite each other at our coffee table. The native servants crept about quietly with downcast eyes – clearly sad, and uncertain as to what was happening. Where only a short time before, eight persons were engaged in lively discussion, now only a deadly silence reigned."[5]

Some Boers, who were regarded as anti-British, were interned along with the Germans. All the German men from the surrounding farms and plantations were also arrested and brought to Arusha and interned in the hotel. Armed British askari troops guarded the hotel and patrolled the streets and no one was allowed to leave the hotel complex. The men were kept there for three days before being moved to the newly constructed camp several 100 meters from the hotel in the buildings and grounds of the Usagara Trading Company in Arusha. The men were crowded onto trucks and driven to the camp watched by the natives of Arusha.[6]

The camp was a 200 meter square surrounded by a three meter high fence made of corrugated iron sheets. The living quarters, storage sheds and other buildings inside the camp were empty with no furniture or any other fittings except for a few empty petrol drums, which provided some seating. Three water taps had been installed to provide for the needs of the camp, which was to house 200 prisoners-of-war. The 'kitchen' was in the open and several trestles for food preparation and three ovens were covered by a corrugated iron roof. Two trees provided some shade in the hot tropical sun – the heat within the compound was intense as the high fence reflected the heat and no breeze could disperse it. The elected camp leaders protested to the British authorities about these conditions with little success. Soon "unofficial" channels were found and some bedding and chairs were smuggled in by friends and family from outside the camp. The camp routine was to get up at 6am, and lights out at 10pm. The camp was guarded at all times by askaris armed with rifles and mounted bayonets.[7]

1. Ruth Blaich and Eberhard Assmus in front of Jakob Blaich's farmhouse January 1940

The number of inmates increased when another contingent of male prisoners was brought to the camp. They were the plantation settlers from the German community at Oldeani. The Oldeani region was the mountainous area to the west of Arusha where some young German settlers, including some Templer families, had started farms after World War I. The Red Cross had built a small hospital and, during the Third Reich period, a school had been built there with German Government assistance. Most of these plantation settlers spoke little English because they spoke German in their homes and with their neighbours. However, from conversing with the native workers, they were fluent in Swahili.[8]

196

THE GERMAN WOMEN AND CHILDREN IN THE ARUSHA AREA WERE NOT INTERNED IN CAMPS BUT WERE KEPT UNDER OBSERVATION IN THEIR HOMES

The German women and children in the Arusha area were not interned in camps but were kept under observation in their homes. After some time, the British authorities allowed the women and children to visit their husbands and brothers on Sundays between 3.00pm and 5.00pm. They were permitted to bring clean clothing and some fresh food to their loved ones. Many of the German women and children from outlying areas came to Arusha to visit their menfolk and nearly every German-owned house in Arusha was utilised to accommodate these families. The Blaichs' houses in Arusha were totally occupied by strangers – Karl Blaich was in Germany with his four children, Otto was interned, and Frieda had left to be with her elderly parents at Oldonyo Sambu. Initially, the elderly Jakob Blaich (aged 80) had been interned in Arusha but was later released on humanitarian grounds and allowed to return to his home. Paula Assmus and her son Eberhard came and stayed with the Bauers on several occasions to visit their husband and father.[9]

At the outbreak of war the British authorities froze all bank accounts and assets of the German nationals. In order for the non-interned German women and children to at least be able to buy some food, the authorities paid them monthly two pounds per adult and one pound per child up to age 18. To compensate the cost of accommodating families from outlying areas, the visiting families paid two shillings per adult and one shilling per child for each day that accommodation was provided.[10]

Gotthilf Blaich was interned in a similar camp at Moshi.

After several weeks in the Arusha camp the internees were told that they would be transferred to a large camp at Dar-es-Salaam. The authorities granted one more visit, a farewell visit to the men's wives, mothers and friends who came from near and far to say good-bye.

IT WAS A SAD TIME AS LEAVE WAS TAKEN FROM LOVED ONES AND NO ONE KNEW WHAT THE FUTURE WOULD BRING OR WHEN THEY WOULD SEE EACH OTHER AGAIN

It was a sad time as leave was taken from loved ones and no one knew what the future would bring or when they would see each other again. After packing up their few belongings, the 200 internees were taken by trucks, 30 to 40 men standing on the back of each truck, through Arusha to the railway station. One hundred heavily armed askaris surrounded the train and after checking each individual, the internees were allocated to specific carriages. They were squeezed into the narrow-seated carriages normally used by the natives, whilst the askari guards travelled in the comfortably upholstered second class compartments. At Moshi, more carriages with German internees were hitched to the train. After travelling all night in the tight,

2. The coastal steamer Askari *took male internees from Tanga to Dar-es-Salaam*

IT WAS MIDDAY AND THE HEAT WITH 300 MEN IN THE HOLD BECAME UNBEARABLE

uncomfortable, smoke-filled compartments, the train reached Tanga the next morning. Again under heavy guard, the internees walked to 'Internment Camp Tanga'. After only a few hours in the camp, they had to return to the train and were taken to the port where two small steamers lay at anchor. The men were not allowed to stay on deck but were immediately taken below. It was midday and the heat with 300 men in the hold became unbearable. Most men stripped down to their underpants and demanded relief, as many of them became groggy in the stifling conditions. After several hours, the ships finally weighed anchor and the men were allowed to take turns in spending time on the deck. The ships sailed through the night in choppy seas and many of the internees became seasick. No water was provided for washing and only bread and tea was served for meals. By mid morning the ships berthed at Dar-es-Salaam and the internees were taken ashore and, in the heat of the day, were marched in groups through the town to the internment camp on the outskirts of town.[11]

The fence surrounding the camp in Dar-es-Salaam was of corrugated iron sheets with another high barbed wire fence on the inside and several guard towers. Entry to the camp was by a series of locked gates, which led to the administration building. On arrival, the men were forced to wait in the hot sun for several hours as formalities for their admittance were completed. Each internee was asked whether he was a member of the Nazi Party or whether he had fled Nazi Germany. Once inside, the newly arrived internees were greeted by other previously interned men, among them Helmut Bauer, who, after being captured on a hunting trip, was immediately transferred to Dar-es-Salaam because he had 'resisted internment'.[12] The camp comprised six very large sleeping barracks and two large halls which served both as eating areas and for general meeting purposes. A notable internee at Dar-es-Salaam was Kai-Uwe von Hassel, a clerk on a plantation who, in 1963, became a Minister in the Cabinet of Konrad Adenauer's government in Germany. The internees were assigned to areas corresponding to the regions from where they had come. Only stretcher beds were provided – there were no chairs or tables for the internees. An area in the camp was set aside for a first aid facility and laundry. Initially the food rations for the internees were so inadequate and rotten that they even resorted to digging for worms to supplement their rations. The first meal consisted of a watery soup with bread, coffee and an orange but, gradually, the food improved.[13]

The Neef family, who lived near Tanga, were part of a similar internment process. Walter Neef was interned on 3 September 1939 and then taken to the Dar-es-Salaam camp before further internment in South Africa. His wife, Anne, who was pregnant (Werner was born in 1940) and her daughter were also interned and in 1941 taken to Rhodesia – Tanganyika Camp 2 near Salisbury.[14]

In early November 1939, the camp authorities interviewed each internee to assess his chances of repatriation through an exchange of civilian prisoners. A list of 150 names for repatriation was circulated in the camp. At first it seemed evident that only unskilled men would be repatriated. Twenty men were called up and advised to get ready to leave. This was increased to 120 men who were told they would be repatriated with their wives and families. They were to be sent to Italy on a ship named *Palestine*.[15]

ON ARRIVAL, THE MEN WERE FORCED TO WAIT IN THE HOT SUN FOR SEVERAL HOURS AS FORMALITIES FOR THEIR ADMITTANCE WERE COMPLETED

INITIALLY THE FOOD RATIONS FOR THE INTERNEES WERE SO INADEQUATE AND ROTTEN THAT THEY EVEN RESORTED TO DIGGING FOR WORMS TO SUPPLEMENT THEIR RATIONS

```
Helmut  B a u e r
Moshi.

              V e r m ö g e n s a u f s t e l l u n g .
              ========================================

   1    Reise - Schreibmaschine
              Urania - Piccolo  neuwertig          Shs.    220.--
   1    Photo-Apparat  4 x 6,5 cm für Roll-
        filme, Filmpack- und Platten -
        Kasetten, Lichtstärke 2,9 und
        eingebautem Selbstauslöser, Bereitschafts-
        tasche, Vorsatzlinsen, Stativ , voll -
        ständige Dunkelkammereinrichtung          Shs     350.--
   1    Photo - Album mit ca. 300 Aufnahmen
        einschl. Negative                         Shs     150.--
        Wäsche, Schuhe und Anzüge                 Shs     250.--
        Haushaltungs- Gegenstände                 Shs      30.--
   1    Tischuhr                                   Shs      15.--
   1    Rolle neuer Hühnerdraht                    Shs      15.--
        Gehalts-Guthaben b.Firma H. Bueb,Moshi ca.Shs     450.--
                                                  Shs   1.480.--

        S c h u l d e n :

        Rechnung Hotel Windler in Moshi   Shs. 15.--
        Rechnung   "   Stender  "   "     Shs. 10.--
        Rechnung Moledina,Inder-Duka ,Moshi
                 für Kleider u.Wäsche     Shs. 90.--
        Rechnung Rhambhai,Kifumbu/Moshi
                 für Lebensmittel         Shs. 60.--
        Rechnung Ostafrikanischer Reise-
        dienst in Mombasa für Ueber -
        weisungen an Willi Bauer,Rastatt Shs. 150.-- Shs.  325.--

                                                  Shs.  1.155.--
        ==============================================

        Die Richtigkeit obiger Angaben kann als Zeuge bestätigen:
        Herr  Dr. Bergold, Moshi
        ...W. Lermt.T.Bergold..

        Obige Angaben nach bestem Wissen und Gewissen gemacht zu haben,
        bestätigt:

        Daressalaam, den 1.Dezember 1939.
                                              ( Helmut Bauer)
```

3. Copy of inventory of Helmut Bauer's personal belongings, prepared on 1 December 1939 before his deportation

Christmas 1939 was celebrated by the internees with a small concert in one of the halls. New Year's Eve was also celebrated with beer and an especially composed "operetta". A further list of 180 internees for repatriation was announced and this was followed by a list of 50 single men. The group of 180 was to be repatriated on 16 January 1940 on the Italian ship *Urania* and the 50 single men on board the British ship *Durban Castle*.[16]

Similarly, in the Nairobi area in Kenya, the German nationals were interned from the day the war broke out. By six o'clock in the evening, the British sent trucks to the farms owned by the Germans and the families were instructed to take with them what ever they could carry. The women and children were interned in a hotel and the men were taken to a native prison with bare cement floors, before being moved to an internment camp where they were allowed to be visited by their families.[17]

In the other remote and outlying farms and plantations, the German farmers were placed under house arrest. This was the case with the Goetze family near Bukoba. Throughout the war they needed a permit to leave their property and their car was immobilised: the generator was dismantled and taken away to prevent them from travelling.[18]

When the German farmers and their families were interned, the British authorities appointed caretaker farmers, often Boers, to manage and look after the farms and the livestock.[19]

DEPORTATION TO GERMANY

During the early war years a number of German civilians were exchanged with foreign national civilians held in Germany.

When the time for the exchange came the wives and children of the interned men selected for repatriation were told of their imminent deportation and to pack their belongings.

The Kopp family, interned in Kenya, was with the group that was deported in November 1939. To add to the internees' trauma of being deported when they reached the port, the authorities refused to allow all their luggage on board and seized numerous items just prior to embarking. To the dismay of the deportees, this included their warm clothing, feather doonas and the warm woollen blankets they had packed for the cold European winter. All the seized goods were thrown on to a large heap and set alight. As they watched their possessions being burnt, the authorities told them that they would be issued with warm clothing once they reached Germany.[20]

On 16 January 1940, a second contingent of civilian internees was repatriated, including Fritz and Irene Blaich, their daughter Ruth-Karin and baby daughter Gudrun, as well as Helmut and Herbert Bauer.[21]

At Dar-es-Salaam, the men's luggage was checked for prohibited items such as money, typewriters, musical instruments and cameras. On departure, the men had to undergo a body search to ensure that none of these items was taken; the search included having to take off boots, shoes and tropical helmets, all of which were closely exam-

N THE OTHER REMOTE AND OUTLYING FARMS AND PLANTATIONS, THE GERMAN FARMERS WERE PLACED UNDER HOUSE ARREST

CERTIFICATE OF DEPORTATION FROM
TANGANYIKA TERRITORY

I, MARK AITCHISON YOUNG, Knight Commander of the Most Distinguished

Order of Saint Michael and Saint George, Governor and Commander-in-Chief

of the Tanganyika Territory, hereby certify that in pursuance of a Deportation

Order dated at Dar es Salaam the ....12th.... day of .....January....., 19.40.,

directions have been issued by me that.....Mr. H. Bauer.....

of the......Northern......Province of the Tanganyika Territory,

a German subject, ...

....

....

....

....

should be placed on board the......s.s. "Urania"......in order

that......he......may proceed as soon as may be to Germany via......Venice.

GIVEN UNDER MY HAND and the Public Seal of the Territory at Dar es Salaam

this......12th......day of......January......, 19 40

Governor

CHAPTER NINE

Left: 4. Helmut Bauer's Certificate of Deportation from Tanganyika Territory in January 1940

ined. The men were marched under heavy guard to the port where they boarded the steamship *Urania*.[22]

The ship called at Tanga, where a special train had brought the women and children to be repatriated. It was a happy reunion for many. The *Urania*, however, had not been built for 450 passengers and conditions on board were very crowded and cramped. The voyage to Suez went smoothly and no storms were encountered. In Suez, the *Urania* was moored next to the *Durban Castle* with the 50 single German men from East Africa on board. As mines had been laid at the entrance to the Suez Canal, special pilots came on board to navigate the next leg of the journey through the Canal to Port Said. From Port Said, the *Urania* went to Brindisi in Italy, their first European port; the deportees in their light tropical clothing were greeted by a cold winter wind. After a three-week voyage, with a short stop at Venice, they reached Trieste, where finally they were issued with their warm winter clothing and footwear.[23]

5. *The ship* Urania *took the deportees from East Africa to Italy in January 1940*

Accompanied by German officials and relief workers, the deportees continued their journey by train via Villach through the snow-covered countryside to Berchtesgaden in Bavaria. At Berchtesgaden a garrison type complex had been established to house all the Germans who were repatriated from all over the world.[24]

THE NEWLY ARRIVED PERSONS WERE ENCOURAGED TO IMMEDIATELY CONTACT ANY RELATIVES OR FRIENDS THEY MIGHT HAVE IN GERMANY

The newly arrived persons were encouraged to immediately contact any relatives or friends they might have in Germany and to seek accommodation away from Berchtesgaden.[25]

After an initial settling-in period, men of military age were conscripted into the German armed forces. These young men now found themselves fighting the British with whom many had been friends in Africa before the war. They were fighting for a regime and country which was really foreign to them – it was not their home. Several of the men, including Fritz Blaich and Willi Bauer, fell during the war; whilst others, including Werner Uhlherr, were severely wounded. Walter Blaich and Herbert Bauer became prisoners-of-war and were held in Russia and Yugoslavia for several years after the war had finished before they were discharged and returned to Germany.[26]

INTERNMENT AT MT KILIMANJARO 1940–1941

Most of the German women and children from the farms and plantations in the Arusha and Oldeani areas were taken via Italy to Germany as part of the exchange program and their former homes were now empty. The remaining settlers in the rural areas including Jakob and Marie Blaich, and Paula Assmus and her son Eberhard, were taken to a nearby camp before being moved to the Oldeani camp.[27]

In May 1940 the six German women and five children, who were still in Arusha, were ordered to pack their belongings. They were going to be relocated and could take with them whatever they could carry. Certain items such as cameras, typewriters and musical instruments could however not be taken.[28]

Elise Bauer and her daughter Irmgard were amongst these last Germans to leave the Arusha region. They packed a large trunk with essential needs and some of their most cherished possessions. Some valuables were hidden under the roof of their house and some were left with their trusted native gardener for safekeeping. At night, he would take these items to his hut on the slopes of Mt Meru. In 1941 the interned Germans believed that Germany would win the war and they would be able to return to their properties once the war was over. When the truck came to pick up the German families, the British at first refused to take Elise's trunk, but Elise, a large middle-aged lady, threatened that they would have to physically carry her unless her trunk went as well. In the end the British relented.[29]

This group from Arusha was taken to a hunting lodge at Mt Kilimanjaro. The area there was very remote, the rations small and poor (illness due to food poisoning occurred) and during the night the temperatures were low and the inhabitants were very cold.[30]

After six weeks in this lonely location, this group of internees was moved again. This time the British authorities had decided to clear the entire Kilimanjaro/Meru region of Germans, including the German mission stations. They were taken to Moshi to board a train to Arusha. They had to spend a night in Arusha and this gave Elise and Irmgard Bauer a last opportunity to visit their home. Irmgard describes the scene as follows, *"We found all rooms totally emptied of our possessions, but many bedsteads had been cramped into them instead. The bush telegraph (bush drums) signalled our arrival and we were met by our loyal gardener, Jeremias, who told us that the British had even cleaned out the shed and had taken away everything, even the last petrol can. Every so often, troops from South Africa and Rhodesia had been billeted here for short periods. These troops were no doubt on their way to the front in northern Africa."*[31]

The next day the women and children and their luggage were taken to Oldeani in a long convoy of trucks. There they were allocated to the empty homes of the German settlers. Those who could not be accommodated in the homes were placed in the schoolhouse. The octogenarian Jakob Blaich, his wife Marie, and daughter Frieda were brought from their farm at Oldonyo Sambu and placed in a cottage at the very perimeter of the settlement. Elise and Irmgard Bauer were pleased to meet up with the Blaichs again and they often visited them. The cottage where the Blaichs were housed was on the edge of impenetrable bush and a sign had been erected by the former German settlers "Territory of the Wanderbo – enter at your own risk". The Wanderbo were much-feared dwarfish forest people who used poisoned arrows for hunting.[32]

Near the homes of the internees there was a general store where some goods could be purchased for everyday needs. A Greek would come to the plantation settlement on a monthly basis to pay the German internees their government allowance.

During their stay, the internees regularly saw leopards at night and watched buffalo herds making their way in the evening through the coffee plantations to the grasslands in the lower regions and returning early in the morning to find shelter and shade in the bush during the hot daylight hours. Again, Irmgard Schoer provides a good description of the surrounding countryside, *"From the jungle around the Ngoro-ngoro crater there are rivers that had eroded deep gorges into the soft volcanic soil, these are known as* korongos. *These gorges were shady and cool, heavily timbered with trees and bushes, in which jungle vines were intertwined in artistic beauty. During the day, leopards would rest there. The well-trodden native tracks led from one farm or plantation to another but all eventually came to the centre where the store, a Red Cross station and a school were located. The shortest route to the centre was therefore along these tracks."*[33]

The German women and children were interned at Oldeani for nine months. The children had to go to school and many had to walk along the *korongos* to get there. Women with their small children often walked along these narrow tracks as well. Fortunately, no one was injured or attacked despite the constant presence of leopards, buffaloes, rhinoceros, elephants and poisonous snakes. No medical help would have been available if an incident had occurred. During their stay at Oldeani, the internees experienced a significant earthquake (Author: probably a volcanic eruption), which was followed by several days of falling ash and sulphur until a severe thunderstorm with large hailstones cleared the air.[34]

NO ONE WAS INJURED OR ATTACKED DESPITE THE CONSTANT PRESENCE OF LEOPARDS, BUFFALOES, RHINOCEROS, ELEPHANTS AND POISONOUS SNAKES

At the beginning of March 1941, the Oldeani internees were once again ordered to pack their belongings and to assemble with their luggage at the schoolhouse as they were about to be moved. The only persons who were allowed to remain were two elderly couples, the Blaichs and the von Hohwalds, and a daughter from each couple. The internees, on this occasion, were not allowed to take their photo albums or any other framed pictures with them. They left them behind with the Blaichs for safekeeping. As their third deportation was about to begin, most of the internees still believed that Germany would win the war and that they would return once this had occurred.[35]

Jakob and Marie Blaich and their daughter Frieda continued to be interned at the Oldeani camp. Jakob passed away in 1943 and was buried in the camp cemetery. His wife Marie died shortly after the war in 1947. Frieda Blaich eventually migrated to Australia in 1952.[36]

CHAPTER NINE

Deportation to Rhodesia in 1941 [37]

The mood amongst the women and children was low and depressed as they were concerned what would happen to them next. They were taken by truck convoy to the Arusha Railway Station where a train was waiting. To their dismay, they saw that all the windows in the carriages were boarded up. The whole station area had been fenced off with a large mesh wire fence. Outside the fence many natives had gathered to watch what was happening. The Bauers heard their name being called from the crowd and saw their loyal servant Jeremias making signs to them. As they went over, he passed his hands through the fence and with tears in his eyes bade them farewell. It must have been an emotional parting.

After travelling on the train all night, the internees reached Tanga the next morning. Under heavy guard, small groups of women and children were taken to a large barrack type shed where they were body-searched by British female officials. After the search, the internees walked to the port and were taken by a small boat to a troop transport lying at anchor some distance offshore. This process took hours and for those waiting in the enclosed crowded railway carriages the heat became unbearable.

THE CAPTAIN HAD ORDERED HIS CREW TO TREAT THE GERMAN WOMEN AND CHILDREN DECENTLY

Once on board the troop carrier, the internees were allowed to stay on deck. The captain had ordered his crew to treat the German women and children decently. As night fell, all internees were ordered below deck where the ship's crew did their utmost to provide food and drinks for the hungry and very thirsty internees. After steaming to Dar-es-Salaam, the ship took on board all the German women and children who had been interned in southern Tanganyika. From there, the ship left for an undisclosed destination. During this journey into the unknown, the ship's crew kept a sharp lookout for U-boats.

After nearly two weeks at sea, the ship berthed at Durban in South Africa. A train was waiting at the port to take the approximately 400 women and 200 children to their next destination. The train journey took four days and often, when the train stopped at stations, kind women distributed food, drinks and fruit to the internees, who were not allowed to leave the train.

TANGANYIKA INTERNMENT CAMP NO. 2 IN RHODESIA[38]

In April 1941 the train reached its destination on the outskirts of Salisbury, Southern Rhodesia (now Harare, Zimbabwe). An area had been fenced off with a three-metre high barbed wire fence. A double row of corrugated iron barracks, several large brick buildings, many small brick buildings and several toilet and ablution blocks greeted the weary internees on their arrival. Many of the camp buildings and facilities were incomplete, and men were still busily at work. A camp kitchen staffed by an English crew provided meals for the internees. The camp was known as Tanganyika Internment Camp No 2. A similar camp on the other side of Salisbury was Camp 1 and that is where the German civilians from Rhodesia were interned.

6. Picture of women and children in Tanganyika Internment Camp No 2 Rhodesia
(L to R) Back row: Mrs Voss, Mrs Rittmeister, Irene Schlottmann
Third Row: Mrs Habes, Unknown, Unknown, Unknown, Mrs Baron von Eppinghoven, Gesa Bundies
Second Row: Miss von Tischka, Alarich von Eppinghoven, Paula Assmus,
Mrs Bächers, Mrs Bächer's son, Irmgard Bauer, Sister Erika Müller
Front row: Ursula Ruthenbeck, Miss Rodtice,? Ruthenbeck, Reinhold Ruthenbeck, Mrs Schlottmann, Mrs
Schlottmann's son, ? Gromeltski, Glennie Heine, Conny Heine

CHAPTER NINE

Badehaus.

7. Paintings of buildings in Tanganyika Internment Camp 2 Top to bottom: Amenities Block, Barracks, Tennis Court, Kitchen

Shortly after arrival a bad outbreak of diarrhoea occurred. The toilet blocks were unfinished and a long distance from the living quarters and could not cope with the needs of the internees. The British authorities decided to distribute chamber pots to each adult in an effort to overcome the crisis. Mothers with children were given several pots. The camp was next to a main road and, particularly on weekends, many Salisbury residents would pass by looking at the internees to see what was happening. When they observed so many women carrying toilet pots, they called the camp 'chamber pot camp'!

Irmgard Schoer describes the camp as follows *"[...] The small brick homes were double sided and each half had two rooms connected by a doorway as well as a small kitchen area. Two persons were accommodated in each of these rooms. In the 'kitchen' single ladies or older children were allowed to stay [...]The barracks were partitioned and some parts occupied by the missionary sisters, and other parts were used for school rooms. The camp kitchen and dining hall were located in another large building. The middle room of a further large brick building was used as a church. On the left side of the building, a shop (canteen), a reading room and a sewing room with two sewing machines were located. Later, a library and a radio room were set up on the other side."*

The internees suffered another setback just as they had settled in. An outbreak of measles occurred and most children contracted the illness. The small hospital could not cope with the influx of sick children and they had to be bedded down on mattresses in the church. Salisbury is 1,700 meters above sea level and can be quite cold. A number of the children became more ill by developing pneumonia and, tragically, two small boys from one family died. This was an enormous shock to the internees.

During the first two years of internment, the British soldiers kept tight control of the camp. Inside, the camp was patrolled by female military personnel, armed with pistols, clubs and whistles. Persons over 16 years of age had to present for roll call every day, and the German camp leaders had to report any sick persons not attending roll calls. Every internee was given a number that had to be quoted on incoming or outgoing letters, all of which were censored. At the entrance to the camp there was a large administration building with guards and the camp's perimeter was patrolled day and night. The quartermaster store was staffed by British male personnel. The store provided shoes, cutlery, soap, woollen blankets, sheets, pillowcases and material to the internees on a needs basis. The women were able to sew clothing for their children.

209

*8. Paintings of buildings in
Tanganyika Internment Camp 2
Top to bottom: Kitchen, Hospital, Exit
to Camp*

At times, excursions to the countryside adjoining the camp were allowed. Groups of ten internees would be allowed to leave the camp, closely guarded by female personnel, who would shepherd the group 'like sheep' and anyone straying from the 'flock' would be whistled at and brought back into line immediately. This type of excursion was soon abandoned as it was not popular with the internees.

Life in the camp settled down and the interned women started to organise their own camp routine – they gradually took over the servicing of the hospital, the home visits to sick internees, the kitchen and food preparation, the canteen and the internal running of the camp. Children from 6 to 17 were given schooling. A grass building with a thatched roof was built as a kindergarten for younger children.

THE ATTITUDE OF THE BRITISH TOWARDS THE GERMAN INTERNEES SEEMED TO CHANGE AFTER THIS TRAGIC EVENT

A tragedy occurred when two young children set the kindergarten ablaze. The two kindergarten teachers risked their lives to save most of the children but, unfortunately, eleven children were burned to death, and two suffered severe burns. By the time the fire brigade arrived from Salisbury, the building had burnt down. The attitude of the British towards the German internees seemed to change after this tragic event. Ministers from the Anglican Church and other denominations came to the camp for the funeral services. The fathers of the deceased children were allowed to come from the camp in South Africa where they were interned to be with their families at this time of sorrow. Mission stations offered to take in the German families in order to help them overcome their grief.

A number of people with a Templer background and friends of Templers were in the camp. They included Mrs Bäuerle, Elise Bauer and her daughter Irmgard, Hanna Blaich, Paula Assmus and her son Eberhard, Anna Neef with daughter Rosemarie and son Werner, a Mrs Polenz (nee Kappus) and her unmarried sister.

During 1942, two more groups were organised for exchange with civilian internees from Germany. In most cases families were brought together for the exchange which meant the male members of the families were released from their internment in South Africa. Mrs Polenz and her sister were amongst the first exchange group. The second group's return to Germany was disrupted, because of the war situation in the Mediterranean, which caused the ship with the internees to be diverted to Jaffa in Palestine. From there, the exchange internees were taken to the Sarona perimeter camp and held until their exchange could be affected. The Sarona camp held Templers as well as other German civilians.

9. Names of women and children in Tanganyika Internment Camp 2

1. Mrs von Eberhardt ?
2. Mrs Blaich, (Sanja)
3. Ulla von Brandis
4. ?
5. Ilse Eckstein
6. Anneliese Ziegler
7. Mrs Müller (Logeloge)
8. Klaus Harries
9. Mrs Harries (Mutter von Klaus)
10. Inge Minssen
11. ?
12. ?
13. Miss Zink
14. Mrs Lindemann
15. Mrs Peschel
16. Frau Herms
17. ?
18. ?
19. Bahati Ranninger
20. ?
21. Mrs Anni Schoer
22. ?
23. Elisabeth Schoer
24. ?
25. Rosemarie Neef

26. Mrs Hartmann
27. Waldtraut Lindemann
28. ?
29. Manfred Kirschner
30. Anna Neef
31. Werner Neef
32. ?
33. Child Klasbrummel
34. Mrs Klasbrummel
35. Mrs Schneemann
36. Mrs Kosmala
37. Cornelia Kosmala
38. Mrs Linke
39. Sigrid von Eberhardt
40. Mrs Kirschner
41. ?
42. ?
43. ?
44. Child Klasbrummel ?
45. Child Klasbrummel ?
46. Child Schneemann
47. Child Linke
48. Ibo von Eberhardt
49. ?

10. Letter sent by Paula Assmus to her husband in the Baviaanaspoort Internment Camp in Pretoria, South Africa

CHAPTER NINE

Most of the original internees had either been deported to Australia in 1941 or exchanged in 1941 and 1942 for civilian internees in Germany when the exchange group from Africa arrived.

In March 1944, married men – fathers and husbands – were allowed to come from internment camps in South Africa to be with their wives and children. In September unmarried men – brothers and sons – were allowed to also visit the Salisbury camp as well. It was a happy, yet at times sad reunion, as most realised that a return to Tanganyika was now most unlikely. During this time, Elise Bauer met her son Theo after a five-year separation.

For the Neef family it was a very special reunion, as Walter Neef, who had been interned separately from his wife since September 1939, was able to see his son, Werner, for the first time. Werner was nearly five years old when father and son were united.[39]

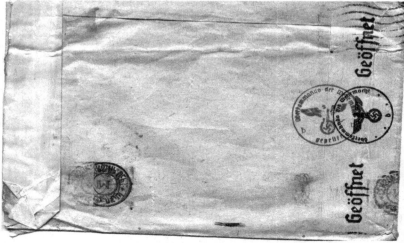

11. Envelope of letter sent from Germany to Internment Camp II at Salisbury, Rhodesia in 1942. It was opened and censored by the Oberkommando der Wehrmacht (Command of the German Defence Forces) and also by the Censorship Department at the camp

Gotthilf Blaich, who was middle aged had been interned in the Andalusia camp in South Africa, was reunited with his wife, Hanna.[40]

The Assmus family, separated during internment – Erwin Assmus was interned at Baviaanspoort, Pretoria in South Africa and Paula Assmus in Camp Tanganyika II at Salisbury, Rhodesia – were also reunited.[41]

Luise Korntheuer remained interned and passed away during the war years.[42]

Anton Asentorfer and his son Tony, after their initial internment in Kenya, were transferred to an internment camp near Johannesburg in South Africa. After the war they were released and returned to Germany.[43]

As the war drew to a close, life in the camp became easier - roll calls were discontinued and the internees were allowed to leave camp, without having to be accompanied by a guard, as long as they notified the officials and returned by a given time.

CHAPTER TEN

RETURN TO GERMANY AND INDEPENDENCE FOR TANGANYIKA 1946 TO 1961

INTERNMENT CAMP NORTON NEAR SALISBURY, RHODESIA 1945 - 1947[1]

When the European theatre of war finished in May 1945 the internees were not released.

In November 1945 the two internment camps near Salisbury were cleared and all internees were transferred to a disused air force base at Norton, not far from Salisbury. Hostilities towards the Germans by the surrounding farming communities waned soon after the internees arrived. There was no barbed wire fence impounding the internees and whenever opportunities arose to get a lift to Salisbury they were allowed to go unaccompanied for a few hours.

In early 1946, as internment camps in South Africa closed down, the remaining single men, who had been interned there, were brought to the Norton camp. With the influx of these men, several initiatives were undertaken – new clay mud brick houses were built, various trades were practised and bakers and slaughtermen soon started small businesses with some of the local farmers. It even seemed possible that a small German community could be established near Norton. However, those hopes were dashed when the British government in London directed that all German citizens from Tanganyika be repatriated to Germany.

THE BRITISH GOVERNMENT IN LONDON DIRECTED THAT ALL GERMAN CITIZENS FROM TANGANYIKA BE REPATRIATED TO GERMANY

The Neef family left the Norton Camp on their own accord and went to Mozambique, the Portuguese colony. Walter Neef had heard that a factory situated next to the Zambezi River needed to be relocated. After a short stay in Mozambique, the Neefs were forced to return to Norton to seek treatment for their son, Werner, who had contracted malaria. Their stay in "freedom" was short-lived![2]

REPATRIATION TO GERMANY 1947[3]

In May 1947, the former settlers from East Africa were moved once again. This time they were taken on a four-day train journey to Cape Town, South Africa. There they boarded a large former Castle Line ship, *Winchester Castle,* which was still fitted out as a troop transport from the war years. They were taken to the port of Southampton, where specialised pilots boarded the ship to navigate it through the uncleared minefields of the North Sea.

1. The ship Winchester Castle *which took the former German settlers back to Germnay in 1947*

RETURN TO GERMANY AND INDEPENDENCE
FOR TANGANYIKA 1946 TO 1961 - CHAPTER TEN

At Hamburg, the former settlers were 'welcomed' by British military personnel in armoured vehicles. Several men were taken into custody by the military police as soon as they stepped ashore. The former settlers were put on a train, but this time in cattle cars with an armed soldier at each end of the carriage. The train had to travel very slowly through the war-ravaged city as the train tracks around Hamburg were still damaged from Allied wartime bombings. Their next stop was at the former SS prison Neuengamme, where the settlers were put through a de-nazification program for several days. Each individual also had to appear before a tribunal of three officers, who had a file on each person and knew exactly whether anyone had belonged to the National Socialist German Workers Party or whether they had any connection or affiliation to it through any other organisation.

2. Camp Neuengamme 1945 near Hamburg

After this process, the settlers were taken in small groups to the Jahnhalle in Hamburg where they were asked to nominate a town or destination they wanted to go to and were then given an appropriate railway pass. Each adult was given 5 *Reichsmark* and each child 2.50 *Reichsmark*. The future in post war Germany, a country foreign to nearly all the former African settlers, appeared grim – accommodation was scarce and food supplies extremely short and barely at subsistence level.

In the years 1947 to 1950, the former settlers went about rebuilding their lives in a new country. The Bauer family remained in touch with the Blaich family. They met Walter Blaich after he returned from years of captivity in Russia. Walter Blaich migrated to Australia in the 1950s. They had contact with Otto Blaich, who had married during the war, and lived with his wife and young son in Tübingen. Otto and his family also migrated to Australia. In 1950, the Bauers went to Stuttgart to farewell their former 'African friends' Irene Blaich and her children, and Walter and Anna Neef and their children, all of whom were going to Australia.

After the war, the elderly Frieda Blaich, who had remained in Tanganyika, was cared for by a Boer family until she found residence in a room at a mission station and later in a hospital. In 1952, Trudi Blaich went from England to Tanganyika, and brought Frieda to Australia where she could be with her family. Frieda Blaich was the last member of the Blaich family to leave Tanganyika.[4]

Gotthilf Blaich and his wife were released from camp in 1947 and went to South Africa to start a new life there. The Assmus family wanted to stay on, but their request was refused by the authorities and they were transferred to Germany.[5]

Irmgard Schoer (née Bauer) and her husband and family migrated to Namibia in the 1950s.[6]

Erwin and Luise Kopp with their family migrated to the USA. One of their daughters, Lieselotte, had gone to live the USA in 1952 and the family joined her in 1955.[7]

Dorothea, a daughter of Helmut Bauer, moved with her husband Wulf Gatter and her young family to Zwedru in the interior of Liberia in West Africa in the early 1980s.[8]

3 Friedrich, Luise, Erika and Alfred Goetze in the 1950s

The British authorities offered the confiscated German farms in Tanganyika for sale to the caretakers. Eventually the former owners received only a very small amount of compensation for their properties – from the German government.[9]

The Goetze family were allowed to stay on their farm after the war. They improved the farm and continued to grow coffee and grain crops, raised cattle and developed a good dairy herd. Another generation of children were born after Friedrich married in 1954.

4. The Goetze coffee plantation – coffee trees in bloom

5. Picking coffee on the Goetze coffee plantation

6. & 7. Loading coffee on the Goetze coffee plantation

In 1961, with the coming of independence to Tanganyika, the Goetzes feared the new government would dispossess them. They were able to sell their property to the Protestant Bethel Mission, which was staffed mainly by Swedish and Danish personnel. They were given 'British Protected Persons' status by the British authorities and were able to migrate to Australia via Germany.[10]

The Goetze family was the last family with any connections to the Templers to leave Tanganyika, the former colony of German East Africa.

8. Friedrich Goetze, his father Alfred Goetze, a visitor and several workers

9. Cutting meat at Goetze's farm

10. Visit by ministers from nearby mission stations

END OF BRITISH RULE – AN INDEPENDENT TANGANYIKA

Although there was no actual war in Tanganyika, the effects of World War II were significant. The Tanganyikans who went to war and fought with the Allies were told that they were fighting against tyranny and for their freedom.[11]

Towards the end of the war, the United Nations was established and the development of a new world in international relations started to emerge. This was reflected in the United Nations charter on Trust Territories with an emphasis on 'self government and independence'. The pre-World War II colonial powers did not have to hand over their colonies and mandate territories to the newly established United Nations Trusteeship Council, but the territories under the Trusteeship Agreements were subject to scrutiny by the Council. This scrutiny was far greater than the previous supervision by the League of Nations under the mandate agreement. The Trusteeship Council comprised delegates from various nations, which outnumbered the delegates of the administering authorities (Great Britain in Tanganyika's case). Rather than relying on reports from the administering authorities, the Trusteeship Council sent regular missions to the trust territories to monitor progress. The immediate post war period saw a worldwide move against colonialism generally. Furthermore, the growth and influence of communism amongst developing (emerging) nations created additional political pressure in the development of Tanganyika and its move towards independence.[12]

THE IMMEDIATE POST WAR PERIOD SAW A WORLDWIDE MOVE AGAINST COLONIALISM GENERALLY

Throughout the 1950s, progress towards independence continued. In 1951, Chief Kidaha was the first African to join the Executive Council. The former pre-World War II Executive Council and Legislative Council's structure and membership gradually changed to provide for racial parity. In 1955, the Legislative Council was enlarged to include nine representatives of each race plus one representative of each race was also appointed for a special interest to the unofficial members side.[13]

Of particular significance during the 1950s was the formation in July 1954 of the Tanganyika African National Union (TANU). The TANU developed from the former Tanganyika African Association which had been established in 1929. The aims of the TANU were to prepare the people of Tanganyika for self-government and independence, to combat tribalism and to build a unified sense of nationalism. TANU opposed the alienation of land to non-Africans and encouraged the growth of an African business community. During the latter 1950s,

RETURN TO GERMANY AND INDEPENDENCE

FOR TANGANYIKA 1946 TO 1961 - CHAPTER TEN

TANU had grown into a substantial organisation, but its policy of a rapid move to independence was not in line with that of the administrative authority (government) of Tanganyika, which was for slower and more gradual progress towards independence. The TANU also petitioned the United Nations' visiting missions and established links with anti-colonial groups at the United Nations. Its views gradually received more recognition.[14]

To counter the TANU, the government supported the growth of the United Tanganyika Party (UTP), which was formed in 1956. Although advocating independence, the UTP maintained that the established government and the traditional authorities be respected and opposed the potential domination of one racial group over another. The UTP's Chairman, Ivor Bayldon, went as far as declaring that the United Nations had no right to interfere with Tanganyika's affairs.[15]

In 1958, another political party with more racial policies was formed, the African National Congress, which promoted citizenship for black Africans only and the 'Africanisation' of the Legislative Council and the Public Service.[16]

11. Arusha Town Centre in the mid 1950s

In the general elections of 1958/59, the TANU crushed the opposing political parties and emerged as the dominant political force in Tanganyika. Independence discussions continued between the TANU and the British authorities to provide for a peaceful progress to independence. In October 1959, the government announced that the existing Legislative Council would be dissolved in 1960, and that Tanganyika would have responsible self-government.[17]

Following the 1960 general elections, the Governor, Sir Richard Turnbull, asked Julius Kambarage Nyerere, leader of the TANU, to form a government. The Governor told the Legislative Council that Great Britain supported a quick move to independence. Further discussions followed between Britain and the newly elected government of Tanganyika, covering the financial aspects and Great Britain's contribution to assist Tanganyika in the initial stages following independence. On 1 May 1961 Nyerere became the first Prime Minister of Tanganyika, most of the Governor's powers were abolished and the Legislative Council was renamed the National Assembly.[18]

In June 1961, the National Assembly formally requested independence from Great Britain by December 1961 and a constitution was drafted. On 9 December 1961, Great Britain relinquished its control and Tanganyika became an independent nation. Tanganyika remained a member of the Commonwealth.[19]

*   *   *   *

The remaining former East Africa settlers and their descendants now live all over the world – in Germany, USA, South Africa, Namibia and Australia. None of the former settlers, covered in this book, are now living in Tanzania where once their forefathers toiled to establish a better life. World events beyond the control of individuals deal bitter blows to the best intentions and aspirations. Nevertheless, a proud legacy of the work of these hardworking, adventurous and pioneering settlers remains to this day and is worthy of the admiration of the present and future generations.

APPENDICES

APPENDIX 1- GOVERNORS AND ADMINISTRATORS OF GERMAN EAST AFRICA AND TANGANYIKA

27 May 1885 – 8 Feb1888 ....Carl Peters ....Administrator

8 Feb 1888 – 21 Feb 1891...................................Hermann von Wissmann....................................Reichskommissar

GERMAN GOVERNORS

14 Feb 1891 – 15 Sep 1893...................................Julius Freiherr von Soden

15 Sep 1893 – 26 Apr 1895...................................Friedrich Radbold Freiherr von Schele

26 Apr 1895 – 3 Dec 1896...................................Hermann von Wissmann

3 Dec 1896 – 12 Mar 1901 ....Eduard von Liebert

12 Mar 1901– 15 Apr 1906...................................Gustav Adolf Graf von Goetzen

15 Apr 1906 – 22 Apr 1912 ....Georg Albrecht Freiherr von Rechenberg

22 Apr 1912 – 14 Nov 1918 ....Albert Heinrich Schnee (with virtually no authority from Oct. 1916 when British forces occupied northern German East Africa).

9 Oct 1916 – 22 Jul 1920...................................Horace Archer Byatt (Sir Horace after 1918).........................Administrator

BRITISH GOVERNORS

22 Jul 1920 – 5 Mar 1925 ....Sir Horace Archer Byatt

5 Mar 1925 – Jan 1931...................................Donald Charles Cameron

Jan 1931 – 19 Feb 1934 ....George Stewart Symes

19 Feb 1934 – 8 Jul 1938...................................Sir Harold Alfred MacMichael

8 Jul 1938 – 19 Jun 1941 ....Sir Mark Aitchinson Young

19 Jun 1941 - 28 Apr 1945...................................Sir Wilfrid Edward Francis Jackson

28 Apr 1945 – 18 Jun 1949...................................Sir William Denis Battershill

18 Jun 1949 – 15 Jul 1958 ....Sir Edward Francis Twining

15 Jul 1958 – 9 Dec 1961 ....Sir Richard Gordon Turnbull

9 Dec 1961 – 9 Dec 1962...................................Sir Richard Gordon Turnbull.........................(Governor-General)

APPENDIX 2 - FAMILY TREES OF THE MAIN FAMILIES THAT MIGRATED TO GERMAN EAST AFRICA BEFORE WORLD WAR I

The Bauer Family

The Bauer family migrated from Höfen near Winnenden (Würrtemberg)
to Palestine in 1869. Descendants settled in German East Africa in 1910.

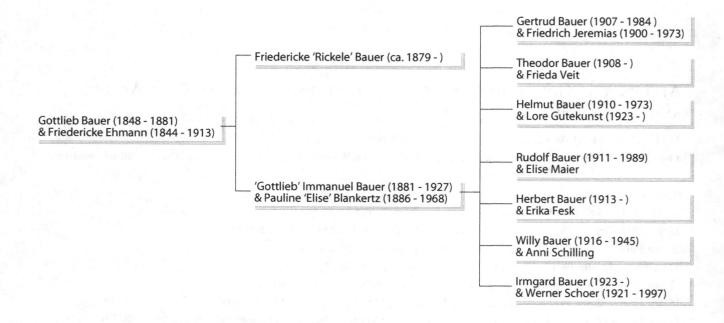

The Bäuerle Family

The Bäuerle family migrated from Weilimdorf (Würrtemberg) to Palestine in the 1870s.
Descendants settled in German East Africa in 1910/11.

The Blaich Family

The Blaich family migrated from Neuweiler in the Blackforest (Württemberg) to Palestine in 1870. Descendants settled in German East Africa in 1910.

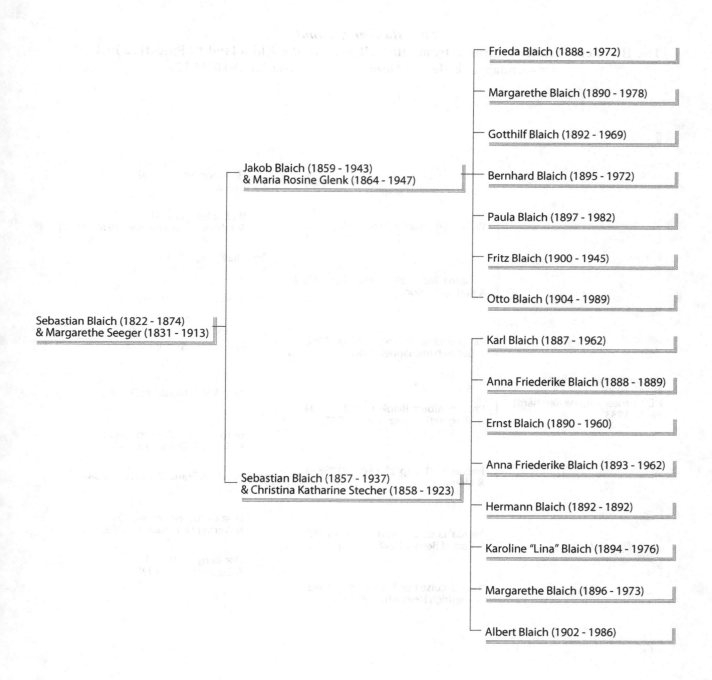

Sebastian Blaich (1822 - 1874)
& Margarethe Seeger (1831 - 1913)

Jakob Blaich (1859 - 1943)
& Maria Rosine Glenk (1864 - 1947)

- Frieda Blaich (1888 - 1972)
- Margarethe Blaich (1890 - 1978)
- Gotthilf Blaich (1892 - 1969)
- Bernhard Blaich (1895 - 1972)
- Paula Blaich (1897 - 1982)
- Fritz Blaich (1900 - 1945)
- Otto Blaich (1904 - 1989)

Sebastian Blaich (1857 - 1937)
& Christina Katharine Stecher (1858 - 1923)

- Karl Blaich (1887 - 1962)
- Anna Friederike Blaich (1888 - 1889)
- Ernst Blaich (1890 - 1960)
- Anna Friederike Blaich (1893 - 1962)
- Hermann Blaich (1892 - 1892)
- Karoline "Lina" Blaich (1894 - 1976)
- Margarethe Blaich (1896 - 1973)
- Albert Blaich (1902 - 1986)

The Blankertz Family

The Blankertz family migrated from Hückelhoven in the Rhineland to Palestine in 1858.
Descendants settled in German East Africa in 1910-1912.

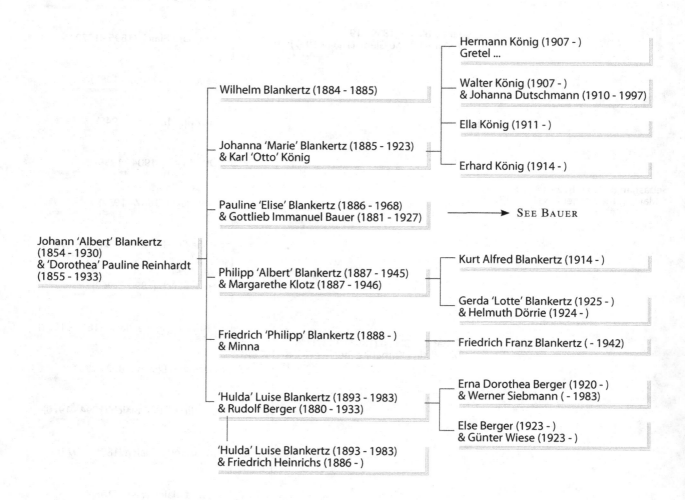

The Glenk Family
The Glenk family migrated from Standorf (Württemberg) to Palestine in 1875. Descendants settled in German East Africa in 1909/10.

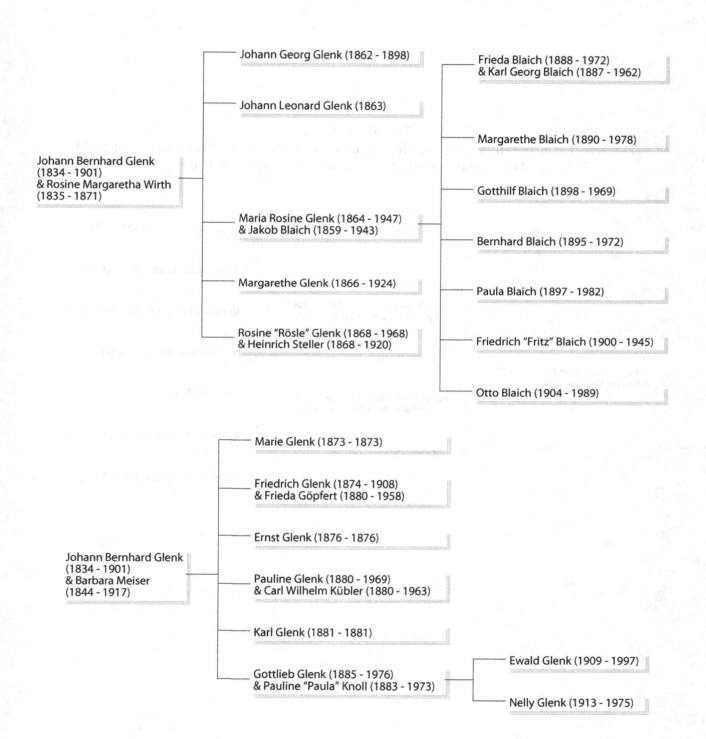

The Knoll Family

The Knoll family migrated from Möglingen (Württemberg) to Palestine in the 1870s.
Descendants settled in German East Africa in 1909.

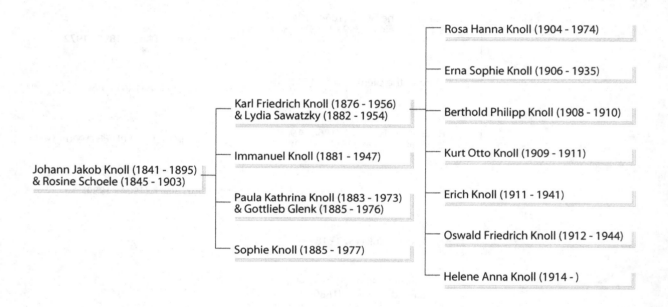

Johann Jakob Knoll (1841 - 1895)
& Rosine Schoele (1845 - 1903)

- Karl Friedrich Knoll (1876 - 1956)
  & Lydia Sawatzky (1882 - 1954)
  - Rosa Hanna Knoll (1904 - 1974)
  - Erna Sophie Knoll (1906 - 1935)
  - Berthold Philipp Knoll (1908 - 1910)
  - Kurt Otto Knoll (1909 - 1911)
  - Erich Knoll (1911 - 1941)
  - Oswald Friedrich Knoll (1912 - 1944)
  - Helene Anna Knoll (1914 -)
- Immanuel Knoll (1881 - 1947)
- Paula Kathrina Knoll (1883 - 1973)
  & Gottlieb Glenk (1885 - 1976)
- Sophie Knoll (1885 - 1977)

The Reinhardt Family

The Reinhardt family migrated from Oberkollwangen in the Blackforest (Württemberg) to Palestine in 1869. Descendants settled in German East Africa in 1890, 1896 and 1910/11.

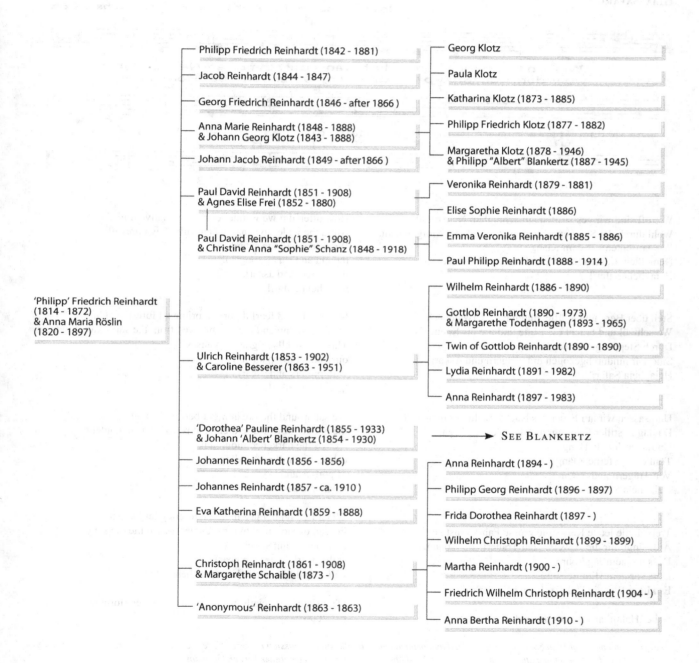

APPENDIX 3 - AFRICA SONG, 'HEIA SAFARI'

This was a very popular song amongst the German settlers in East Africa. It was written after World War I. The song is about the life and experiences of the men with the Schutztruppe (Protection Force), who served in East Africa in World War I.

HEIA SAFARI

Wie oft sind wir geschritten auf schmalem Negerpfad,
Wohl durch der Steppen Mitten, wenn früh der Morgen naht,
Wie lauschten wir dem Klange,
Dem alten, trauten Sange der Träger und Askari
Heia, heia Safari!

How often did we wander on narrow native trails.
Amid the wide savannah when early dawn prevails.
We listened to the sounds of
the old and trusty songs of
the porters and askari,
heia. heia Safari!

Steil über Berg und Klüfte, durch tiefe Urwaldnacht,
Wo schwül und feucht die Lüfte und nie die Sonne lacht,
Durch Steppengräserwogen
Sind wir hindurchgezogen mit Trägern und Askari
Heia, heia Safari!

Steep hills and fearful gorges, primeval forest's night,
the air is damp and muggy, blocked from the sun's sweet light.
Through swells of grass expanses,
our valiant troop advances
with porters and askari,
heia, heia safari!

Und sassen wir am Feuer des Nachts wohl vor dem Zelt,
Da lag in stiller Feier um uns die nächt'ge Welt,
Und über dunkle Hänge
Tönt es wie ferne Klänge
Von Trägern und Askari
Heia, heia Safari!

We sat around the fire at night before the tent,
the nocturnal world rejoicing, at peace, at rest, content.
Across the darkened mountain,
echoes are still resounding
of porters and askari:
heia, heia safari!

Tret ich die letzte Reise, die grosse Fahrt, einst an,
Auf, singt mir diese Weise statt Trauerliedern dann,
Dass meinem Jägerohre,
Dort vor dem Himmelstore,
Es klingt Wie ein Halali*, heia, heia Safari!

When I go on my last trek, the journey far beyond,
instead of mournful hymns, come, sing to me the song
that to my hunter's ear
- (the pearly gates are near)
will sound like one halali: heia, heia safari!

*(the 'Halali' announces the end of the hunt)

(Translated especially for this book by Peter Hornung, December 2006)

*The lyrics and music of Heia Safari are copyrighted and printed here with the kind permission of Voggenreiter Verlag, Bonn, Germany.
Words: Robert Götz after A. Aschenborn and Music by Robert Götz. © Voggenreiter Verlag, Germany*

ABOUT THE AUTHORS

Helmut Glenk

Helmut was born in 1943 at Tatura, Victoria, Australia where his parents were interned during World War II. He is a descendant of the Glenks who migrated to Palestine in 1876 and who settled in the German Templer settlement of Sarona as one of the pioneering families. His paternal grandfather and grandmother, Gottlieb and Paula (nee Knoll) were both born in Sarona, Palestine in the 1880s and migrated to German East Africa in 1910 for a short period of time. His father Ewald was born in Palestine in 1909. His mother Anne (nee Schurr), came from Geislingen, Germany and went to Palestine in the 1930s. Helmut's brother, Dieter, was also born in Palestine before World War II. The Glenks were part of the contingent of deportees who were brought to Australia in 1941.

After the war the Glenks settled in Bayswater, Victoria, Australia. They were the first Templers from Camp in Tatura to settle in Bayswater in November 1946. Helmut grew up there and finished his primary and secondary education in the local area.

On completion of secondary schooling he joined the Victorian Public Service and studied Public Administration at the Royal Melbourne Institute of Technology graduating with a Diploma. After a career spanning nearly 40 years with the Victorian Public Service, during which he held a number of senior positions in several departments as well as being Chief Executive Officer of a Statutory Authority, he left the service in 2000 to pursue other interests. On leaving the VPS he was awarded Life Membership of the Institute of Public Administration for "outstanding contribution to the achievement of the Institute's objectives and for exemplary service to the Victorian Community".

In the period 2001 to 2005 he researched and wrote a book titled *From Desert Sands to Golden Oranges*. This book, which has received international recognition, is an historical account of the former German Templer settlement of Sarona and the achievements of the settlers and their contribution to the modernisation of Palestine. In 2006 he was interviewed and featured in an Israeli TV documentary on the former Sarona settlement. He has also been interviewed on that subject by the Australian National Special Broadcasting Service.

He has co-authored a short history of the Glenk family in Bayswater (published in *The Fruits of Bayswater/Wantirna* and contributed other articles for *Bayswater Inside Out* (a local newsletter). He was contributor to *Ringwood Recalls* (a History of the first 50 years of Ringwood High School/ Ringwood Secondary College). He was interviewed on the local Community Radio on some of his childhood experiences in Bayswater. In 2005/06 he was a finalist in the *Exiles and Emigrants* short story writing competition conducted by the Leader Newspaper Group.

After extensive personal research, and in conjunction with input from Horst Blaich and Peer Gatter, he wrote the text as well as the captions for the illustrations of this publication.

Helmut lives in the Eastern suburbs of Melbourne with his wife Lorraine. They have three children and six grandchildren.

His interests are his family, history, travelling and reading. He is a keen vegetable gardener and likes the outdoors especially fishing and hunting.

Horst Blaich

Horst was born in 1932 in Haifa, Palestine. His parents, Albert and Hertha (née Katz) were both born in Palestine. During World War II, Horst, his mother and brother were interned in the Waldheim Camp before being exchanged to Germany in November 1942. After the war Horst completed an apprenticeship as a colour-photo lithographer and emigrated to Australia with his family and settled in Bayswater a suburb of Melbourne.

Horst furthered his education and skills by completing an Advanced Printing Technology Course and then proceeding to study management and industrial engineering. He served on the committee of the Institute of Industrial Engineers for several years.

Horst developed an interest in quality and productivity, in particular with the Quality Circle concept and in 1978 undertook a comprehensive study on the industrial boom in Japan. Horst was one of the "pioneers" in introducing the Quality Circles concept to Australian industry. In 1982 he successfully introduced the concept at W D and HO Wills (Australia) a major company with the Amatil Group of companies. He was instrumental in developing the first Quality Circles chapter in Australia and when the Chapter became the Australian Quality Circle Association, Horst was its inaugural President.

In 1985 Horst formed his own company – Horst Blaich Pty Ltd – Total Quality Management Consultants and Publishers. He undertook large consultancy projects with major organisations in industry, with government authorities and the defence forces. In conjunction with Donald Dewar, of the USA, he published *Team Leader Manual* on statistical problem solving techniques for employee participative team work.

Horst has a keen interest in family history and maintains his "Albert Blaich Family Archive" with a large database of Templer families and an historical photographic database with over 25,000 images. This archive has been a major source of information for historians and academics, especially from Israel, the Tel Aviv City Council Restoration and Preservation Department and the Eretz Israel Museum. In 2006 Horst was instrumental in the museum mounting a major exhibition on the Templers. He provided a significant amount of material for display at the exhibition.

Horst, with his keen interest in genealogy, has trained persons and lectured in genealogy for over 25 years. He has been an adviser on genealogy to the Church of Jesus Christ of Latter Day Saints. For many years Horst has served in leadership positions in the Church and as a Bishop of the Church.

Horst is married to Irene they have five children and twelve grandchildren.

In recent years Horst formed the Temple Society Australia Heritage Group and is leading the group into the modern archival and historical recording of the Temple Society's history. This work also includes the translation and publication of historical books and texts. He is a regular contributor to the heritage segment in the Temple Society's monthly publication the Templer Record. Horst has organised a number of visual displays and exhibitions of Templer history in Australia at Melbourne, Sydney and Tanunda, South Australia. Recently he has organised a permanent 'Templer Gallery' with photographic displays at Tabulum and Templer Home for the Aged in Bayswater.

He has researched and published a series of family history books. In 2007, Horst, in conjunction with his wife, published a book titled *The Wennagel Family.* A comprehensive and wide ranging history and achievements of the Wennagel family.

Horst worked in conjunction with Helmut Glenk in the publication of the book *From Desert Sands to Golden Oranges* published in 2005, a historical account of the German Templer settlement of Sarona.

For this book Horst helped with researching material and interviewing family members and friends both in Australia and overseas. He designed the cover and co-ordinated the maps and illustrations for the book.

Peer Gatter

Peer was born in 1968 in Kirchheim unter Teck, Württemberg, Germany, not far from the villages that his Templer ancestors had left for their pious quest to the Holy Land a century earlier.

He is a descendant of the Temple Elder Philipp Friedrich Reinhardt (1814-1872), who arrived in Palestine in 1869 and was among the founding settlers of the Haifa settlement. Four of his children later emigrated to German East Africa. His sons Johannes, Ulrich and Christof were the first known Templers to settle in the new German colony in the late 19th century.

His daughter Dorothea Pauline Reinhardt (1855-1933) married the Jaffa brewer Johann Albert Blankertz, whose family had come to the Orient from the Rhineland in 1858, and had founded Jerusalem's first brewery.

With three of their children, the Blankertz's left Palestine in 1911 to plant tobacco at Mount Meru in the African interior. A fourth daughter, Elise Blankertz, had already settled near Arusha with husband Gottlieb Immanuel Bauer a year earlier. Their son Helmut Bauer (Peer's grandfather) returned to East Africa after the First World War and until he was deported during the Second World War to Germany, managed the Coffee Plantation Kifumbu at Mt Kilimanjaro. Today members of the Bauer family live in Germany, Namibia, South-Africa and Australia.

Peer spent part of his childhood in the hinterland of Liberia (West Africa), where his parents worked during the 1980s. The stories on the family's African past were always present and familiar to Peer. At age 13, he visited the Kilimanjaro region with his parents and his younger sister Carola, then started to record the family's history, tracing it back to Palestine and Germany.

ABOUT THE AUTHORS

From 1989-1991, Peer lived in Israel, where he worked in a Palestinian relief project in Akko, just across the bay from the former Templer Colony Haifa. Here he found the houses and graves of his ancestors and was encouraged by the late Professor Alex Carmel (author of the book *Die Siedlungen der württembergischen Templer in Palästina 1868-1918)* to record their life stories.

Peer studied Political Science and Middle Eastern Studies in Tübingen, Teheran and Georgetown. At Tübingen University he became friends with Dr Jakob Eisler, an expert on Templer history, who introduced him to the historical sources and provided, from his own personal archive, a wealth of information and records about Peer's ancestors.

Peer's prime source of information was however his great aunt, Irmgard Schoer (née Bauer) who grew up in Tanganyika and who had spent many years of her younger life in British internment camps in Rhodesia. Despite all the hardships she suffered, she never became tired of sharing her fascinating African stories.

From 1991 to 1999, Peer worked as a journalist for *Der Spiegel, Die Zeit* and *Focus,* and reported from Iran, Kurdistan, Afghanistan and Northern Ireland. In 1998, his book *Khomeinis Erben* (Khomeini's Heirs) was published, which documents the fruitless economic reforms of Iranian President Rafsanjani and his power struggle with Islamist hardliners.

In 1999, Peer joined the World Bank Country Office in Yemen, where he worked on decentralization reform and drug policies. From 2001 to 2005 he worked with the United Nations Development Programme in Sana'a, Yemen, and was an adviser to the Minister of Water and Environment, on water management and community development.

Today, Peer lives in Phnom Penh, Cambodia, where his wife Nathalie heads an HIV/AIDS project of Doctors without Borders. They have two children, Ruben and Lea. Peer is finalizing a PhD on the Political Economy of Qat, a drug widely consumed in Yemen and most of eastern and southern Africa. For the World Bank in Yemen he is currently preparing a strategy on this drug.

BIBLIOGRAPHY AND REFERENCES

ARCHIVES

Albert Blaich Family Archives, Bayswater, Victoria, Australia
Helmut Glenk Personal Records, Ringwood East, Victoria, Australia
Jakob Eisler Personal Archives, Stuttgart, Germany
Peer Gatter Personal Family Archives, Lenningen, Germany
Temple Society Australia Archives, Bentleigh, Victoria, Australia
Tempelgesellschaft Deutschland Archiv, Stuttgart, Germany

PUBLISHED SOURCES
(BOOKS, ARTICLES AND NEWSPAPERS)

Ben-Artzi, Yossi, 1992, *Religious Ideology and Landscape Formation: The Case of the Templers in Eretz-Israel*, Cambridge University Press

Buckwitz, Harry, 1940, *Vertrieben aus deutschem Land in Afrika, Tatsachenbericht eines Heimkehrers aus Deutsch-Ostafrika* (Driven out of German Land in Africa, A factual report of a "homecomer" from German East Africa), published in the journal Kolonie und Heimat, 1940

Carmel, Alex, 1973, *Die Siedlungen der württembergischen Templer in Palästina 1868-1918* (The settlements of the Württemberg Templers in Palestine 1868-1918), W. Kohlhammer Verlag, Stuttgart

Carmel, Alex. and Eisler, Jakob, 1999, *Der Kaiser reist ins Heilige Land* (The Kaiser travels to the Holy Land) W. Kohlhammer Verlag, Stuttgart

De Haas, Rudolf, 1927, *Im Sattel für Deutsch-Ost – Auf Wildpfad und Feindesfährten* (In the Saddle for German-East – On Wildlife Trails and on the Tracks of the Enemy) Brunnen-Verlag Karl Winckler, Berlin

Eisler, Jakob 1997, *Der deutsche Beitrag zum Aufstieg Jaffas 1850-1914 – Zur Geschichte Palästinas im 19. Jahrhundert* (The German Contribution to the rise of Jaffa 1850-1914 – On the history of Palestine in the 19th Century) – Harrassowitz Verlag, Wiesbaden, Germany

BIBLIOGRAPHY AND REFERENCES

Eisler, Jakob 1999, *Peter Martin Metzler – Ein christlicher Missionar im Heiligen Land* (Peter Martin Metzler – A Christian Missionary in the Holy Land), Universität Haifa, Israel

Encyclopedia Britannica – Volume 21, (1962), William Benton Publisher, Chicago,USA

Glenk, Helmut, et al, 2005, *From Desert Sands to Golden Oranges, The history of the German Templer Settlement of Sarona in Palestine 1871 – 1948*, Trafford Publishing, Victoria, BC, Canada

Götz, Robert, *Wir fahren in die Welt*, Voggenreiter Verlag, Bad Godesberg, Germany

Haenicke, Alex, et al, 1937, *Das Buch der deutschen Kolonien* (The Book of German Colonies) Wilhelm Goldmann Verlag, Leipzig, Germany

Hughes, Anthony (Tony), 1963, *East Africa – Kenya, Tanzania, Uganda*, Penguin Books, Great Britain

Knauss, Adolf Anton, 1942, *Im Schatten des Ruwenzori* (In the Shadow of Mt Ruwenzori), Steiniger Verlag, Berlin

LeBor, Adam, 2006, *City of Oranges – Arabs and Jews in Jaffa*, Bloomsbury Publishing, London

Lettow-Vorbeck, Gerd von, 1957, *Am Fuße des Meru* (At the Foot Mt Meru), Verlag Paul Parey, Hamburg und Berlin

Limpert, Wilhelm, Buchgestaltung, 1939 – *Deutsche Heimat in Afrika* (German Homeland in Africa), Wilhelm Limpert Verlag, Berlin

Rooney, David, 2000, *Military Mavericks: Extraordinary Men of Battle*, Sterling

Samler Brown, and Gordon Brown, G, 1920 – *South and East Africa Year Book and Guide for 1920*, 26th Edition, Union Castle Line, London

Sauer, Paul 1991, *The Holy Land Called - The Story of the Temple Society* – Temple Society Australia (TSA), Melbourne, Australia

Schlicht, C 1908, *Neuste Nachrichten aus dem Morgenland* (Latest News from the Orient), Journal published in Germany, June 1908

Schmidt, Rochus 1898, republished 1999, *Deutschlands Kolonien* (Germany's Colonies) – Verlag des Vereins der Bücherfreunde Schall & Grund 1898, republished by Weltbild Verlag GmbH, Augsburg, Germany

Tempelgesellschaft in Deutschland (TGD) 1961, *100 Jahre Tempelgesellschaft* (100 years Temple Society)

Temple Society Australia (TSA), *The Temple Society – An Overview: Templer Handbook*

TGD 1961, TSA 1974, *in memory of those who have gone before us*

Temple Society Periodical Publications
    Süddeutsche Warte, (South German Sentinel) – various editions
    Jerusalemer Warte, (Jerusalem Sentinel) – various editions
    Warte des Tempels, (Temple Sentinel) – various editions

The New Encyclopaedia Britannica, Volumes 2 and 5, 1997, Encyclopaedia Britannica, Chicago, USA

Unpublished Manuscripts

Bauer, Lore, *Life of the Bauer Family in East Africa*
Bauer, Rudolf, *Eine Familie – Drei Kontinente* (One Family – Three Continents)
Blaich, Gerhard, *Life Story*
Blaich, Gotthilf, *Life Story*
Gatter, Peer, *History of the Reinhardt, Blankertz and Bauer Families in Germany, Palestine and East Africa*
Kopp, Luise, *Lebenslauf* (Life Story – Reminiscences of Mine)
Schoer, Irmgard, *History of the Bauer Family in East Africa and Germany (1915-1947).* 2006

Wieland, Rudolf, *What Father Rudolf told us Children in regard to his German East Africa Report*

INTERNET REFERENCES

www.ntz.info/genb00274
www.smithsonianmagazine.com.smithsonian/issue02/Oct02/leakey
www.mnsu.edu/museum/archaeology/sites/africa/olduvai-gorge
www.kenyalogy.com/eng/info/histo6.html
www.ntz.info/gen/n0/n1214.html
http.africanhistory,about,com/cs/biography/p/bio_peters.htm
www.hs.uni-hamburg.de?DE/ins/Per/Kueh/Wissm/wissmann
www.dhm.de/lemo/htm/biografen/WissmannHermann
www.ntz.info/gen/n0023.html
www.ntz.info/gen/b00628.htm1
http://en.wikipedia.org/wiki/Heligoland-Zanibar_Treaty
http://en.wikipedia.org/wiki/Paul Erich von Lettow-Vorbeck
www.dikigoros.150mcom/lettowvorbeck.htm
www.tokencoins.com/gea04a.htm
www.firstworldwar.com/bio/lettowvorbeck

ABBREVIATIONS

ABFA	Albert Blaich Family Archives
CZA	Central Zionist Archives
HGPA	Helmut Glenk Personal Archives
PGPA	Peer Gatter Personal Archives
TANU	Tanganyika Africa National Union
TGD	Tempelgesellschaft Deutschland
TSA	Temple Society Australia
TTB	Tanzania Tourist Board
UTP	United Tanganyika Party

ACKNOWLEDGEMENTS

We acknowledge the help, encouragement and information provided by the following persons. Without their wonderful recollections, photographs and items of interest this historical documentation could not have been compiled in such detail.

Assmus, Eberhard
Asenstorfer, Ulrich
Bauer, Christel
Bauer, Gert
Bauer, Liesel
Bauer, Lore
Beilharz, Renate
Ben-Artzi, Yossi
Besemer, Bettina
Blaich, Anita
Blaich, Herta
Blaich, Horst
Blaich, Irene
Blaich, Walter (the late)
Blaich, Gerhard
Brain, John
Brenner, Erna
Danon, Ruth
Dörrie, Gerda Lotte
Dravenicks, Charlotte
Eisler, Jakob
Evans, Trevor
Fisher, David
Gatter, Dorothea
Glenk, Dieter
Goldman, Danny
Goetze, Erika
Goetze, Friedrich
Haar, Gisela

Heinrich, Ilse
Herrmann, Christine
Higgins, Martin
Hornung, Peter G.
Klingbeil, Karin
Klink, Ursula
Kneher, Brigitte
Kuebler, Helene
Kopp, Luise
Laemmle, Charlotte
Lange, Peter
Moritz, Heinke (the late)
Neef, Herbert
Neef, Werner
Plink, Rainer
Plink, Ruth-Karin
Reinhardt, Hedwig
Reinhardt, Klaus
Reinhardt, Helmuth
Ruff, Ernst
Ruff, Helmut
Shilony, Zvi
Schoer, Irmgard
Siebmann, Erna
Uhlherr, Hermann
Uhlherr, Michael
Wagner, Doris
Weller, Theo
Wiese, Else

Endnotes

Chapter One

[1] Tanzania Tourist Board (TTB), *Map and Guide to Tanzania,* 1995 (internet reference   *www.ntz.info/genb00274.*

Internet reference, *www.smithsonianmagazine.com.smithsonian/issue02/Oct02/leakey.*

Internet reference, *www.mnsu.edu/museum/archaeology/sites/africa/olduvai-gorge.*

[2] TTB, 1995.

Encyclopaedia Britannica, Volume 21,1962 – p 6299.

The New Encyclopaedia Britannica Volume 2, 1997 – p 528.

Haenicke, Alex – *Das Buch der Deutschen Kolonien (The Book of the German Colonies),* Wilhelm Goldmann Verlag, Leipzig, 1937, p 137.

[3] TTB, 1995.

[4] Ibid.

[5] Ibid.

Encyclopaedia Britannica, 1962.

Haenicke, 1937, pp 138, 139.

[6] Ibid.

[7] Ibid.

Eisler, Jakob –*Peter Martin Metzler – Ein christlicher Missionar im Heiligen Land (Peter Martin Metzler – A Christian Missionary in the Holy Land),* Universität Haifa 1999, pp 16-17. Clauss 1882 (Aanm.17), pp 137-149; Krapf 1858 (Anm.20), pp 448-449, *Die Missionare Johann Jakob Erhardt und Johannes Rebmann waren mit J. L. Krapf Pioniere der Ostafrika- Mission (The Missionaries Johann Jakob Erhardt and Johannes Rebmann were, with J. L. Krapf, Pioneers of the East Africa Mission).* Regarding Rebmann also Ringwald, Walter – *Johannes Rebmann 1820-1876, Missionar – Endecker – Sprachforscher (Missionary – Explorer – Language Researcher), in the" Lugwigsburger Geschichtsblätter, Heft 29", pp. 87-109, 1977;* regarding Erhardt also Mayer, E., *Missionar Johann Erhardt aus Boennigheim 1823-1901 (Missionary Jakob Erhardt from Boennigheim 1823-1901) in "Zeitschrift des Zabergäuvereins, Nr.3, pp 33-48, 1960.*

[8] TTB, 1995.

Encyclopaedia Britannica, 1962.

The New Encyclopaedia Britannica

Haenicke, 1937 – p 139.

Internet reference, *www.kenyalogy.com/eng/info/histo6.htmml.*

Internet reference, www.ntz.info/gen/n01214.html.

Internet reference, *www.ewpnet.cm/kilimanjaro..htm.*

[9] TTB, 1995.

Haenicke, 1937 – p 140.

Ludwig Gerhardt – Roscher, Albrecht. In "Historische Kommission bei der Bayerischen Akademie der Wissenschaft" (Hrsg.): Neue Deutsche Biographie, Bd.22. (In "Historical Commision at the Bavarian Academy of Science": New German Biography) Dunker and Humblot, Berlin 2005, pp 41-42.

Internet "ewpnet".

Internet"ntz.info/gen".

[10] Internet "ewpnet";.

[11] TTB, 1995.

Schmidt, Rochus – *Deutschlands Kolonien (Germany's Colonies),* Verlag des Vereins der Bücherfreunde Schall & Grund, Berlin 1898, republished by Weltbild Verlag GmbH, Augsburg 1999, pp 1-6.

Internet reference, *http.africanhistory.about.com/cs/biography/p/bio_peters.htm.*

[12] Ibid.

Schmidt, 1999 – pp 6-12.

Haenicke, 1937 – p 141.

[13] Internet "africanhistory".

[14] TTB, 1995.

Haenicke, 1937 – pp 141,142.

[15] Ibid;.

Schmidt, 1999 – pp 14-16,40,41.

Encyclopaedia Britannica, 1962.

The New Encyclopaedia Britannica.

[16] Schmidt,1999 – pp 16-17.

Haenicke, 1937 – p 143.

[17] Schmidt, 1999 – p 19.

[18] Ibid – p 39.

[19] Ibid – p 40.

[20] Ibid – pp 39,40,58.

[21] Ibid - pp 40, 43-45.

Internet, *"africanhistory".*

Haenicke, 1937 p 143.

[22] Schmidt, 1999 – pp 45,46, 54-59.

[23] Ibid – pp 60,61.

Internet reference, *www.hs.uni-hamburg.de/DE/Ins/Per/Kueh/Wissm/wissmann.*

Internet reference, *www.infoplease.com/ce6/people/a0852535.*

Internet reference, *www.dhm.de/lemo/htm/biografen/WissmanHermann.*

[24] Schmidt, 1999 – pp 61-121.

Internet, *"infoplease"*.

[25]Schmidt, 1999 – pp 122-124.

Internet, *"africanhistory"*.

Internet reference, *"www.ntz.info/gen/n0023.html*.

Internet reference, *http://en.wikipedia.org/wiki/Heligoland-Zanzibar_Treaty.*

[26] Schmidt, 1999 – pp 124 – 127.

Haenicke, 1937 – pp 144,145.

[27] Schmidt, p 127.

Haenicke, 1937 – p 144.

Internet, *"africanhistory"*.

[28] Limpert, Wilhelm, 1939 –*Deutsche Heimat in Afrika (German Homeland in Africa).*

[29] Schmidt, pp 128 -133.

Internet, *"ntz.info"*.

[30] Internet, *"ntz.info"*.

Hughes, pp 41,42.

[31] Hughes;, - p42.

[32] Haenicke, 1937 – p 168,313,314.

Chapter Two

[1] Tempelgesellschaft in Deutschland (TGD)1961, *100 Jahre Tempelgesellschaft (100 years Temple Society*

Temple Society Australia (TSA), *The Temple Society – An Overview; Templer Handbook*

Glenk, H., 2004, *From Desert Sands to Golden Oranges, p 1*

Sauer , P., 1991, *The Holy Land Called, chapter 1*

Carmel, A., *Die Siedlungen der württembergischen Templer in Palästina 1868-1918,* 1973

[2] Ibid

[3] TGD, 1961; TSA, 1974, ~~in~~ In memory of those who have gone before us; Sauer, P, 1991.

[4] Glenk, H., p 4

[5] Ben-Artzi, Y., 1992, *Religious Ideology and Landscape Formation: The Case of the Templers in Eretz-Israel*, pp83-106

[6] Glenk, H., 2004

[7] Eisler, J., 1997, *Der deutsche Beitrag zum Aufstieg Jaffas 1850-1914 (The German Contribution to the Rise of Jaffa 1850-1914)*

Chapt 4, Sauer, P., 1991, p47

TSA, 1974, *In memory of those who have gone before us;*

[8] Ibid

LeBor, Adam, 2006, *City of Oranges – Arabs and Jews in Jaffa*, pp29,30

[9] Eisler, J., 1997, pp118-120, 124

Sauer, P., 1991, p71,

[10] Sauer, P,1991, p96

[11] Carmel, A.

[12] Glenk, H. p 9

Goldman, D., *Sarona – Settlement Design*

[13] Glenk, H., p10

[14] Ibid., p11

Süddeutsche Warte (Warte),No. 47-23 November 1871, p184 (Southern German Sentinel)

[15] Glenk, H, pp13-18

TSA-A, A07-46

Warte No. 32 – 9 August 1873, p126 and No. 33 – 14 August1873, pp129-130

[16] Glenk, H, pp19-40

[17] Sauer, P., p96

[18] Ibid, pp 64, 68-77

[19] Ibid, p 62

[20] Ibid, p 71

[21] Ibid, pp 71-73,

Carmel, A/Eisler, EJ., *Der Kaiser reist ins Heilige Land (The Kaiser travels to the Holy Land)*

[22] Sauer, p 75

[23] Ibid, p 76

[24] Ibid, p 76

Carmel, A.

[25] *Warte* No 21 – 21 May 1868, pp 81-82, *Warte* No 22 – 28 May 1868, pp 86-87, *Warte* No 23 -4 June 1868, pp 90-91

[26] *Warte* No 7 – 18 February 1869, pp27-28, *Warte* No 8 – 25 February 1869

[27] *Warte* No 16 – 22 April 1869, pp61-62

Chapter Three

[1] Eisler, 1999 – pp 16,17,29 and email of 20 October 2006

[2] Ibid

[3] Ibid – pp30 – 44

LeBor, 2006 – p29

[4] Eisler,1999 – pp 44-46

[5] Albert Blaich Family Archives – *Life story of Josef Wennagel*

[6] Shilony, Zvi – personal records and email of 20 December 2006

[7]Wennagel, Hugo interview March 2005

ABFA

[8] Central Zionist Archives (CZA), Jerusalem, L1/125

Shilony – email of 16 November 2006

ENDNOTES

9 CZA, L1/125 (Translated by H Glenk)

10 Peer Gatter, Private Archives of the Reinhardt, Blankertz, Bauer, and Ehmann families. Interview with Konrad Reinhardt by Peer Gatter in 1997.

11 Ibid

12 Lange, Peter, email 5 September 2006

13 Gatter

Gisela Haar interview January 2005

14 Gatter.

15 Sauer, P, 1991, The Holy Land Called (THLC), P 70

16 Carmel, A, 1973, Die Siedlungen der württembergischen Templer in Palästina 1868-1918 (The Settlements of the Templers from Württemberg in Palestine 1868-1918), p 156

17 Ibid

18 ABFA

19 *Warte* No.8 -20 February 1908, pp 61-63

20 Ibid

21 Ibid

22 Carmel, A, 1973, p 68-87

23 *Warte* No 8 – 20 February 1908, pp 61-63

24 Ibid

25 Glenk, pps 26-30

26 Carmel, pp 69-71

27 Sauer, pps 79-82

Carmel, Chapter III

28 *Warte* No. 12 – 19 March 1908, pp 92-93

29 *Warte* No 13 – 26 March 1908, pp 100-101

30 Ibid

31 *Warte* No 11 – 12 March 1908, pp 86-87

32 Carmel,1973, p 71;

Sauer, 1991, p106

33 *Warte* Nos. 11, pp 86-87; 12; 13, pp 100-101; and 25, pp 195-196 of 1908

34 *Warte* No. 13- 26 March 1908, pp 100-101

35 *Warte* No 25 – 18 June 1908, pp195-196

36 Ibid

37 *Warte* Nos 17 -23 April 1908, pp 130-131; 35 – 2 September 1909, pp 275-276

38 *Warte* No 17 23 April 1908, pp 130-131

39 Ibid

40 Sauer, 1991, p105;

Warte No. 8 – 20 February 1908, pp 61-63

41 Ibid,

Sauer, 1991, p283

42 *Warte* No 18 – 30 April 1908 (Translation by H. Glenk), pp141-143

43 *Warte* No. 8 - 20 February 1908, pp 61-63

44 Ibid

Chapter Four

1 *Warte* No. 9 – 27 February 1908, pp 69-71

2 Ibid

Internet, "ntz.info"

3 *Warte* No. 9 – 27 February 1908, pp 69-71

Internet, "www.zum.de/psm/imperialismus/kolonialatlas09"

4 *Warte* No. 9 – 27 February 1908, pp 69-71

5 Ibid

6 *Warte* No. 24 – 16 June 1908, p 191

7 *Warte* No. 9 – 27 February 1908, pp 69-71

8 Ibid

9 Ibid

10 *Warte* No. 10 – 5 March 1908, pp 78-79

11 Ibid

12 Ibid

13 Ibid

14 Ibid

15 Ibid

16 *Warte* No. 11 – 12 March 1908, pp 84-86

17 Ibid

18 Ibid

19 *Warte* No. 12 – 19 March 1908, p 92

20 Ibid

21 *Warte* No. 13 – 26 March 1908, pp 99-100

22 Ibid

23 Ibid

24 *Warte* No.14 – 2 April 1908, pp 106-107

25 Ibid

26 Ibid

27 Ibid

28 Ibid

29 August Leue came to German East Africa in 1885 as part of von Wissmann's expedition. He was an officer stationed at Bayamoyo and later in Dar--es--Salaam. After leaving the *Schutztruppe* in 1901, he returned to German East Africa in 1905 and started a settlement on Mt Meru, which became known as Leuedorf (known today as Ngare Sero). Internet reference *http://ntz. info/gen/n)1614.html*

30 *Warte* No. 15 – 9 April 1908, pp 117-118

31 Ibid

[32] Ibid

[33] *Warte* No.16 – 16 April 1908, pp 127-128

[34] *Warte* No. 17 – 23 April 1908, p 135

[35] Ibid

[36] *Warte* No. 18 – 30 April 1908, pp 141-143

[37] Ibid

[38] Ibid

[39] Ibid

[40] *Warte* No. 19 – 7 May 1908, pp 150-151

Chapter Five

[1] *Warte* No. 32 – 6 August 1908 (Translated by H. Glenk), pp 252-253.

[2] *Warte* No. 33 – 13 August 1908 (Translated by H. Glenk), p 267.

[3] H. Glenk Personal Archives (Taped interview with Ewald Glenk).

Herta Blaich interview 10 November 2004.

[4] Ibid.

[5] Helene Kuebler (nee Knoll) interviews 27 September 2004 and 2 August 2006.

[6] Ibid.

[7] Erna Brenner advice in email from Ursula Klink 2 May 2006.

[8] Blaich interview.

[9] Albert Blaich Family Archives, Bayswater, Victoria, Australia.

[10] Herta Blaich interview 10 November 2004.

[11] HGPA.

[12] Ibid.

Warte No. 36 – 7 September 1911, pp 284-285.

Warte No. 37 – 14 September 1911, pp 293-294.

[13] *Warte* No. 38 – 21 September 1911, pp 300-301.

[14] *Warte* No. 40 – 5 October 1911, pp 308-309.

[15] The Bauer family segment is based on the unpublished private manuscript by Peer Gatter, grandson of- Helmut Bauer (born 1910 in Jaffa).

[16] Peer Gatter, Personal Archives of the Reinhardt, Blankertz, Bauer, and Ehmann families.

[17] Bauer, Rudolf, *Eine Familie – 3 Kontinente (One Family – 3 Continents)* – Unpublished private manuscript.

[18] PGPA.

[19] *Warte* No. 8 - 20. February 1908, p 62.

Warte No. 18 - 30 April 1908, pp 141-143.

[20] Interview with Irmgard Schoer (nee née Bauer) by Peer Gatter in 1996.

[21] PGPA.

[22] Ibid, *Warte* No. 8 - 20. February 1908, pp.61-63.

[23] PGPA.

[24] Ibid.

Bauer, R.

[25] PGPA.

[26] PGPA.

[27] The Blankertz family segment is based on the unpublished private manuscript by Peer Gatter, great-grandson of Elise Blankertz (born 1886 in Jaffa).

[28] Ibid.

[29] PGPA.

[30] During his frequent stopovers with pilgrims on the Jerusalem Road at the Hotel Reinhardt in Ramleh, he met his wife Dorothea Pauline, who was working there alongside her brother, the hotel owner Paul Reinhardt.

[31] PGPA.

[32] Ibid.

[33] Ibid.

[34] Bauer.

[35] Kopp, Luise, *Reminiscences of Mine* - Unpublished private manuscript.

[36] Herta Blaich interview 10 November 2004.

[37] Kopp.

; ABFA.;

Higgins.

[38] Glenk, 2005;

Kopp.

[39] Kopp.

Blaich November 2004 and May 2005.

[40] Bauer (Translated by Peer Gatter).

[41] Ibid.

[42] Ibid.

PGPA.

[43] Blaich.

[44] Blaich.

Bauer (Translated by H. Glenk).

[45] Blaich.

[46] Ibid.

;HGPA.

[47] Ibid.

[48] Gatter, Peer – unpublished private manuscript.

[49] Bauer.

[50] Kornthal was a village near Stuttgart where in 1823, under – Gottlieb Wilhelm Hoffmann, the *apostolische Brüdergemeinde* [Community of Brethren] took its beginnings.

[51] PGPA.

[52] von Lettow-Vorbeck, Gerd 1957, *Am Fuße des Meru* (At the foot of Meru), p 13

In February 2005 Rolf Ackermann's book *Die Weiße Jägerin* (the White Huntress) was published by Droemer-Knaur Verlag (Germany). It is the biographical story of the legendary German huntress Margarete Trappe.

[53] Ibid, pp 15,16.

[54] Ibid.

[55] Ibid, p 20.

[56] Ibid.

[57] Ibid, pp 27-29.

[58] Ibid.

[59] Blaich.

HGPA.

[60] Ibid.

[61] Ibid.

[62] Kopp.

[63] *Warte* 10 – 10 March 1913, pp 76-77.

HGPA.

Kuebler.

[64] Ibid.

[65] Haar, G – interview January 2005.

HGPA.

[66] Jakob Eisler Personal Archives, *Was Vater Rudolf uns Kinder erzählte und zwar in Anlehnung an seinen Deutsch-Ost-Afrika-Bericht* [What father Rudolf told us children in regard to his German East Africa report] unpublished private manuscript.

[67] Ibid (Translated by H. Glenk).

[68] Ibid.

[69] *Warte* 10 – 10 March 1913, pp 76-77.

[70] Ibid (Translated by H. Glenk).

[71] Neef, Walter, *Kurzgefasster Lebenslauf* (abbreviated Life Story) *by Walter Neef 1950,* unpublished private manuscript.

Chapter Six

[1] Internet – dikigoros.150m.com/lettowvorbeck.htm

Rooney, D – 2000, Military Mavericks: extraordinary men of battle, pp 99-101

[2] Rooney, D – 2000, pp 99,100

[3] Ibid

[4] Internet – www.tokencoins.com/gea04a.htm, Summary of Oberst Paul von Lettow-Vorbeck's extraordinary military campaigns against the aAllies

[5] Samler Brown, A and Gordon Brown, G – 1920, *South and East African Year Book and Guide for 1920,* Union Castle Line, London

Internet – www.ntz.info/gen/b00628.html

[6] Rooney, D – 2000, p103

Internet – www.firstworldwar.com/bio/lettowvorbeck

De Haas, Rudolf – 1927, *Im Sattel fuer Deutsch Ost (In the Saddle for German East),* pp12,13

[7] Internet - tokencoins etc

Internet – en.wikipedia.org/wiki/Paul Erich von Lettow-Vorbeck

[8] De Haas, 1927, p 17

[9] Ibid, 1927 – pp 123,124

[10] Blaich, Herta – 2004, interview 2 December 2004

[11] Blaich, Herta - 2004, interview 10 November 2004

De Haas, 1927, pp 14-16

[12] De Haas, 1927, pp 12 - 120

Blaich, Herta – 2004, Interviews

Gatter, Peer, email 3 December 2006

[13] Von Lettow-Vorbeck, -1957, pp56,57

Blaich, Herta – 2004, interviews

[14] Von Lettow-Vorbeck, pp 49,50,53,54

[15] Rooney, p 102

[16] De Haas, 1927 – pp 14 – 16, 17-19,23,28,46,95, 123,124

[17] Ibid – p 97, 285 (Translated by H. Glenk)

[18] Ibid – pp22-27,38-62,92

Kopp, letter December 2005

[19] Rooney, 2000, pp 102 -103

Internet – "tokencoins"

[20] De Haas, 1927 – pp 121,177

[21] Ibid – pp 14-16,17-19,23-28,46,69,84,95

Internet – "tokencoins"

Rooney,2000 – p 103

[22] Rooney, 2000 – p 103

[23] Samler Brown, 1920

Internet – "ntz.Info"

[24] Boell, L – 1951, *Die Operationen in Ostafrika.Ostafrika im Weltkrieg 1914-1918. Der Lettow-Feldzug* (Operations in East Africa. East Afrika during the First World War 1914-1918. The Lettow Campaign), p109.

25 Internet -"tokencoins"

Internet –"firstworldwar"

26 De Haas, 1927 – pp 114 -116,122,256,257

27 Rooney, 2000 – p 104

Samler Brown, 1920

Internet, "ntz,info"

28 De Haas, 1927 – pp 175,178,192,345

29 Rooney, 2000 – p 105

internet –"firstworldwar"

30 Ibid

31 Ibid – p 105,106

De Haas, 1927 – pp 262,263

Blaich, H - interview

32 De Haas, 1927 – pp 265,266

33 Bauer, Rudolf (Translated by H. Glenk)

34 Schoer, Irmgard, - *History of the Bauer Family in East Africa and Germany (1915-1947).* Completed and corrected by Lore Bauer (née Gutekunst), Dorothea Gatter (née Bauer) and Peer Gatter 2006, Unpublished private manuscript

35 Samler Brown, 1920

Internet,"ntz.info"

36 Blaich, H – interview November 2004

Lettow-Vorbeck, 1957 – pp72,73,123

Schoer, 2006

37 Schoer, 2006

38 Rooney, 2000 – p106

De Haas,1927 – p270

39 Hughes, A J, – *East Africa* - Penguin Books,1963– pp42,43

40 Blaich, H – interview November 2004

Lettow-Vorbeck, 1957 – pp 60,73

Schoer, 2006

41 Blaich, H

42 De Haas,1927 – p307

43 Lettow-Vorbeck, 1957 – p57

44 Rooney, 2000 – p107, 108

De Haas,1927 – pp254,279

45 De Haas,1927 – p133

46 Rooney, 2000 - pp108 -111

De Haas, 1927 – pp280,287

Internet, "tokencoins"

47 Rooney,2000

Internet, "tokencoins"

48 Ibid

49 De Haas, 1927 – pp280,306,335

50 Rooney, 2000

Internet, "tokencoins"

51 Ibid

De Haas, 1927 – p357

52 Ibid

De Haas,1927 – pp341,343

Samler Brown,1920

Internet, "ntz.info."

53 Ibid

Chapter Seven

1 Hughes,1963 – pp 42,43.

von Lettow-Vorbeck, 1957 – p 126.

2 von Lettow-Vorbeck,1957 – p 114.

3 Ibid, pp 60-73.

Blaich, H. – interview December 2004.

4 Blaich, ;H. – interview.

5 von Lettow-Vorbeck, p 125.

Blaich, ; H.- interview.

6 Ibid, p 126-128.

Blaich ,H. – interview.

Schoer, I.

7 Ibid.

8 Schoer, ;I.

9 Ibid.

10 Ibid.

11 Ibid.

12 Ibid.

13 Blaich, H. – interview.

14 Ibid.

15 Glenk, H., 2005 – pp 67-73.

16 *Warte des Tempels*, [Templer Sentinel], No. 15 – 20 August 1922, pp 63-65.

17 HGPA-Interview with Ewald Glenk.

18 Ibid.

19 Ibid.

20 Ibid.

21 Ibid.

22 Ibid.

Glenk, 2005 – p 78.

23 Ibid.

Glenk, 2005 –p 79.

24 Haar, Gisela – Interview January 2005.

Kopp, Luise – *Lebenslauf* [Life Story] – unpublished private manuscript.

Blaich, H. – Interview.-

[25] Blaich ,H. – Interview.

[26] Schoer, I.

[27] Ibid.

Chapter Eight

[1] Hughes, 1963 – p 43

[2] Ibid

Samler Brown, 1920

Internet, "*ntz.info*"

[3] Hughes, pp 44,49

- Internet, "*www.ntz.info/gen/b00274*"

[4] Ibid, p 44

[5] Ibid, pp 45-47

Internet, "ntz.info"

[6] Internet, "ntz.info"

[7] Hughes, pp 48,49

Blaich, H., - interview

[8] Ibid, p 47

Blaich, H., – interview

Von Lettow-Vorbeck, 1957 - pp

[9] *Warte des Temples*, No. 23-15 December 1926, pp 179-181

[10] Ibid

[11] Ibid

[12] Ibid, Translated by H. Glenk

[13] The Blaich family segment is based on interviews with Herta Blaich, the late Walter Blaich, the unpublished private manuscripts of their lives by Gotthilf Blaich and Gerhard Blaich and correspondence from Karin-Ruth Plink (née Blaich)

[14] Assmus, Eberhard – interview –with Horst Blaich - June 2006

[15] Ibid

[16] The Blankertz family segment is based on the unpublished private manuscript by Irmgard Schoer, *History of the Bauer Family in German East*[17] Interviews with Irmgard Schoer, Lore Bauer and Dorothea Gatter by Peer Gatter.

[18] The Bäeuerle family segment is based on the unpublished private manuscript of her life by Luise Kopp

[19] The Goetze family segment is based on interviews with Erika Goetze and Friedrich Goetze

[20] The Trappe family segment was researched in the von Lettow-Vorbeck book, 1957 – pp 131-140

[21] Neef, Werner, *Kurzgefasster Lebenslauf* (abbreviated Life Story) *by Walter Neef, 1950,* unpublished private manuscript

[22] Uhlherr, M. – Interview January 2006

Uhlherr, H. – Interview January 2006

-Draveanieeks, C.– Interview October 2005

[23] Glenk, 2005 – pp 197-200

[24] Draveanieeks, C. – interview October 2005

Asenstorfer, Ulrich – interview August 2006

[25] Ibid

Chapter Nine

[1] Buckwitz, H, 1940 *Vertrieben aus deutschem Land in Afrika (Expelled from German Land in Africa)-Kolonie und Heimat"*, 1940.

[2] Knauss, Adolf A, – "*Im Schatten des Ruwenzori (In the Shadow of Mt Ruwenzori)*", 1942, Steiniger Verlage, Berlin.

[3] Bauer, Lore, interview by Peer Gatter

[4] Buckwitz, H.

[5] Schoer, I. (Translated by H. Glenk)

[6] Buckwitz, H.

Schoer, I.

[7] Ibid.

[8] Ibid.

Blaich, H. – interview May 2005.

[9] Schoer, I.

Buckwitz, H.

[10] Schoer, I.

[11] Buckwitz, 1940.

Plink, R-K., letter February 2006.

[12] Bauer, L. – interview Peer Gatter

[13] Buckwitz, 1940.

Bauer, L.- interview Peer Gatter.

[14] Neef, W.

[15] Buckwitz, H.

[16] Ibid.

Plink, R-K.

Bauer, L.

[17] Kopp, L.

[18] Goetze, F. – interview October 2004.

Goetze, E. – interview October 2004.

[19] Blaich, H.

[20] Kopp, L.

[21] Bauer, L.

[22] Buckhwitz, 1940.

Plink, R-K.

[23] Buckhwitz, 1940.

[24] Ibid.

Plink, R-K.

[25] Kopp, L.

[26] Bauer, L.

Uhlherr, W.

Blaich, H.

[27] Blaich, H.

[28] Schoer, I.

[29] Ibid.

[30] Ibid.

[31] Ibid, (Translated by H Glenk).

[32] Ibid.

[33] Ibid, (Translated by H Glenk).

[34] Ibid.

[35] Ibid.

[36] Blaich, H.

[37] This segment is mainly based on Irmgard Schoer's unpublished manuscript of the history of the Bauer-Family (see above) — she was amongst those deported with this group to Rhodesia — and interview with Werner Neef, 24 November 2006.

[38] This segment is based on Irmgard Schoer's unpublished manuscript of the history of the Bauer Family (see above) and interview with Werner Neef. They were both interned in this camp in 1941.

[39] Neef, W.

[40] Blaich, H.

Blaich, G, 1963 – *Lebenslauf (Life Story)* – unpublished private manuscript.

[41] Blaich, H.

[42] Ibid.

[43] Asenstorfer, 2006.

Chapter Ten

[1] Schoer, I.

Neef, W. – interview 24 November 2006.

[2] Neef, W.

[3] Schoer, I.

Neef, W-.

[4] Blaich, H.

[5] Ibid.

Blaich, G.

[6] Ibid .

[7] Kopp, L.

[8] Gatter, P. – email of 5 January 2007.

[9] Blaich, H.

Schoer, I.

[10] Goetze, F.

[11] Hughes, 1963 – p 47.

[12] Ibid – pp 47-51.

[13] Ibid – pp 54,55.

[14] Ibid – pp 56-63.

[15] Ibid – pp 63,64.

[16] Ibid – p 65.

[17] Ibid – pp 65,71.

[18] Ibid – pp 80-83.

Internet – www.ntz.info/gen.

[19] Ibid.-

LIST OF ILLUSTRATIONS

LIST OF ILLUSTRATIONS

Chapter 9

258

SOURCES OF ILLUSTRATIONS

The first number refers to the illustration; the second number to the page and the third number to the chapter where the illustration is printed,.for example 6:19:2 is illustration 6 on page 19 chapter 2.

Albert Blaich Family Archives: 1:16:2, 2:16:2, 4:18:2, 8:21:2, 9:21:2, 3:27:3, 5:49:4, 9:55:4, 10:55:4, 13:59:4, 14:59:4, 4:74:5, 26:101:5, 27:101:5, 38:111:5, 5:114:6, 6:125:6, 7:126:6, 8:126:6, 9:127:6, 15:132:6, 17:136:6, 19:137:6, 20:138:6, 20:138:6, 5:147:7, 7:160:8, 8:161:8, 9:162:8, 14:164.8, 15:164:8,

Aliza Ehemann-Amir (Mrs) (daughter of Josef Treidel): 2:27:3

Charlotte Dravenicks: 53:191:8

David Fisher: 1:1:1, 6:50:4, 8:53:4, 12:58:4, 15:60:4, 1:71:5, 7:76:5, 10:162:8,

Eberhard Assmus: 29:103:5, 17:164:8, 20:168:8, 21:168:8, 22:169:8, 23:169:8, 24:169:8, 29:174:8, 1:196:9, 6:208:9, 10:214:9

Friedrich Goetze: 11:56:4, 43:116:5, 38:181:8, 39:182:8, 40:183:8, 41:184:8, 3:221:10, 4:222:10, 5:222:10, 6:223:10, 7:223:10, 8:224:10, 9:225:10, 10:225:10

Helmut Glenk: 5:75:5, 6:75:5, 35:108:5, 36:109:36, 44:186:8,

Herta Blaich: 11:12:1, 28:102:5, 30:103:5, 39:112:5, 10:128:6, 22:139:6, 3:157:8, 4:158:8, 5:159:8, 18:166:8, 19:167:8, 31:175:8, 42:184:8, 43:185:8,

Ilse Heinrich: 7:51:4, 3:73:5, 18:65:4, 31:103:5, 37:110:5, 2:119:6, 3:119:6, 4:120:6, 11:163:8, 12:163:8, 13:163:8, 16:165:8,

Jakob Eisler: 1:26:3, 6:20:2, 7:20:2

Karin Klingbeil: 41:114:5

Karin Plink: 40:113:5

Luise Kopp: 25:98:5

Martin Higgins: 37:181:8

Peer Gatter Personal Archives: 4:29:3, 19:68:4, 5:30:3, 6:30:3, 7:31:3, 8:31:3, 9:33:3, 10:34:3, 11:43:3, 2:46:4, 19:68:4, 9:80:5, 10:83:5, 11:84:5, 12:85:5, 13:87:5, 14:88:5, 15:89:5, 16:89:5,17:90:5, 18:91:5,19:92:5, 20:93:5, 21:95:5, 22:96:5, 23:97:5, 24:97:5, 32:104:5, 33:105:5, 34:106:5, 42:115:5,11:129:6, 12:130:6, 13:131:6, 14:131:6,

16:134:6, 18:137:6, 1:142:7, 2:143:7, 3:144:7, 4:146:7, 6:150:7, 7:150:7, 25:170:8, 26:171:8, 27:171:8, 28:172:8, 30:174:8, 32:175:8, 33:177:8, 34:178:8, 35:178:8, 36:179:8, 3:200:9, 4:202:9, 5:202:9, 2:219:10, 11:227:10

Royal Geographical Society, London, England: 4:5:1, 5:5:1,

State Library of Victoria, Melbourne, Australia – Heritage Room
(Maps from *The History of Africa et al* modified and adopted for book by Horst Blaich): 2:2:1, 3:3:1, 7:8:1, 4:48:4, 1:152:8

Tempelgesellschaft Deutschland, Stuttgart, Germany: 3:17:2, 5:19:2, 10:22.2

Ursula Klink: 1:46:4, 2:72:5,

Werner (Roland) Neef: 45:187:8, 46:188:8, 47:188:8, 48:188:8, 49:189:8, 50:189:8, 2:198:9, 7:209:9, 8:210:9, 9:212:9, 11:215:9, 1:218:10,

Werner Uhlherr: 16:62:4, 17:60:4, 2:156:8, 6:159:8, 51:190:8, 52:190:8,

Theo Weller: 8:78:5

www.nationalherbarium.nl: 3:47:4
www.wikipedia.org: 6:6:1, 8:10:1, 1:118:6
www.zum.de: 9:11:1, 10:11:1

INDEX

Page numbers in italic refer to illustrations.

Ladies who are referred to, in different parts of the text, by both their maiden name and their married name, have been entered
in the index under their married name, with a reference from their maiden name.

Subheadings are arranged alphabetically.

INDEX

INDEX